QMUL

Europe and
International Migration

Europe and International Migration

Sarah Collinson

Pinter Publishers, London and New York
for
Royal Institute of International Affairs, London

Distributed in the United States and Canada by St. Martin's Press

© Royal Institute of International Affairs, 1993

First published in Great Britain in 1993 by
Pinter Publishers Limited
25 Floral Street, London WC2E 9DS

British Library Cataloguing in Publication Data

A CIP catalogue record for this book is available from the British Library.

ISBN 1 85567 049 6

Text designed and set by Hannah Doe
Printed and bound in Great Britain by Biddles Ltd, Guildford and Kings Lynn

Distributed exclusively in the United States and Canada by St. Martin's Press, Inc.
400, 175 Fifth Avenue, New York, NY 10010, USA

Library of Congress Cataloging–in–Publication Data
A CIP catalog record for this book is available from the Library of Congress

For my parents

Contents

Foreword

This book is the first substantial piece of research on international migration to be published by the Royal Institute of International Affairs since the two classic studies of 1939 by Sir John Hope Simpson – *Refugees: A Review of the Situation Since 1938* and *The Refugee Problem: Report of a Survey*. We decided that the most important initial contribution the Institute could make would be to step back from the often rather emotive nature of the contemporary public policy debate to give some historical and geographical depth to the migration issue. This book is therefore an attempt to give perspective to many of Europe's immediate preoccupations with the subject, and thus, it is hoped, greater depth of understanding. Moreover, this work appears at an extremely opportune time. In Britain the new asylum bill is the subject of intense controversy. In Germany there is great concern over the social disruption immigration can create, as witnessed by the increase in violence aimed at recent immigrants. With the now free movement of peoples throughout much of the European Community the migration debate is set to intensify.

I would like to congratulate Sarah Collinson, the Institute's Research Fellow working on migration, for having produced such a readable and well-argued piece of work. Most significantly, this book will introduce an essentially lay readership to a wide range of primary and secondary material. Her handling of extensive though uneven source material is a particular strength.

Without our sponsors none of this research would have been undertaken, so we thank the Le Poer Power Trust for generously supporting this project. Already a second project is under way, sponsored by the Le Poer Power Trust and the Wyndham Place Trust. This study, also to be written by Sarah and to be published in the summer of 1993, will focus squarely on the issues of the day such as refugees and asylum policy.

January 1993   Dr Philip Robins

Preface

Introduction

Since the end of the cold war, international migration has risen rapidly up the political agenda in Western Europe. A number of developments have coalesced to create a high degree of anxiety over the issue, an anxiety which is not confined to political circles, but now stretches across virtually every sector of society. The lifting of emigration restrictions in the former Eastern bloc, coupled with growing economic instability in the region, appeared to set the scene for millions of economic migrants moving from East to West in search of a better life. More recent events in the former Yugoslavia have raised the spectre of further future mass dislocations of population in Europe stemming from a resurgence in ethnic tensions and generalized political instability following in the wake of the collapse of the Soviet Empire. In addition, an increase in asylum applications and illegal immigration from outside Europe, together with a rise in extreme anti-immigrant attitudes in Western Europe, have intensified longer-standing worries about migration from the 'South', particularly from the less-developed countries of the Mediterranean rim and sub-Saharan Africa. Suddenly it appears that Western Europe is under siege from its poorer and less stable neighbours, and that a new threat of mass population movements has come to replace the old and more distant peril of a Communist Eastern bloc.

To an extent, fears of a 'mass influx' have served to obfuscate level-headed analysis of the migration issue in Western Europe, and have therefore worked against balanced appraisals of just what kind of migration challenges Europe might come to face in the decades to come. All attention is focused on the innumerable pressures building up in existing and potential 'sending' regions that are deemed likely to drive movement into Western Europe in the future, such as rapid population growth, growing unemployment and falling incomes. As a result, other factors which are important for shaping migration have not received the kind of attention that they might seem to deserve. Migration policy is one of these. While it has been the subject of some considerable debate in a wide range of intergovernmental, media and other public sectors, the direction, focus and impetus of discussions have been determined more by immediate immigration fears and concerns than by efforts to assess just how state action has influenced, and will continue to influence, the outcome of intensifying migration pressures in the past and in the future. This deficit is also reflected in the academic literature, which, although vast, is curiously disjointed. Surprisingly little attention has been paid to the international and national politics of migration, and to the role of state intervention in the migration process. As Myron Weiner observes, a number of important questions remain inadequately explored: 'How do state actions shape population movements, when do such movements lead to conflicts and when to cooperation, and what do governments do in their domestic policies to adjust to or influence population flows'?[1]

The intention of this study is to take a step back from many of the preoccupations dominating current discussions of the issue in Western Europe. By tackling the question from a historical, and to a lesser extent global, perspective, the study aims to contribute contructively to a debate which has in many ways tended to treat international migration as a new phenomenon and as a problem unique to Western Europe. More specifically, by focusing on state action and inaction – on migration policies and the role that such policies (or the lack of them) have played in shaping migration flows in the past – it aims to draw attention to the part that states now have to play to influence migration flows.

The purpose of the book is not to downgrade the importance of migration pressures acting around Western Europe and throughout the world. Indeed, it is emphasized in the conclusion that those very pressures which hold the *potential* for creating large-scale migration – whether resulting in migration or not – need to be addressed urgently, if for no other reason than to avoid the prospect of much wider economic and political destabilization in Europe and in other regions of the world in the years to come. It is argued, however, that when action is taken in the future, it is likely to prove most effective when based on an understanding and recognition of states' capacity and responsibility to deal with migration pressures and to cope with migration flows.

The subject of international migration crosses numerous disciplinary boundaries and presents a bewildering array of different levels, directions and methods of possible approach. All this study, like any in the field, can hope to do is throw light on one corner of what is a much larger and more complex picture. Certain omissions have proved inescapable and a number of issue areas have not benefited from the close attention that they might seem to merit. The main focus of the book is on state action in respect of voluntary, as opposed to involuntary, migration. It therefore follows that emphasis has been placed on migration which may be broadly categorized as 'economic' (and voluntary) in motivation, and migration which is connected directly with such flows (family migration), rather than on refugee flows and other forms of forced movement. While it is sometimes difficult to make a clear distinction between refugees and migrants or between voluntary and involuntary flows, the distinction is an important one, and, when separated conceptually, the two phenomena raise very different questions. The scope of this book is not sufficient to do justice to both issues. Therefore, with the exception of Chapter 3, discussion touches on refugee issues only in so far as they have recently become entangled with policy questions relating to international migration more generally (Chapters 2 and 7).

The study begins by setting out the major types of international migration in the world today, outlining current broad trends in international 'economic' migration, and providing some pointers as to how these trends have affected migration into Western Europe in recent decades. The second chapter looks at three specific categories of international migration in an attempt to determine to what extent current trends reflect the singular position of Western Europe as compared with other regions of the world. This comparative perspective is developed further in Chapter 3, which examines major historical trends in European migration since the emergence of sovereign states (and thus the first strictly 'interstate' population movements) in Europe after the thirteenth century. This chapter looks, in particular, at the role of the state in influencing migration, and, in so doing, highlights elements of continuity and change in states' involvement in the migration process. The theme of state action is expanded in Chapters 4 and 5, which concentrate on how the policies of certain major migrant-receiving and migrant-sending states of the postwar period have influenced trends in voluntary international migration in Western Europe over the past four decades. This theme is also developed in Chapter 6, which focuses on policy influencing the settlement of immigrant communities in receiving countries (as opposed to the migration process itself). All three chapters throw light on aspects of similarity and difference in the policies of different states in Western Europe, and thereby provide a backdrop for Chapter 7, which critically examines current moves towards the harmonization of migration policy within the European Community and wider groupings in Western Europe. While this chapter considers in some detail a number of specific obstacles lying in the way of harmonization, the concluding chapter suggests that the single greatest obstacle to the future development of an effective European migration policy might prove to be states' reluctance to look beyond traditional concepts of migration control – concepts which have guided state policy for decades, and to some extent centuries, but which in the late twentieth century and beyond are likely to prove increasingly ill-equipped to deal with a phenomenon that has the potential for taking on a scale and complexity wholly unprecedented in the history of international migration.

I would like to thank a number of people for their help in the preparation of this study. First and foremost, my departmental head, Dr Philip Robins, who read and commented upon every draft, and who, with our programme administrator, Jill Kalawoun, demonstrated untiring support and commitment throughout the project. I must also thank my colleagues Professor Helen Wallace and Professor Jack Spence for their many valuable suggestions, and Pauline Wickham and Hannah Doe for all their patient work on the publications side of the project. I am also grateful to the numerous academics, officials and practitioners who were consulted during the course of the study, and whose comments proved invaluable. Needless to say, I take ultimate responsibility for all the ideas and views expressed in the book. The study, of course, would not have been feasible without the continuing support of the sponsor, the Le Poer Power Trust, which I would like to thank not only for financing the project, but also for its help in developing the shape and focus of the study. Finally, I would like to add a special personal thanks to Chris Sylge, Jenny Wilson and my family for all their encouragement.

January 1993   Sarah Collinson

Chapter 1

Introduction

'The migratory movement is at once perpetual, partial and universal. It never ceases, it affects every people ... [and although] at a given moment it sets in motion only a small number of each population ... in fact there is never a moment of immobility for any people, because no migration remains isolated.'[1] Eugene Kulischer wrote these words in 1943 when Europe was still suffering the ravages of war and a massive dislocation of millions of people across the whole continent. By that time, Europe had experienced virtually every kind of international migration discernible in the world today – forced and voluntary, economic and political, seasonal and permanent, regional and transcontinental, bonded and free. Moreover, Europe was not the only continent of the world to have experienced massive population movements, nor, indeed, were population movements in Europe isolated from developments elsewhere in the world. And now, in what is a world more interdependent than at any previous time in history, these words are as true as they have ever been.

The international migrations of people have always been complex. The worldwide picture today reveals millions of people displaced by war and conflict and persecution – some within countries, others across borders, some with assistance, others with none, some crossing land borders, others fleeing by air. Millions more are displaced by desertification and other kinds of ecological degradation and disaster – some natural, some man-made. Incalculable numbers of people move periodically across borders, as seasonal or frontier workers or as transient traders. More and more businessmen and professionals move from one country to another, sometimes for short periods, sometimes for years. And as international communications develop further and the mobility of and contacts between individuals of different countries and continents increase and multiply, so more and more people migrate as foreign spouses and foreign-born children of 'indigenous' residents. As always, there is the international migration of labour – some permanent, some temporary, some legal, some illegal, some skilled, some unskilled, some headed for agriculture, some headed for industry; and, as often with the movement of labour, there is an accompanying movement of families, some outward, some returning.

Towards a classification of types

International migration is so complex a phenomenon that any attempt to categorize the many different types inevitably proves a reductionist exercise. Nevertheless, for the purposes of discussion and analysis, a degree of classification is called for. An approach which is central to the process of policy formulation is that which distinguishes migrants according to the basic cause and intention of movement. Thus it is common to distinguish between migration which is caused by factors that can be described as being broadly 'political', and that which is caused or motivated by economic factors. It is this distinction, for example, which guides the definitional division between refugees and other kinds of migrants. The distinction between migration which is essentially voluntary in motivation and that which is involuntary is also useful.

Taking the two dimensions together, one can visualize a matrix within which to place the many different migration types. The extremes would be (1) migration which is strongly economic and voluntary in cause and motivation (e.g. worker migration); (2) that which is strongly political and voluntary (e.g. migration of Jews to Israel); (3) that which is strongly political and involuntary (e.g. 'classic' refugee flows); and (4) that which is strongly economic and involuntary (e.g. refugees from famine and ecological disaster). It should be stressed that such categories are always blurred and that most migration flows fall somewhere between the four extremes. Thus, for example, the expulsion of workers from the Arab Gulf, or the movement of 'distress' migrants in the Horn of Africa would, though for different reasons, fall somewhere between categories (3) and (4). Similarly, the 'economic' and 'voluntary' movement of migrant workers never takes place in a political vacuum, and thus worker migration incorporates elements of category (2). Furthermore, the fact that many worker migrants move to escape or avoid extreme economic hardship means that category (1) frequently overlaps with category (4).[2]

Although excluded from this matrix, certain factors which may be broadly defined as 'social' and/or 'cultural' usually impact on migration to a very significant degree. Thus the migration of families and dependants may be described as 'socially' determined, although the original migration which gives rise to this movement (and, sometimes, the family migration itself) may be largely economic in motivation. Even worker migration itself is very heavily influenced by the operation of social and cultural factors such as networks of communication between migrant-sending and migrant-receiving countries, or by more general cultural and linguistic links between sending and receiving countries. It is also worth mentioning that the increase in 'South/North' migration witnessed over recent decades has almost certainly been influenced by the spread of Western culture throughout the world.

One can take the categorization a stage further by distinguishing, for example, between the movements of professional and the movements of unskilled workers, between documented or undocumented (illegal) movements, and between transient, seasonal, temporary and permanent migrants.[3] All fall within the same broad category by virtue of being 'economic' and 'voluntary' in character, but all are very different in terms of specific causes, motivations and impacts. Each general category includes a myriad of specific types. This diversity is important, and has led some analysts to argue that the causes and consequences of international migration should be evaluated only within the context of specific countries and specific migratory situations.[4] Indeed, even in a specific migratory context, factors determining and arising from migration may be very difficult to identify. It is perhaps this more than anything else that explains why international migration has eluded researchers and policy-makers for so long, and why clear policies are so difficult to formulate and clear conclusions so hard to reach.

Global trends

Like international capital and product flows, the international flow of people has undergone a marked expansion over the past four decades. One estimate puts the number of people currently resident outside their country of citizenship at some 80 million.[5] If account is taken of (1) high numbers of people who are or have become citizens of the receiving country, (2) those who are now outside their country of origin after the collapse of the Soviet Union, and (3) huge numbers of seasonal, frontier and transient migrants worldwide, the figure can be assumed to be much higher (upwards of 100 million).[6] The international significance of the phenomenon is most easily demonstrated in economic terms. Although the total revenue created by international labour flows is impossible to evaluate, crude estimates of the scale of international remittance flows (capital sent by migrants from their country of residence to their country of origin) provide a rough indication: in the late 1980s, the total value of international remittances, put at some US$60.9 billion in 1989, came second only to trade in crude oil. Its value exceeded both global flows of official development aid (US$51 billion in 1988) and the global value of trade in coffee (US$9 billion).[7] Given this scale, it is somewhat surprising that it is only in the past few years that the issue has received the level of international attention that it would seem to deserve.

Although migration has affected all regions of the world throughout history, it is only in recent decades that international flows can be said to have become truly global. With the spread and advancement of modern communications, the expansion of the global economy, and the intensification of regional and international economic and demographic disparities, every continent of the world is now touched by the phenomenon. Furthermore, the past few decades have seen a remarkable expansion and diversification in transcontinental flows, such as from Africa and the Caribbean to Europe, and from Asia to North America and the Middle East. Much of this migration is driven by economic and political forces – such as world trading patterns and capital flows – which have become increasingly global in their genesis and development. The global causes and impacts of international migration have become increasingly intertwined. Thus, for example, migration flows from Asia to the Middle East have caused both economic and social changes in the sending regions, which in turn have given rise to further migration flows, e.g. migration into areas benefiting from development on the basis of remittances, or out of areas where a migration 'psyche' has developed or where traditional social and economic structures have been eroded by prolonged emigration.

However, while it has become progressively global in scope, the process has also undergone a degree of regionalization. To begin with, certain established patterns of movement between contiguous and proximal states have become entrenched, such as that between Mexico and the United States, or that between states in West Africa. At the same time, a number of new regional patterns have emerged or are expected to develop in conjunction with the strengthening of particular regional economic groupings. For example, the past decade has witnessed a marked diversification and increase in levels of migration between East and Southeast Asian states, and the next few years may witness higher levels of migration within the so-called 'European

Economic Area'. As described by one analyst, 'we are observing ... the same phenomenon as in the global product market, namely a combination of globalization and regionalization, of outward-orientation and inward-orientation, of free movement and barriers, analogous to the combination of free trade and protectionism'.[8]

In connection with the process of regionalization, it is perhaps most important to note that over the past few decades international migration has become progressively concentrated in just a few areas of the world. Out of the estimated 100 million international migrants worldwide, over a third are in sub-Saharan Africa (at least 35 million), and of the remaining 65 million, most are concentrated in the Middle East and South and Southeast Asia (15 million) and in North America and Western Europe (15 and 13 million respectively).[9] Concentrations are often particularly marked in the case of particular countries. Saudi Arabia, for example, accounted for around 4.5 million of the estimated 6–7 million international migrants in the Arab Gulf prior to the Iraqi invasion of Kuwait; of the total 7 million or so refugees in South Asia, over 6.5 million are concentrated in Pakistan and Iran; of the 17 million or so people in Central and North America who are citizens of a country other than that in which they are resident, over 14 million are in the United States; and of the some 13 million 'foreigners' resident in Western Europe, roughly 8 million[10] are in Germany, France and Britain.[11] Furthermore, many transcontinental migration flows, although indicative of a globalization in migration, are, on closer examination, highly regionalized in terms of sources as well as destinations. Thus particular sending countries tend to dominate flows to particular receiving countries (e.g. Egypt to Saudi Arabia, Algeria and Morocco to France), and flows out of any one sending country may be dominated by emigration from particular regions of that country (e.g. Kerala in India).

Trends affecting Western Europe

Each of the three principal global migration trends outlined above – escalation, globalization, and regionalization[12] – have characterized migration to Western Europe over recent decades. However, these trends are not entirely new or clear-cut. For example, inflows of workers from other regions of the world rose at an unprecedented rate during the two to three decades following the Second World War, reflecting both an escalation and a globalization in international movements of migrant labour. But this was not Europe's first experience of large-scale transcontinental labour migration. Indeed, Western

Europe had already been directly involved in two of the largest transcontinental migrations to have taken place in history – the Atlantic slave trade and the subsequent population of the New World. Nor did the postwar arrival of foreign workers signify an entirely new phenomenon, since migration patterns in Europe before the two World Wars were characterized by high levels of international labour movement, including that out of areas of Eastern and Central Europe.

International migration, however, is a phenomemenon which is simultaneously constant and ever-changing. Although sharing many attributes of earlier flows, recent migration to Western Europe has departed from previous trends in a number of important ways. It was not until the postwar years, for example, that any West European states experienced large-scale inflows of foreign workers from geographically, ethnically and/or culturally 'distant' countries outside Europe. Hence this was the first time that a globalization in migration flows (coupled with regionalization) had come substantially to affect migration patterns *into*, rather than out of, Western Europe. While not signifying the emergence of a new region of immigration, this influx brought about new migration patterns. Poorer Mediterranean countries which were hitherto isolated from the labour markets of Western Europe became linked into the West European migration 'network'. These links subsequently gave rise to new migration patterns, such as flows to Southern Europe from North Africa. And while the overall magnitude of, and the generally negative reaction to, the immigrant populations of the postwar years may not have been substantially different from those of earlier years, the implications of migration changed considerably owing to shifting economic, political and social conditions in both sending and receiving areas.

Migration trends have undergone further changes in Western Europe since the period of labour immigration following the Second World War. Although many of the same countries are involved, new players have entered the fray. Eastern Europe, separated from the labour markets of Western Europe for some thirty years, is once again a source of economic migration to Western Europe. At the same time, improved global communications and intensifying migration pressures outside Europe are giving rise to a diversification in flows from more distant regions, such as sub-Saharan Africa. Much of this migration is now directed to Southern Europe – Italy, Spain, Portugal, Greece – which has traditionally sent migrants abroad, rather than receiving them from elsewhere. Moreover, while postwar labour immigration took place at a time of economic boom in the most advanced industrialized countries of Western Europe, the environment today is one of economic recession and rising unemployment. Whereas migration during the postwar years was encouraged, or at least sanctioned, by the receiving states, most of that taking place today is 'unwanted' and, to some extent, uncontrolled by the receivers.

Nevertheless, current migration trends should not be divorced from the patterns of previous periods. First, as already discussed, the fundamental forces shaping migration have remained remarkably similar over decades and centuries. This applies not only to voluntary economic migration, but also to involuntary refugee movements, as discussed in Chapter 3. Second, migration flows and the policies that shape them are frequently linked very directly to previous patterns. One can point, for example, to the importance of Mediterranean migration in current flows to Western Europe – flows which may be attributable as much to past policies of labour recruitment as to current migration pressures operating in the sending regions. Third, a consideration of past trends and policies can prove informative for the formulation of new responses. Reference to the past may not only demonstrate areas in which state policy has had, or could have, a decisive role in shaping migration; it may also reveal areas of convergence and divergence in the positions of different states – an important consideration at a time when moves are being made to harmonize a wide range of laws and procedures relating to international migration in Western Europe.

Chapter 2

Western Europe in a World of International Migration

As noted in the Introduction, migration is now a global phenomenon, which affects virtually every country of the world, whether it be the movement of workers, refugees, highly skilled professionals or traders, or other forms of migration. This chapter aims to look a little beyond the confines of Western Europe to consider, on a broad level, to what extent trends today reflect the singular position of the West European region. It concentrates on three main migration categories: documented labour migration, illegal or 'irregular' migration, and asylum flows.

The first category is one that dominates the postwar history of migration into Western Europe (as detailed in following chapters), but which has come to affect the region less and less in recent years. Despite this decline, Western Europe continues to be seen – at least by many among its own population – as the most important destination for economic migrants in the contemporary world. By focusing on the emergence of new areas of international labour migration elsewhere in the world, the first section challenges this perception, demonstrating that Western Europe and other advanced industrialized countries can no longer claim to be the sole or primary 'honeypots' of international economic migration.

Nevertheless, economic migration into Western Europe continues today. Apart from the (increasing) international movement of highly skilled and professional workers, 'economic' migration to Western Europe now takes place principally through illegal or 'irregular' channels. In addition, escalating inflows of asylum-seekers are perceived as being comprised more and more of economic migrants as opposed to refugees. These two categories have become increasingly important in the European setting over the past decade, and now dominate current concerns over migration in Europe's receiving states. Like the legal movement of labour, illegal migration and asylum/refugee flows are now worldwide phenomena, and thus the challenges they pose for a number of West European states are in many ways not unique. However, the situation in one region can never be compared directly with that in another. The second and third sections of this chapter compare some of the particular problems facing Western Europe in connection with illegal and asylum flows with those encountered by receiving countries in other regions in the world.

Documented labour migration

According to World Bank data, the world's main destination countries for international migrants in the late 1980s, or, more precisely, those countries which experienced the highest rates of net (documented) immigration during this period, were (in descending order) the United States, Australia, Saudi Arabia, Canada and Côte d'Ivoire.[1] This list supports the perception that countries of the industrialized 'North' are a major pole of attraction for international migrants in the contemporary world, but challenges the common impression that these are necessarily today's most important immigration countries.

The level of net migration to the United States during the second half of the 1980s was higher than total net immigration in all other countries of the world combined, reaching 2.9 million during the period 1985 to 1990.[2] Indeed, the United States took in almost the same number of permanent settlers and temporary workers in the 1980s as it did during the first decades of this century (around 7 million compared with 8.8 million in the period 1900–10).[3] But, although standing out in terms of overall numbers, recent migration trends to the US reflect general patterns that are common, to a greater or lesser extent, to all the Western industrialized immigration states. All these countries have introduced policies which leave little room for the legal and independent immigration of most classes of migrant worker. As a result, immigration is now dominated by family (including foreign family-members of 'indigenous' residents) and asylum migration flows. What worker migration persists is now largely accounted for by legal movements of highly skilled and professional workers (much of which is temporary or transient), and by illegal and clandestine migration (discussed below). According to SOPEMI estimates, seven selected West European countries – Belgium, Germany, Luxembourg, the Netherlands, Norway, Sweden and Switzerland – experienced an inflow of nearly 4 million and an outflow of some 2.5 million foreign nationals between 1985 and 1989, indicating a net immigration of around 1.5 million foreigners during that period.[4] Nevertheless, stocks of documented foreign *labour* in Northwestern Europe remained relatively stable during the 1980s, increasing by less than 350,000 between 1980 and 1989 (6% of the total stock of foreign labour at the beginning of the decade).[5]

Although the documented migration of labour from 'South' to 'North' has declined, this has not implied a worldwide reduction in levels of international labour migration. Indeed, the number of people working outside their country of origin today is likely to be significantly larger than that of twenty years ago. This increase is due less to rising levels of illegal or 'irregular' migration to Western Europe or North America than to the growing importance of so-called 'South/South' flows, i.e., labour migration which is not directed to the most advanced Western industrialized countries. Today, the numbers of international migrants in Western Europe and North America represent around 30% of the estimated 100 million international migrants worldwide. Of the remaining 70 million or so, at least half are accounted for by people moving within the sub-Saharan African region (both 'economic' migrants and refugees), and a quarter by migrants in the Middle East and Southeast Asia.[6] Indeed, contemporary migration patterns suggest that if intensifying pressures to migrate are to translate into an actual increase in migration in the future, labour movement is likely to be characterized more and more by flows within the confines of the 'third world'. It is worth noting, for example, that of the total estimated number of sub-Saharan African migrants living and/or working outside their state of origin, less than 1.5% are currently resident in the European Community.[7] A relative increase in 'South/South' migration will be reinforced by the restrictive stance of the industrialized countries on immigration, and by growing economic and demographic disparities between those countries which are collectively defined as 'less developed'. This was illustrated most graphically by the sudden expansion of the international migrant labour market in the Arab Gulf following the oil crisis of 1973.

The quadrupling of world oil prices in 1973 led to an economic downturn in the industrialized North, but brought unprecedented economic growth to the world's most important oil-producing states. On the basis of an explosion in export revenues, the Middle East oil-producers opted for a rapid development of their physical and socio-economic infrastructures. This necessitated a supply of workers that could not be satisfied by the indigenous labour force, since the affected populations were both small (with the exception of Iraq) and unsuited to meet the new demand.[8] Within two years of the oil crisis, huge numbers of foreign workers were flowing into the Gulf and Libya. This influx was initially dominated by flows from other Arab countries (Egypt, South Yemen and Jordan), but these were soon joined by rising levels of migration from Asia (particularly from India and Pakistan, and, later, from Bangladesh, the Philippines, Sri Lanka, Korea and Thailand). This development accompanied a progressive commercialization of the Middle East labour markets, and reflected the great importance of transcontinental migration flows in the world today. Asian countries were able to compete aggressively with Arab sending countries by providing cheaper and more regulated labour, such that between 1975 and 1985 the proportion of Asian workers in the non-national workforce of the Gulf Cooperation Council states had increased from 20% to around 63%. The overall populations of the Arab oil-producing states more than doubled between 1975 and 1985 as a result of immigration.[9]

Those sending states which managed to win a share in the Arab Gulf and Libyan labour markets were not the same countries as those which had previously sent migrants to Western Europe (with the partial exceptions of Pakistan, Bangladesh and Turkey). The reasons for this are complex, and include the fact that many of the traditional sending countries (including the North African and Caribbean states) were geographically, economically, linguistically and/or politically disadvantaged for competing in the Middle East. The shift from Arab to Asian labour sources reflected, among other things, the outstanding importance of Asia as a migrant-sending region in the world today. The Philippines, for example, is now the largest labour exporter in the world. In the period between 1975 and 1987, over 3 million Filipinos had worked abroad,[10] a figure equal to 5% of the country's population in 1989.[11] Like other sending countries in the region, it has become highly reliant on the ability to export labour. As Manolo Abella observes, 'few developments have had a more profound impact on the economic conditions in a number of ... Asian countries than the overseas migration of labour'. In 1987, emigration represented almost 10% of the total GDP of Pakistan, and 60% of the value of total merchandise exports in Bangladesh.[12]

Although there are small migration flows from Asia to Western Europe, and more substantial flows to North America, the majority of Asian worker migration continues to be that to the Middle East oil-producers.[13] There has, however, been a slow-down in the migrant labour markets of the Arab Gulf since the mid-1980s, and this has been accompanied by an escalation and diversification of flows within East and Southeast Asia itself. The recent expansion of Asian migrant labour markets reflects both a growth in the volume of trade and capital flows, and a marked variation in rates and patterns of economic and demographic development in the region. Competition among migrant-sending countries to win a share in these new labour markets is fierce. The most successful labour-exporters are the Philippines, Indonesia and Thailand. The main centres of attraction are Japan and the four 'Asian dragons': Hong Kong, Taiwan, the Republic of Korea and Singapore. Malaysia and oil-rich Brunei Darussalam also receive foreign workers. The picture is not straightforward, however, since a number of countries experience high levels of both emigration and immigration (Hong Kong, Korea and Malaysia). This reflects the fact that almost no country in the world today can claim to be exclusively a 'sender' or 'receiver' of migrants.

In terms of immigration pressures, the position of Asia's most-developed economies is in many respects more extreme than that of Western Europe's receivers. Japan, for example, is suffering acute labour shortages caused by steep economic growth, negligible population growth (an annual rate of roughly 0.4%) and a rapidly ageing population. Taiwan is experiencing spectacular per capita income growth (around 14% annually) and close to zero unemployment. These countries provide a striking contrast with sending countries such as the Philippines, where population growth has been running at an annual rate of nearly 3%[14] (close to world's highest rate), and where, despite emigration, labour force growth is placing severe strains on the absorptive capacity of the national labour market. Pronounced demographic and economic imbalances,[15] combined with shifting patterns of trade and investment,[16] an active promotion of emigration by sending governments and intermediaries (recruitment agents, transnational corporations, etc.), and a failure of both migrant-sending and migrant-receiving countries to adjust their labour markets to cope with their respective demographic problems, have all contributed to the recent acceleration of international labour migration within East and Southeast Asia.

In common with the West European immigration countries, the Asian receiving states share a generally negative and restrictive stance towards most kinds of immigration, irrespective of patterns of labour demand. Japan, for example, is experiencing shortages at both ends of the labour spectrum, but, although relatively open to the immigration of highly skilled workers and professionals, the government remains committed to keeping its doors shut to other categories of foreign workers. A senior Japanese official recently stated that: 'It is our government's policy that we permit the entry and stay of the foreign nationals seeking employment with professional skills, technique or knowledge ... on the other hand, we will not ... allow in principle the entry of unskilled workers and we will maintain our principle of not allowing them at present.'[17] Japan's reasons for preventing the entry of unskilled workers reflect a concern to avoid all the problems that are seen to have plagued Western Europe ever since the full-scale recruitment of foreign labour in the 1960s and 1970s. The same official goes on to state that 'if in the future the question of foreign unskilled labour should be considered ... most careful consideration would be needed, taking into [account] ... the past experience of other developed countries, to work out measures to avoid the problems that other countries have been experiencing from the introduction of foreign labour.'[18] To meet what is a growing demand for unskilled labour in the Japanese economy, the preferred policy is that of encouraging overseas investment and the transfer of technology to labour-surplus (labour-cheap) countries. This is a preference shared – at least theoretically – by West European states.

In comparison with other receiving countries in the region, Japan's opposition to unskilled worker immigration may be somewhat extreme. However, all the receiving countries in East and Southeast Asia, like those in Western Europe, are firmly committed to preventing unregulated immigration, as illustrated by the harsh measures implemented by Hong Kong to turn back illegal Chinese immigrants, and by Singapore's recent introduction of mandatory corporal punishment for illegal immigrants, their employers and agents.

'Irregular' or 'undocumented' worker migration

A rise in illegal or 'irregular' migration is an issue of growing concern in the advanced industrialized world. More and more migration is classified as illegal because states have opted to control migration by applying increasingly stringent immigration laws. In addition, and contrary to the restrictionist stance of the industrialized receiving states, an intensification of regional and global economic, demographic, political and social disparities has meant that the pressure or potential for international migration is probably greater today than ever before. Although restrictive migration policies mitigate strongly against the direct translation of migration pressures into migration flows, a growth in economic and other inequalities will inevitably give rise to higher migration levels. If there are fewer and fewer opportunities for legal migration, one can expect more and more migration to take place through 'irregular' channels.

If, as economistic models would suggest, migration is determined predominantly by conditions of supply and demand, or 'push' and 'pull' factors, then illegal migration probably fits the traditional models more closely than other kinds of (international) migration,[19] representing a very direct response to 'push' and 'pull' in which competing state interests play little part.* However, in conjunction with the worldwide increase in illegal migration, there is a growing perception that international movements are determined increasingly by 'push' rather than 'pull' factors,[20] a perception which serves to fuel paranoia in Western Europe about the intensification of migration pressures in surrounding sending states. It is a mistake to think that immigration controls in Western Europe and elsewhere are on the verge of collapse, but it is true that, in determining the shape and composition of migration flows, receiving-state regulation has to some extent been superseded by supply conditions in sending regions. The increasing importance of such conditions, however, may be due less to a decline in demand from receiving areas, than to a change in the intervening mechanisms linking the two factors in the migration process. When receiving states attempt to close off old migration channels or prevent the emergence of new ones without eradicating demand, they relinquish a significant degree of control over the pattern and direction of migration flows, since they are no longer in a position to regulate the satisfaction of demand by choosing who should come and where they should come from. In Western Europe, it is this loss in regulative power that largely accounts for the perception that immigration has been imposed on receiving states by the countries of North Africa or Eastern Europe.[21]

The dynamics shaping irregular migration are extremely complex, however, and there is considerable evidence that illegal immigration flows themselves generate certain patterns of demand which in turn stimulate further immigration. It is this argument which underpins the view that irregular migration has a distorting effect on receiving labour markets because employers in certain sectors come to rely increasingly on sources of cheap, flexible and exploitable labour which are not available in the national labour supply. This does not necessarily imply a damaging effect on the receiving economy, since many enterprises which depend on irregular labour supplies, particularly those in certain labour-sensitive service sectors, would

*Note that 'push-pull' models were originally based on movement within countries, i.e. migration that is not influenced by classic forms of migration control.

not exist in the absence of illegal immigration flows – a point which counters the view that illegal immigration necessarily displaces indigenous workers. The fact that the United States and some West European states have at times turned a blind eye to illegal immigration pays heed to an implicit recognition of the economic benefits of undocumented immigration – at least during periods of economic boom.

Nevertheless, undocumented or irregular immigration is generally viewed negatively in the West, reflecting concerns which may have little to do with the objective economic costs or benefits of the phenomenon. As Myron Weiner observes, 'access rules are not merely the political expression of economic forces, however important these may be ... economic changes may induce governments to change their access rules ... but it would be a mistake to think that the choices governments make are necessarily dictated by economic considerations'.[22] Since it reflects a lack of control on the part of the state, anxiety over illegal immigration is often particularly pronounced at a time when a country's sovereignty seems challenged in wider terms. As Demetrious Papademetriou argues in relation to the restrictive US Immigration Reform and Control Act of 1986,

> The passage of IRCA was in many respects the US Congress' immigration response to an ideology of limits. The 1970s and early 1980s had given rise to, and had subsequently fuelled, perceptions of extreme US vulnerability to foreign political and economic events. These perceptions had reinforced a US self-image of an eroding ability to control its own fate. This self-image, in turn, resulted in a 'defensive' approach to immigration policy reform.[23]

Although a general feeling of vulnerability may provide an atmosphere conducive to a fear of immigration (legal and illegal), the concrete basis of concern is usually expressed in more tangible terms, such as worries over the economic and social order or the national identity. Since responses to 'unwanted' immigration are not shaped purely by economic considerations, they are to a large extent subjective. They vary considerably from country to country and from region to region, reflecting differing political traditions and immigration histories, and changing perceptions of national, regional and international economic, political and social conditions. This is demonstrated clearly in the context of expulsions. Weiner observes that 'any country can expel illegals, but such expulsion is obviously politically easier for authoritarian countries than for democracies'.[24] Thus, for example, the Gulf states have scarcely flinched at the prospect of carrying out mass expulsions when political or economic conditions have seemed to demand (e.g. some 88,000 illegal residents were expelled from Saudi Arabia within a three-month period in 1979, around 18,000 from Kuwait in 1980,[25] and over two million workers were expelled from Saudi Arabia, Iraq and Kuwait in 1990/91). Similarly, one can point to Nigeria's expulsion of two million Ghanaian and other West African illegal immigrants in the early 1980s, Ghana's retaliatory expulsion of 500,000 Nigerians and other aliens, and Algeria's expulsion of some 10,000 nationals of Niger and Mali in the spring of 1986.

The Western democracies face rather different problems to those of the receiving countries in the Middle East or Africa. These include the fact that governments of the Western liberal democracies cannot endorse policies that sanction the *de facto* formation of an illegal immigrant underclass (whatever the actual outcome of the policies pursued). Still less could they tolerate policies of out-and-out segregation and periodic mass expulsion comparable with those practised by the Middle East oil-producing states. Instead – and in common with the Asian receiving states – the Western democracies have looked to enhanced control and enforcement measures to prevent the arrival and settlement of undocumented immigrants: border controls, stricter visa regulations, employer and carrier sanctions,* stiff penalties for traffickers, etc. But there are limits to how far these states can take such measures without infringing the rights of legal immigrants, without straining relations with the countries from which the immigrants come, or, indeed, without generating opposition within certain sectors of the national electorate (such as immigrant-dependent employers).[26] Furthermore, however harsh they may be, enforcement mechanisms are never likely to prove entirely successful as long as employment opportunities exist in the receiving countries. There will always be some migrants able and willing to surmount legal and procedural barriers if opportunities on the other side are markedly better than those at home. In response to the presence of illegal immigrant populations, these states have waivered between practising small-scale expulsions and deportations, and carrying out occasional large-scale legalizations[27] and other programmes designed to integrate (previously) undocumented immigrants into mainstream society.

Western Europe's immigration states face particular problems in comparison with the United States and Asia's receiving states. Like all these countries, receiving states in Western Europe are faced with growing levels

*Penalties for airlines or other carriers transporting passengers lacking necessary documentation or using false documentation.

of illegal immigration as a function of a variety of economic and demographic pressures. The number of illegally present non-nationals in Western Europe is not known, although some estimates have been put forward that suggest a figure of at least 2.6 million. It is estimated that 1.5 million, or over 50%, of Europe's illegals are in the new immigration countries of Southern Europe, particularly Italy and Spain,[28] and that the greater proportion of this immigration is only a few years old. Whereas undocumented immigrant population in the US (estimated at between 2 and 3 million after the 'amnesty' of 1987/8) is comprised almost entirely of Hispanics (of which some 80% are from Mexico),[29] that of Southern Europe is of very mixed origins, including large numbers from North Africa, sub-Saharan Africa, Asia and the Middle East. Illegal flows often follow the same patterns and directions as current or previous documented flows, as has been the dominant pattern in illegal migration to the United States. Sometimes, however, undocumented flows dominate over, and even precede, channels of authorized migration. This is the case with most current migration into Southern Europe, although it may be based to some extent on previous flows to other destinations in Western Europe, or shaped considerably by colonial or other historical links with migrant-sending countries. As a result, receiving states which have no history of immigration are now faced with changing immigrant communities of a kind that, given a greater degree of control, they would probably choose to avoid – i.e. immigrant groups that are perceived to be culturally and ethnically different from receiving populations, and thus considered difficult to integrate.

In contrast to the Asian receivers, the West European immigration states cannot enforce draconian immigration control measures without risking serious negative repercussions for the integration of existing (legally resident) immigrant populations. On the other hand, the absence of a powerful immigrant lobby in Western Europe might seem to imply that European governments have greater room for manoeuvre than the United States. However, unlike North America, Western Europe is currently facing a significant upsurge in xenophobic and anti-immigrant opinion, and this is forcing a number of receiving governments into a corner. Harsh control measures might satisfy certain demands of the extreme right, but they are more likely to fuel anti-immigrant attitudes by drawing attention to the immigrant 'problem', and by appearing to endorse anti-immigrant opinion. On the other hand, to allow illegal immigration to continue unchecked will do nothing to help integrate minorities, nor to quell rising national concerns surrounding all aspects of the issue. Recent policy developments give little indication that receiving states have found a way out of this dilemma.

It is interesting to note that radical right-wing attitudes are on the rise in the United States as well as in Western Europe. However, while there is strong anti-immigrant sentiment among certain sectors of American society, this movement has not as yet taken a significant hold in US public opinion. Indeed, far from fighting immigration, elements of the right have recently found themselves in a curious alliance with a variety of other groups opposing legislation designed to restrict immigration, the success of which largely explains the recent relaxation of US immigration policies in the form of the 1990 Immigration Act, which expanded quotas for certain categories of family and worker immigration.[30] Right-wing support for immigration in the US stems primarily from an ideology which endorses every aspect of the free market, including that of labour, but it also reflects a belief in the fundamental value of immigration which – despite a potential for a resurgence in American nativism[31] – is still widespread in the USA. This attitude has never taken a significant hold in Western Europe, even in those states with a relatively long history of immigration. If one can speak of a nation's self-image, that of the United States is based on the idea of a country built on immigration.[32] Those of the West European immigration states are not, despite the fact that Western Europe now hosts a higher proportion of foreign-born to indigenous population than does the United States.[33] Thus both the United States and Western Europe may be considered 'honeypots' in the contemporary world of international migration, but although this position is on the whole perceived positively in the United States, it is generally perceived negatively in Western Europe. It is perhaps for this reason as much as any other that the fear of an impending immigration 'crisis' – so widespread in Western Europe – is largely absent in the United States.

It is already clear, however, that migration-related pressures currently experienced by Europe's migrant-receiving states cannot be directly compared with those acting on the United States. In addition to differences in the 'immigration heritage' of the two regions, account must be taken of the particular position of Western Europe in relation to the former communist states of Eastern and Central Europe and the ex-Soviet Union. The sudden economic, political and social dislocations that have taken place on the European continent since 1989 have served to heighten anxiety among the general public over Western Europe's perceived vulnerability to all potentially adverse developments in the East, including migration. Anxiety about developments in Eastern and Central Europe and the former Soviet Union has, moreover, introduced an additional element of urgency to what was already brewing as a major political concern from the mid-1980s onwards, that being a dramatic increase in asylum applications and levels of illegal immigration from the South, particularly, in respect of the latter, into countries with no significant prior history of immigration.

Indeed, the unique situation in Europe today indicates that the challenges brought about by migration (actual or potential) differ so much between regions as to render many global or cross-regional comparisons at least partially redundant. This applies as much in relation to flows of asylum-seekers and refugees as it does to those of illegal immigrants.

Asylum flows

It is important to keep in mind the fundamental, although frequently blurred, definitional distinction between asylum-seekers and refugees. In popular usage, the term 'refugee' has a broad meaning, signifying someone in flight from conditions such as war, famine, natural disaster, oppression or persecution. In the context of international law, however, the content of the term is considerably more limited. Although the definitions in force within different national and international jurisdictions are varied, most are based on those adopted by the United Nations in 1950, 1951 and 1967,[34] which identify the refugee as someone who has crossed an international frontier because of a well-founded fear of persecution by reason of his or her race, religion, nationality, political opinion or membership of a social group. Any person arriving in an asylum state claiming to be a refugee can expect to have his or her case examined so as to determine whether he or she fits the accepted refugee definition and therefore deserves the protection attached to that status. Thus, in practice, refugees are not classed as such until their status has been officially recognized by the receiving country. The term 'asylum-seeker', on the other hand, refers to any person seeking asylum on the basis of a claim to being a refugee, irrespective of whether that person's claim is valid or not. Therefore 'asylum-seekers', as a category, includes refugees prior to recognition of their status, and others whose claim to refugee status may be refused.

The number of people seeking asylum in Western Europe has risen dramatically since the mid-1980s, increasing from 134,000 in 1985 to over 400,000 in 1991 (aggregate figures for the EC12).[35] It is commonly assumed that this increase owes less to rising levels of refugee arrivals than it does to increasing numbers of 'economic' migrants seeking to use asylum as a means for migration in the absence of other legal channels. The fact that recognition rates are low, and have fallen in relation to the numbers applying, would seem to support this view (e.g. an EC average of roughly 24.3% in 1989, down to 10.2% in 1991[36]). It is largely because of the growing perception that asylum flows are dominated by economic migrants that asylum issues have become increasingly entangled with broader immigration questions in recent policy debates. The situation is not straightforward, however, since the refugee definition as used in Western Europe has always had its problems as regards application. It is both open to subjective interpretation, and highly restrictive in its field of application. Thus, low rates of recognition within any group of asylum-seekers cannot be taken *prima facie* to imply that all those refused refugee status are automatically 'voluntary' and 'economic' migrants.

To a great extent, the 1950/51 UN definition reflects the cold-war conditions in which it was formulated.[37] Despite the widespread and large-scale displacement of population in Europe during the Second World War, the refugee definition adopted by the United Nations was one applicable to individuals rather than to groups, and one tied to a rather restrictive and subjective idea of persecution. Refugee status became, in essence, a status resulting from a discord between an individual's personal convictions and the tenets of the ruling political system in his or her country of origin – a status which, during the cold war, provided a certain political advantage for Western receiving states when it could be accorded to refugees from the Eastern bloc.[38] Since the early 1950s, however, changing social and political conditions throughout the world have given rise to refugee flows of a rather different nature. Nevertheless, the legal definition applied in Western Europe has remained largely unchanged. As observed by James Hathaway,

> Refugee law as codified in the 1951 Convention and the 1967 Proto-col ... not only continues the original rejection of the notion of com-prehensive assistance for all involuntarily displaced persons, but it allies international law with a series of strategic limitations deter-mined by Western political objectives. It ... defines need in terms which exclude most refugees from the less developed world ... [and is] both substantively and procedurally malleable at the instance of state parties ... [As a result], contemporary international refugee law is marginal to the protection of most persons coerced to migrate.[39]

The best response to such a charge is probably not to call for a wider definition of the refugee, since in today's restrictive climate too broad a conception would certainly threaten the credibility of the refugee's special status vis-à-vis asylum states. But the fact that the 1950/51 UN definition is unsuited to many of today's refugee flows is reflected in the wider and more pragmatic definitions adopted, for example, by the Organization for African Unity (OAU) in 1969 and the Organization of American States (OAS) in 1984 (the Cartegena Declaration),[40] and in what has been a gradual extension of the mandate of the United Nations High Commissioner for Refugees (UNHCR).[41] The 1969 OAU Convention on Refugee Problems in Africa begins with the UN definition, then incorporates every person who 'owing to external aggression, occupation, foreign domination or events seriously disturbing public order, in either part or whole of his country of origin or nationality, is compelled to leave his place of habitual residence in order to seek refuge in another place outside his country of origin or nationality'.[42]

The 1969 OAU Convention was thereby designed to facilitate flexible, humanitarian and pragmatic responses to a wide variety of refugee movements. Such responses became increasingly important over the following decade, which witnessed more and more complex refugee problems in Africa and throughout the Third World. The numbers involved were significantly larger than previously, and, because many movements were caused by repression, poverty and conflict within newly independent states, prospects for the causes of flight to diminish in the short term were not favourable. As today, refugee movements were largely confined to the 'third world'. The only substantial numbers to reach the West were certain groups of Latin American and Indo-Chinese refugees resettled from countries of first asylum.

During the 1980s, the problem changed slightly as growing numbers of asylum-seekers began to flee direct to the West from their countries and regions of origin, owing, perhaps, in part to improvements in air transport services (although it is likely that the dynamics behind this development were/ are extremely complex, comprising, for example, the role of information networks and prior 'economic' migration patterns). 'Spontaneous' arrivals of asylum-seekers in Western Europe had, in fact, been rising steadily since the early 1970s, but it was not until the mid-1980s that numbers began escalating substantially. According to UNHCR data, the numbers increased from around 70,500 in 1983 to 290,650 in 1988.[43] The problem of definition compounded that of sheer numbers, as observed in 1986 by the Independent Commission on International Humanitarian Issues (ICIHI):

Attitudes towards the new influx of asylum-seekers and refugees
might have been more positive if it had been possible to distinguish
them clearly from other immigrant groups. In practice, this has proved
a difficult administrative problem ... Governments now classify
asylum-seekers as 'de facto refugees', 'political or economic immigrants', 'externally displaced persons', 'mandate refugees', 'shuttle
refugees' and 'refugees in orbit'. Even those who have been granted
asylum might find themselves labelled as refugees with 'A' or 'B'
status, with 'tolerance status', or with 'exceptional leave to remain'.
This confusing list of terms derives partly from the inadequacy of the
1951 Convention and 1967 Protocol ... Many of the asylum-seekers
arriving in the developed world left their own country because life had
become intolerably dangerous and insecure. But they cannot prove ...
that they have a well-founded fear of persecution there.[44]

Most of those arriving in Western Europe during the late 1980s came from
countries such as Turkey, Sri Lanka, Somalia, Iran, Ethiopia and Lebanon.[45]
These are not necessarily the poorest countries of the world, but all are
associated with civil conflict and/or poor protection of human rights (although in the case of the Federal Republic of Germany, which had particularly liberal asylum procedures and policies, this pattern was becoming less
clear-cut by the mid- to late 1980s). Many arriving from these states have
been in need of protection despite an inability to demonstrate a well-founded
and/or personalized fear of persecution. In most cases, some form of
protection has been forthcoming, as reflected in the high frequency of
applicants being granted some other kind of humanitarian status such as 'de
facto refugee' or 'refugee B' status (e.g. 94% of applicants in Norway, 92%
in Sweden, 50% in Switzerland and 59% in the United Kingdom in 1991).[46]
Nevertheless, because the countries of origin are without exception economically poor in relation to the receiving countries of Western Europe, politicians
and immigration authorities have been able to justify restrictive measures by
arguing that the majority of the asylum-seekers are 'economic migrants' or
'bogus refugees' seeking a better standard of living in the West.[47]

It is important to note that the acceleration in numbers of arrivals of
asylum-seekers in Western Europe during the 1980s mirrored a worldwide
escalation in the number of refugees and displaced persons. Between 1985
and 1988, arrivals in Europe increased by 70%, or around 120,000.[48] This
is the same percentage change as that witnessed in global refugee populations
between 1985 and 1991 (an increase from approximately 10 million to 17

million).[49] But while reflecting a worldwide increase in refugee numbers, the acceleration in asylum applications in Western Europe during the second half of the 1980s represented less than 5% of the total rise in numbers of refugees worldwide. Rather than flooding to the richer countries of the 'North', over 90% of the world's 17 million refugees (and at least an equal number of 'internally displaced' persons) remain in the 'third world'.[50] Indeed, the highest concentrations of refugees in relation to population occur in some of the world's poorest countries. Thus, for example, in Malawi – a country with a per capita GNP of US$180 – refugees account for 10% of the national population; and in Guinea (per capita GNP of $430), refugees number one in every thirteen residents.[51] These figures may be compared to the situation in Western Europe, where some 1.3 million applications for asylum were lodged between 1983 and 1989.[52] If around 80% of these asylum-seekers have remained resident in their respective countries of asylum, they represent little more than 0.3% of the total population. In these countries, per capita GNP ranges between US$15,000 and US$30,000.[53]

However, as in the cases of illegal and labour migration, direct numerical comparisons between countries or regions may not be the most helpful. It is therefore justified to state that Western Europe is facing severe problems with its asylum systems even though the difficulties it faces are both quantitatively and qualitatively far removed from those experienced by countries such as Malawi. The most obvious basis for such a statement would be the new potential for massive refugee flows in Europe as signalled by the break-up of the former Soviet Union and recent developments in the former Yugoslavia. However, the problems are those relating not only to refugee flows *per se*, but also to the systems and procedures in place to deal with such flows.

First, there is a growing financial problem as a result of the escalation in costs associated with asylum. According to one estimate, the total cost of asylum procedures and refugee protection in the OECD receiving countries rose from under $1 billion in 1983 to $7 billion in 1990, the latter figure being equal to twelve times the total UN budget for refugee assistance worldwide, or one-seventh of total development assistance from the OECD states to the 'third world'.[54] Although this presents a huge financial burden for the Western receiving states,* it may in fact be less of a problem for them than for receiving countries in other regions, since none of this huge expenditure

---

*In point of fact, the costs in real terms may be substantially lower in view of the eventual economic contribution made by asylum-seekers if and when they enter the labour force. Most immigration can be found to be economically advantageous, even in conditions of high unemployment.

is channelled into assisting the far greater and rising number of refugees and displaced persons concentrated in much poorer countries of the world. To a large extent, this problem derives from the costly procedures that the receiving states go through in order to determine the strict classification of applicants according to which, for example, they may be granted so-called 'Convention status' (refugee status) or some less secure humanitarian status. These procedures have come in for criticism from the UNHCR and other concerned bodies on the grounds that such classification makes very little difference to the eventual outcome, i.e. whether asylum-seekers stay or leave: over 90% stay on in the country where their application was lodged, irrespective of the outcome of the screening process.

This issue links in with a second problem concerning basic procedures, for if displacement within and out of the former Yugoslav Republic represents only the first of a new series of mass involuntary displacements in Europe, asylum systems which rely on traditional refugee definitions and individual case-by-case decisions are likely to become increasingly redundant, as they have been for a long time in Africa and parts of Asia. The procedural problem is made more difficult by the high profile of the asylum issue in public debate in Western Europe. Whereas changing refugee problems call for flexibility in current and future responses to refugee flows in Europe, public anxiety will certainly limit policy-makers' room for manoeuvre, since concern for the plight of those forced to flee may be more than balanced by a deep and widespread concern to limit numbers of those arriving on the doorstep.[55] The recent outbreak in attacks on asylum-seekers in Germany, although largely attributable to conditions and developments unique to that country, none the less demonstrate the limits of tolerance discernible throughout Western Europe.

Second, a serious problem of a more humanitarian nature is emerging, for, as the numbers of arrivals of asylum-seekers rise, receiving states are more and more inclined (a) to introduce policies which have the effect of limiting asylum-seekers' initial access to asylum procedures; and (b) to refuse asylum to persons who may not be able to provide a convincing case of a well-founded fear of persecution, but who are none the less in need of protection. Restrictive measures include carrier sanctions, visa requirements for nationals of states generating refugees, and summary rejection of so-called 'manifestly unfounded' applications at the border. Such measures have come under harsh criticism from humanitarian organizations and other non-governmental interest groups on the grounds that they impinge on *bona fide* refugees as much as, or more than, other categories of asylum-seekers. As expressed by Jean-Pierre Hocké, former United Nations High Commissioner for Refugees, this crisis is also one of principles, with restrictive measures causing 'serious concern to those who believe in an international humanitarian order' as 'humanitarian principles are threatened and basic standards of refugee protection lowered in the West'.[56]

None the less, receiving states' responses to the recent Yugoslav refugee crisis, albeit hesitant, might signal an emerging flexibility towards European refugee flows in cases of desperate and immediate humanitarian crisis. However, even when the humanitarian need is considered crucial, the perceived economic, political and social costs of accepting large numbers of asylum-seekers and/or refugees are likely to mitigate against liberal responses. If it is believed that many of those entering a country through asylum channels are not, in fact, in need of protection, but are migrating voluntarily and on the basis of economic interest, the costs are likely to be seen as much higher, and the potential for the survival or implementation of liberal asylum policies will be much lower. This is now the case in Western Europe. Even in Germany – a country which, since the Second World War, has gone to great pains to uphold a liberal stance towards asylum-seekers and refugees – the political tide is sweeping against the liberal asylum policies of the past, as evidenced in growing pressure to amend the country's Basic Law and thereby do away with the right of asylum hitherto applied to all refugees in Germany. A recent publication issued by the German Minister of the Interior states that 'in the past few years, asylum was invoked not only by politically persecuted individuals, but to an increasing extent also by aliens who do not qualify for the status of a person entitled to asylum; they start an asylum procedure only for the purpose of staying in the Federal Republic of Germany and taking up gainful employment ... This development ... faces the Federation, the Länder and local governments with serious problems.'[57]

Given the subjective nature of refugee definition, it is difficult to state categorically that flows of asylum-seekers into Western Europe include a growing proportion of so-called 'economic migrants'. However, given the lack of alternative means of legal migration, it is almost certain that contemporary asylum inflows include migrants whose movement is essentially voluntary. This view is supported by the fact that, since 1989, a significant proportion of asylum flows into certain West European countries have consisted of flows from the former communist states of Eastern and Central Europe – countries which are, with the exception of the former

Yugoslavia, deemed to be 'safe' by receiving governments in the sense that all fundamental political and social rights are now seen to be protected in those countries.

It is therefore in this connection that asylum questions are linked in most directly with immigration questions more generally. The very same pressures quoted as underlying illegal migration flows — growing unemployment in countries of origin, steep income differentials between sending and receiving areas, and stricter immigration policies on the part of receiving states – are increasingly quoted as the underlying causes of rising levels of asylum applications in Western Europe. Indeed, perhaps because the mass irregular economic migration from Eastern to Western Europe which many predicted one or two years ago has not materialized, most attention as regards economic migration from the East has focused on the recent rise in asylum applications. If one looks at a breakdown of asylum figures for 1989 and 1990 (excluding applications from Yugoslavia), it seems apparent that most of the increase in overall numbers was accounted for by applications from the so-called 'safe' countries of Eastern/Central Europe (most notably Romania, Albania and Poland). Thus the overall number of applications in Western Europe increased from 349,000 in 1989 to 445,000 in 1990,[58] but at least 133,000 applicants in 1990 originated in Europe (excluding Yugoslavia), while applications from countries such as Turkey, Sri Lanka, and Ethiopia remained stable or fell.[59] Indeed, in the United Kingdom, a country in which asylum applications are dominated by those from Africa and other countries of the 'third world', asylum applications in 1992 seem to have fallen to less than half the number lodged in 1990.[60]

Excluding flows from the former Yugoslav states, however, asylum flows from Eastern and Central Europe do not seem to have reached crisis point in terms of overall numbers. Germany, perhaps, is the one state where one could talk of a crisis, and moves are now being made to declare a state of emergency in Germany so as to push through an amendment of the country's Basic Law and thus prepare the way for further restrictions in Germany's asylum policy. Germany is expected to receive up to 350,000 asylum-seekers in 1992, representing over half of all applications lodged in Western Europe in that year, and representing an increase of around 100,000 on the figure for the previous year. However, this increase is largely accounted for by applications from the former Yugoslavia, which, at least at present, must be treated as something of a special case. In 1989–90, Germany received almost 180,000 asylum-seekers from other European countries, but during the same period voluntarily admitted nearly one million 'ethnic Germans' from the former GDR (*Übersiedler*) and elsewhere in Eastern/ Central Europe (*Aussiedler*). Switzerland received a maximum of 8,000 European asylum-seekers during the same period, against a total inflow of nearly 60,000 asylum-seekers from other regions and net immigration of approximately 65,000 foreigners through other categories of immigration. Other countries in Western Europe, such as France and the United Kingdom, received negligible numbers of European asylum-seekers compared with those received from other areas of the world.

Nevertheless, asylum applications from nationals of European countries of origin can be said to have reached crisis point in the sense that a growing proportion of applications are deemed to be unfounded. If one accepts that most of the countries in Eastern and Central Europe that these asylum-seekers are attempting to leave are indeed 'safe', it follows that by putting additional strain on already over-burdened and fragile systems of refugee protection, these applications jeopardize protection for so-called '*bona fide*' refugees and other displaced persons who are in desperate need of assistance – both those who reach Western Europe, and those who remain in their region of origin. Moves are now being made throughout Western Europe to streamline asylum procedures so to reduce the cost and 'pull' of a system that, at present, may require a refugee, or allow an asylum-seeker with no good case, to wait up to two years for a decision on his or her status.

Issues such as asylum and illegal immigration have increasingly presented themselves as common problems for all West European countries, and, as a result, pressure has built up over recent years to harmonize certain aspects of immigration and refugee policies at the European level. However, while many immigration problems faced by states in Western Europe are problems shared throughout the region, there are, and indeed always have been, important differences among the positions of individual states. This is a point illustrated most clearly today by Germany's peculiarly heavy asylum burden, or by the illegal immigration problems of the South European states. It is a point that emerges in Chapters 4 and 6, which examine the development of migration policy in Western Europe over the past four decades, and, more explicitly, in Chapter 7, which considers in some detail the process of policy harmonization in Western Europe and questions the extent to which one can talk of common concerns and common aims among Europe's receiving states.

Chapter 3

From Babylon to Berlin: A Historical Overview

No society is static, and the history of Europe, like that of every continent, has been marked by significant migratory movements at every stage. Even after the close of the so-called 'great migration period' which followed the collapse of the Roman Empire, the ethnic map of Europe continued to be transformed by periodic conquests and migratory movements. As Eugene Kulischer observed, by AD 900, 'Europe had entered the "sedentary" era. Yet at that time, not one German was in Berlin, not one Russian in Moscow, not one Hungarian in Budapest ... Constantinople existed ... but the only Turks there were a few slaves and mercenaries.'[1]

Patterns of forced and voluntary migration of the contemporary era are in many respects mirrored in the migratory movements of the past. Forced expulsion as a means of conflict resolution can be traced back at least as far as Old Testament times, as illustrated in the biblical record of the Jews' Babylonian exile. Even during the period of absolutist monarchical rule in Europe, when movement of population was severely curtailed, periodic large-scale forced migrations took place that were not unlike those of the modern era. Although the particular dynamics of every migratory movement are complex and unique, in so far as migration is patterned by the interrelation of social, economic and political change and the efforts of rulers and governments to exercise control over populations, general processes of migration can be seen to have remained fundamentally similar over centuries of societal transformation in Europe. As expressed by the same writer, 'the modern age did not so much invent new forms of migration as alter drastically the means and conditions of the old forms'.[2]

The changes in the 'means and conditions' of migration that have taken place in Europe are inextricably bound up with the economic and political transformation of the state: the expansion of state control, shifts in the relationship between subject or citizen and the state, and changing relations between states. In so far as the freedom to move is determined by political structures controlling any given community or population, the particular pattern of migration that takes place at any one time cannot be understood without reference to the nature of a ruler's or government's control over the migratory process. Furthermore, conditions underlying an original desire to migrate can themselves be related back to the political structures in question and the political, economic and social relations that exist between sending and receiving areas. Migration patterns between states must therefore be related to developments within and among the states which condition the desire, freedom and means of individuals to migrate. In cases of forced migration it can be demonstrated that, although certain fundamental determinants of involuntary movement can be traced back to the time of Nebuchadnezzar,[3] the scale and scope of and responses to refugee movements have changed with the development of the state, the emergence of the 'nation-state', and the expansion of state control over populations.

The aim of this chapter is to trace the overall trends in international migration that have taken place in Europe since the emergence of sovereign and state in Europe after the thirteenth century. It is hoped that aspects of continuity and of change in international migration patterns can be identified, and that, in so doing, some light will be shed on current trends and responses to migration.

The mercantilist era: emigration control and forced expulsion

The expansion of monarchical power after the thirteenth century, the decline of the concept of a universal but non-territorial community of Christendom in Europe and the emergence of state sovereign control over distinct subject communities gave rise to the first strictly 'interstate' migrations in Europe.[4] With the expansion of monarchical power and the emergence of absolutist rule that took place in Europe during the fifteenth and sixteenth centuries came what Adam Smith termed the 'mercantilist' order.[5] As the sovereign gained control over the economy and foreign trade, there emerged ideas of state strategic and economic interests. Because a large population was considered an economic and military asset, rulers did all they could to prevent subjects from travelling abroad. Therefore, just as a large proportion of Europe's population had been tied to a particular landlord and locality under the preceding feudal system, so the new order bound the people to a particular monarch and his territory. As noted by Alan Dowty, 'mercantilism in the service of absolutism – the combination of national economic calculation with the habits of authoritarian rule – produced a strikingly modern system of emigration control.'[6] Unlike today, however, because population was considered a valuable resource the rulers generally welcomed immigration and showed little hostility to in-migration of peoples of diverse ethnic origins.

Although not greatly worried by the ethnic make-up of subject populations, the monarchs of this period were concerned with questions of integration, and sought to consolidate their power by promoting identification with their rule. Their power rested on religion, and so Christianity became the prime instrument of integration. These efforts to render populations more religiously homogeneous gave rise to large-scale migratory movements. Just as authoritarian regimes of the twentieth century have resorted to expulsions of minority groups in the interests of national consolidation, so thousands of non-Christians and 'heretics' were periodically expelled or forced to flee as a result of the totalitarian claims of the Christian rulers of this period. According to one estimate, over one million people were forced to move within Europe between 1492 and 1713.[7]

One of the first large-scale expulsions of this period was that of the Sephardic Jews from Spain in 1492. As noted by Kulischer, since the time of the First Crusade the 'persecution of Jews [had become] a permanent part of the social and political life of Christian Europe.'[8] Towards the end of the thirteenth century Jews had been expelled from England, and in the fourteenth century they suffered expulsions from France and periodic banishment from German feudal domains. Similarly, the efforts of the Spanish monarchy during the fifteenth century to convert the Spanish Jewish population to Catholicism proved largely unsuccessful. The powerful position of the Jewish community in the Spanish economy was considered a threat to the crown and, following the implementation of a series of anti-Jewish measures, a decree was issued in 1492 ordering the Jews to convert or leave. Of the some quarter of a million Jews who had been practising their religion openly in Spain, about 200,000 fled. The largest group settled in the Ottoman Empire,[9] others eventually found refuge in the Netherlands and England.[10] This served as a precedent for the expulsion of the Moorish Muslim community from the Iberian Peninsula in 1609 after the failure of Philip II to enforce cultural and linguistic assimilation. Most fled to North Africa.

It was not only non-Christians who fled or suffered expulsions during this period. Towards the end of the sixteenth century, for example, Philip II forced roughly 175,000 Protestants out of the Spanish Lowlands.[11] Most of these subsequently settled in the northern provinces of the Netherlands when the regions gained independence in 1609. At least 200,000 Huguenots fled France after 1685 when Louis XIV revoked the Edict of Nantes which had granted Protestants freedom of worship since 1598.[12] The English use of the term 'refugee' was first used to denote this group. Migration movements also resulted from religious conflicts in England and Germany. Periodic flights of Catholics and Protestants from the German states continued until 1555 when the Peace of Augsburg instituted the general right of the sovereign to decide the faith of his subjects. Significant movement between German states followed as people sought freedom to practise their religion. Oliver Cromwell's campaign against the Irish Catholics in the mid-seventeenth century caused many to flee to France and Spain, while others, resisting deportation to Western Ireland, were sent as indentured plantation labour to Barbados.[13] State campaigns against religious and political dissent also gave rise to refugee movements from the Habsburg lands, such as the flight of about 150,000 Protestants from Bohemia after the Catholic counter-reformation issued a total ban on Protestantism.[14]

It was during this period that the New World began to be opened up. From the fifteenth up to the eighteenth century, over two million Europeans left to settle in the Americas.[15] Yet a much larger migration process was also taking place at that time which linked the two continents. As Kingsley Davis noted, 'for the first time, the world began to be one migratory network dominated by a single group of technologically advanced and culturally similar states'.[16] Davis was referring to the forced movement of up to ten million slaves from West Africa to Europe and the New World which started at the beginning of the sixteenth century with Spain sending slaves to Haiti, Cuba and Jamaica, and which expanded into a worldwide trading network during the seventeenth and eighteenth centuries.[17] The slave trade must be understood in the context of developments in the more advanced European economies of the time. During the early period of colonization, new territories were seen to have immense potential value, to be exploited for luxuries and precious metals, and subsequently for the production of crops (particularly those areas which could be accessed relatively easily: the Caribbean, the Gulf of Mexico, and the coasts of North and South America). Manpower was needed for crop production, and, since a concern to maintain European population levels still prevailed, labour was sought elsewhere. Because the demand for labour in the colonies exceeded that within Europe, most of the slaves were sent to the New World.

Slave imports were prohibited by Britain, the USA and Denmark during the first decade of the nineteenth century, and slavery abolished altogether in the British Empire in 1833. The demand for plantation labour did not disappear with the changes in the law, however. Plantation owners in the Caribbean and the Indian Ocean found a substitute supply in the form of indentured labour drawn largely from landless Asian populations, particularly from India, Southern China and Java. This system was later extended to supply plantations in Southern and Eastern Africa and Southeast Asia, and continued until the beginning of this century. Kingsley Davis has estimated that as many as 16.8 million Indians left under this system, of whom about 4.4 million never returned.[18] The Atlantic slave trade and the subsequent 'coolie' migration together constituted one of the largest involuntary migratory movements to have taken place in history.

The 'new migration epoch'

Towards the end of the seventeenth century the basis of the monarchs' power came under threat from theorists such as John Locke espousing ideas of the natural rights and the social contract. These thoughts were later expanded by the Enlightenment thinkers, who stressed individual liberty and restraint of state power. These ideas found expression in the French Revolution and 1791 French Constitution, which stipulated the 'freedom of everyone to go, to stay, or to leave, without being halted or arrested unless in accordance with procedures established by the Constitution'.[19] The development of individual social and political freedom at this time was inextricably linked to developments in the economic sphere. The advent of a market economy in Europe was reflected in the emergence of the liberal *laissez-faire* economic thinking of theorists such as Adam Smith, which stressed the importance of individual economic action and the withdrawal of state control over production and consumption.[20] Human mobility was argued to be essential for the proper functioning of the market, as expressed in Frank Knight's typification of the market economy when he asserted that there be 'no exercise of constraint over any individual by another individual or "society"; each controls his own activities with a view to results that accrue to him individually ... [There must be] complete absence of physical obstacles to the making, execution, and changing of plans at will; that is, there must be "perfect mobility".'[21]

Contemporaneous with the rise of market capitalism was the emergence of industrial forms of production, and, in the words of the economic historian Karl Polanyi,

> The more complicated industrial production became, the more numerous were the elements of industry the supply of which had to be safeguarded. Three of these, of course, were of outstanding importance: *labour*, land and money ... they would have to be organized for sale on the market – in other words, as commodities. The extension of the market mechanism to the elements of industry ... was the inevitable consequence of the introduction of the factory system in a commercial society.[22]

This social, economic and political transformation of European society was accompanied by a steady rise in population growth, and for the first time governments began to be concerned about the danger of overpopulation. Malthus published his famous treatise on population growth in 1798[23] which drew attention to the high birth-rate of the time and saw widespread famine as inevitable if nothing could be done to reduce the rate of population growth. Although not initially, Malthus subsequently came to support emigration as a mechanism which might alleviate population pressures in certain areas. More explicit support for emigration came from Adam Smith, who criticized mercantilist (exploitative) colonial policy, and argued that the New World economies would be more valuable to Europe if encouraged to develop into equal trading partners.[24] The following decade witnessed mounting demographic, social, political and economic pressures for the increased movement of individuals within and across state borders.

Aristide Zolberg points to the 'demographic, industrial and democratic revolutions', which took place from the second half of the eighteenth century into the first few decades of the nineteenth century, as heralding a transition to a 'new migration epoch' characterized by a shift from emigration control to a positive encouragement of emigration.[25] Over the eight years preceding Malthus's publication, over 700,000 British citizens had emigrated to North America.[26] By the late 1820s, legal controls hindering exit had been removed from most countries in Europe, and, with a waning in refugee movements, voluntary migration to the New World began to dominate European transnational migrations. For European governments, the benefits of emigration in terms of defusing social tensions that resulted from population increase and from religious conflict played a significant part in this shift in policy. Within ten years of passing an act designed to curb emigration,[27] the British government was supporting emigration to the British colonies. Inspired both by concern over increasing pauperism in England and by a desire to direct flows of emigrants to British possessions overseas rather than to America, the British government conducted a series of experiments in state-supported emigration between 1815 and 1826 designed to encourage members of the Irish and other poor communities to leave.[28] In 1827 Britain established an immigration service in Canada.[29] In fact, these experiments had limited success when compared with the rising levels of independent voluntary migration to the United States. France, which was undergoing only a slow process of industrialization, was to prove an exception through continued concern over population deficit, and was thus the only state in Northwest Europe to maintain restrictions on exit throughout the nineteenth century. By the mid-nineteenth century, France was second only to the USA as a country of immigration.[30]

The migration dynamic at this time seems to have been provided largely by the 'push' factor of population growth and by sectoral social and economic dislocation caused by the industrial revolution in Northwest Europe. As noted by Frank Thistlethwaite, 'nineteenth century migration may have been powerfully attracted to the New World but acquired momentum within Europe itself ... waves of migration surging across the Americas were formed by impulses which were local'.[31] Nevertheless, the migration dynamic must be seen as a complex two-way process – a process intimately bound to the dynamics of the so-called 'Atlantic Economy'. The basis of this economy was the exploitation of the grasslands of North America by means of European capital and labour, described by Thistlethwaite as 'not merely a condition of international trade, but one in which there was such freedom of movement for the factors of production, that we can hardly distinguish the two principal countries concerned ... as two separate, closed economies ... emigrants were essential to its operation.'[32]

The subsequent development of the American economy into a trading partner not only created opportunities for European migrants, but also opened up lines of communication which increased the ability and willingness of potential emigrants to make the journey. By 1915 about 52 million Europeans had emigrated, roughly 34 million of whom left for the United States.[33] The numbers who left during this period equalled approximately one-fifth of the total population of emigration countries at the beginning of the nineteenth century.[34] However, the emigration flow did little to stem population growth in Europe. With an overall population increase in Europe from 194 million in 1840 to 463 million in 1930,[35] the only European country that suffered depopulation as a result of migration was Ireland. Ireland experienced extremely high levels of emigration over the years following the Great Famine. Between 1847 and 1854 over 1.6 million people migrated overseas.[36]

As the migration flow out of Europe continued through the nineteenth century, an increasing proportion of those leaving came from the less-developed areas of Southern and Eastern Europe. This marked the beginnings of a new pattern in international migration flows. Whereas transcontinental flows had previously been characterized by movement from the more developed areas of Europe to the underdeveloped regions of the New World and colonies, the new pattern that was emerging was one dominated by movements out of less-developed areas.[37] This was a pattern which had shaped movements within European states in the form of rural-to-urban migration since the beginnings of industrial development, and towards the end of the nineteenth century had started to characterize migration flows within the United States itself. It is also, of course, the pattern which dominates migration throughout the world today. Thistlethwaite wrote that 'the new immigration can be thought of as rural-to-urban migration which happened to be transoceanic rather than local in character'.[38]

This shift can be explained in part by the fact that as the countries of Northwestern Europe developed further, birth rates fell, social welfare was improved, and the pressure to emigrate declined. Meanwhile, uneven development in the more 'peripheral' European states was beginning to result in the same kinds of pressures that had initially spurred emigration from the 'core' countries of Northwest Europe. In the industrializing regions of the New World, '"areas of concentration" replaced the "great open spaces" as magnets of migration'.[39] Greater numbers of migrants returned home than had previously done so, and in this respect transoceanic migration increasingly resembled the pattern of temporary international labour migration which was becoming a dominant pattern of intra-European migration. As with international migration in the twentieth century, improved transoceanic lines of communication and lower transport costs reinforced this trend.

Towards the end of the nineteenth century, migratory movements within Europe began to exceed the flow to the Americas. During the last two decades before the turn of the century, Germany, England, Scandinavia, France and Switzerland were experiencing net inflows of population as the 'push' factors driving emigration began to decline. With a shift towards heavy industry, the most advanced European economies turned increasingly to foreign labour to satisfy manpower needs which could not be met by the immediate internal labour pool. By 1880 Germany had passed its emigration peak and was attracting workers from Poland. France, which had been experiencing net inflows of population by the mid-nineteenth century, began actively recruiting foreign labour. By 1911 the number of foreign workers in France had reached over one million (Italian, Belgian, Spanish and Polish).[40] Britain continued to depend on Irish labour which, already by the mid-nineteenth century, made up roughly one-quarter of the urban industrial population of England and Scotland.[41] Generally these migrants came from a rural background and filled unskilled positions at the lower end of the labour spectrum. Their work was usually considered temporary, to be taken up or disposed of as dictated by demand. The seasonal nature of much of this migration was made possible by the relatively short distances to be travelled. Nevertheless, just as with later international labour migrations, many workers settled.

From free movement to immigration control and involuntary migration
Alan Dowty writes of the late nineteenth/early twentieth century as the 'closest approximation to an open world in modern times'. Yet at the same as the world had been opening up to free movement in and out of states, the nature of the state in Europe had been changing as it expanded to take on roles affecting all levels of social, economic and political life. With this transformation emerged a deepening national consciousness – nationalism with the concomitant appeal for 'one nation, one state'. Just as the mercantilist rulers of the Middle Ages were troubled by questions of religious integration, so European societies of the late nineteenth and twentieth centuries became increasingly concerned with the problem of integration based on national/ ethnic identity. As noted by Ernest Gellner: 'Industrial society presupposes a mobile population with a shared literate culture ... The state supervises the transmission of that culture ... It is hostile to deep ... culturally marked chasms between its own sub-groups'.[42] While a new relationship was emerging between citizen and state through developments such as the introduction of state education and widening political representation, technological-industrial advances were rendering the centralizing and growing state apparatus increasingly equipped for internal control and external intervention.

Although the nineteenth century had witnessed numerous refugee movements (for example, those resulting from the suppression of the Italian uprisings in 1820–21 and 1833, and the counter-revolutionary upheavals of 1848), Michael Marrus argues that a high proportion of those who sought asylum abroad during this period in many ways resembled exiles rather than refugees. The numbers involved were relatively small and, since most were wealthy enough to travel, most had the means to support themselves until they felt they could return home. According to Marrus, 'so long as the refugees remained few in number and so long as they seemed relatively innocuous guests in the ... countries that were willing to accept them, nothing changed'.[43] Few had any trouble finding refuge. The largest numbers who remained in Europe went to Switzerland or London, which for a time was known as the 'great exile centre of Europe'.

The completion of Italy's unification in 1861 and the proclamation of a German Empire in 1870 contributed to the growth in nationalist sentiment in nineteenth-century Europe. Yet the ideal of the nation-state could never be easily realized, and the presence of minority populations posed a substantial challenge to the integrity of many of Europe's new-style nation-states. Efforts to consolidate new nation-states and conflicts over the internal social and political order of both new and old states began to emerge as the dominant refugee-generating processes in Europe – forces which are as strong today as they were a century ago. Furthermore, the forces giving rise to the flight of many refugees began working to reduce asylum-seekers' chances of finding a safe haven. As expressed by Hannah Arendt, 'Those whom the persecutor had singled out as scum of the earth – Jews, Trotskyites, etc. – actually were received as scum of the earth everywhere; those whom persecution had called undesirable became the "indésirables" of Europe',[44] a statement which, it is worth noting, could describe equally well the situation of many refugees in Europe today.

The nature of refugee movements in Europe began to change with the wars of German unification (1864–71). The nationalist nature of these wars created movement of groups in and out of areas under Bismarckian rule, including 80,000 Germans who were forced to leave France in 1870 and the flight of large numbers of Poles out of the German Reich.[45] These movements were followed two decades later by a much larger refugee flow as Jews began fleeing a series of pogroms in Russia, Austrian Poland, Romania, the Baltics and the Ukraine. Many fled a combination of political discrimination, economic hardship and social disorder, adding to the more generalized emigration out of Eastern and Central Europe, which was being driven by depressed agricultural conditions and overpopulation. The majority travelled to the USA, making use of improved and cheaper transatlantic transport communications. Between 1881 and 1914 over 2.25 million Jews emigrated to the United States[46] and roughly 120,000 settled in Britain.[47]

Liberal immigration policies began to come under question in the receiving countries. The United States was already facing problems in its efforts to return so-called 'coolie' labour migrants to China.[48] The mounting numbers of arrivals from outside Northwest Europe and the influx of Jewish refugees accelerated moves towards immigration control. Although strong pro-immigrationist sentiment persisted within certain sectors of the industrial and business community, the US economy had by this time developed to the point where its dependence on European capital and labour was declining and the state could begin exercising a degree of selective control over who should be allowed to settle. In 1892, a judgment in a US court included the statement that 'It is an accepted maxim of international law, that every sovereign nation has the power, as inherent in sovereignty, and essential to its self-preservation, to forbid the entrance of foreigners within its dominions, or to admit them only in such cases and upon such conditions as it may see fit to prescribe.'[49]

In 1896, the US Congress approved a bill imposing a literacy requirement on immigrants in an attempt to reduce entry of foreigners from less-developed parts of Europe and the Far East. This was followed in 1903 with the passing of an Immigration Law which included provisions for head taxes on immigrants and listed certain categories of prohibited immigrants.[50] A Congress report of 1911 recommended the prohibition of immigration from much of Asia.[51] Similar provisions were introduced in Canada and Australia.[52]

While most Jewish refugees continued to leave Europe for America, European asylum countries could afford to maintain relatively liberal immigration policies. At an international conference held in 1898, Britain, Belgium and Switzerland stated their commitment to existing liberal asylum and immigration policies.[53] However, by the end of the nineteenth century anti-Semitism was widespread in Europe, and with the closing of the American safety-valve it was not long before demands for more restrictive policies began to be heard in these countries. In Britain, growing concern over the numbers of Jewish arrivals generated support for the 1905 Aliens Act designed to limit entry of unwanted immigrants.[54] The shift towards stricter immigration controls in Europe was hastened by the outbreak of war in 1914, as marked by the widespread imposition of passport controls during the first year of conflict. By 1919, systematic immigration regulations and alien control measures were the norm and the 'open world' of the nineteenth century had come to an end.

From the Balkan wars to the Second World War: a new refugee era
A series of new refugee crises emerged with the political upheavals of the first two decades of the twentieth century and the eruption of regional and international conflicts in Europe. As observed by Zolberg et al., refugee flows of the early twentieth century were caused principally by multi-ethnic states 'adopting a mononational formula', which entailed 'some form of exclusion, either extreme segregation or expulsion' of 'unwanted' minorities. Interactions among a number of states 'striving to achieve this monistic objective' tended 'to invite mutual hostility and endless attempts at unmixing nationalities'.[55] With the decline of Ottoman control in the Balkans during the decades preceding the First World War, there arose an increase in nationalist activity and a series of refugee movements dominated by flows of Muslims to the South and Christians to the North. The first large-scale movements took place during the Balkan wars of 1912–13 and included the exodus of some 177,000 Muslims into Turkey and about 70,000 Greeks out of Western Thrace.[56] Struggling to introduce an element of control into the inflow of refugees, Bulgaria reached a population exchange agreement with Turkey in 1913,[57] which resulted in the transfer of roughly 50,000 people from each side. This agreement served as a precedent for much larger population exchanges which took place between Greece and Bulgaria and Greece and Turkey in the mid-1920s. The exchange negotiated between Greece and the new Turkish Republic at the Lausanne Convention of 1923[58] provided for 'a compulsory exchange of Turkish nationals of the Greek orthodox religion in Turkish territory and of Greek nationals of the Muslim religion established in Greek territory',[59] and resulted in the forced transfer of roughly 1.5 million people.[60] Large as these population movements were, they were generally confined to the Balkan region and involved a 'readjustment' of the ethnic map of the area to suit the new nation-states. Unlike today, refugee flows in the Balkans had little effect on the rest of Europe.

A new kind of refugee challenge was soon to appear on the European continent posed by what Hannah Arendt described as 'the most symptomatic group in contemporary politics':[61] refugees for whom no state was willing to accept responsibility. The flight of Russian refugees from persecution, famine, or the upheavals of revolution and civil war in the Soviet Union created one of the first groups of 'stateless' people. Although the main thrust of refugee flows took place within what was or had been tsarist territory, many managed to escape abroad. By 1922 at least three-quarters of a million Russians (including large numbers of Jews) had fled the Soviet Union.[62] While the Soviet government was stripping émigrés of their citizenship, the USA and the European receiving states demonstrated increasing reluctance to extend protection to Russian refugees. In 1921 the International Red Cross Committee appealed to the Council of the League of Nations to take action. Later that year the High Commission on Behalf of the League in Connection with the Problem of Russian Refugees in Europe was established,[63] its main function being to deal with questions of legal status, including (subsequently) the provision of travel documents for denaturalized refugees who had no means of identification. In the mid-1920s, the Soviet Union adopted a no-exit policy which, in the words of one writer, 'immobilized what was at that time probably the largest pool of potential emigrants in the world'.[64]

The Russian emigration was only the first of a series of refugee problems that arose in Europe over the following two decades to which the League of Nations was called upon to respond. The post-First World War peace settlements were intended to satisfy European national aspirations as far as possible, yet with the dissolution of three multinational empires, it was inevitable that groups would emerge who could not assume the nationality of a successor state.[65] In the early 1920s the League Council was requested to extend its services to help the million or so Armenian,[66] Assyrian, Assyro-Chaldean and Kurdish refugees who were fleeing persecution or had been expelled from the newly independent Turkish Republic. According to Zolberg et al., there were as many as 9.5 million refugees in Europe in 1926.[67]

At a time when the grip of nationalist and protectionist sentiments was strengthening throughout Europe and all states were attempting to reduce flows of immigrants, the League proved relatively impotent in its efforts to ensure protection for these refugees. As with its previous efforts to assist Russian refugees, its success was limited to legal rather than humanitarian assistance. The US immigration report of 1911,[68] which had expressed alarm over the 'alien invasion', laid the foundation for a restrictive US national origins quota system, which was first enacted as a temporary measure in 1921 and was made permanent in 1924.[69] The numbers of Europeans to be admitted by the United States was severely curtailed, especially in respect of those from Southern and Eastern Europe. By the 1930s nearly every country of Northwest Europe had followed suit with the introduction of discriminatory immigration policies designed to keep out all but a few self-supporting immigrants.[70]

The problems facing the League in its efforts to encourage protection of refugees became all the more apparent during the Great Depression, when Europe faced the new refugee crisis of thousands of 'non-Aryans' fleeing systematic harassment and persecution in Nazi Germany. By the end of 1937 roughly 165,000 German Jews had emigrated.[71] The conditions of economic depression that prevailed throughout Europe at the time made governments increasingly nervous about the possibility of mass refugee influxes. The League of Nations proved reluctant to lean too heavily on Germany or on receiving states at that time, and sought a compromise in the establishment of the High Commission for Refugees Coming from Germany, which was to work independently of the League in the coordination of relief operations in member states. At an intergovernmental conference held at Evian in 1938, all participants – fearful of a massive Jewish emigration from Poland, Hungary and Romania[72] – stated that they could not accept any additional refugees. Even France, despite not yet having to face large numbers of refugees from the Spanish civil war, was reported as being 'saturated with refugees'.[73] The same year saw the German annexation of Austria, the absorption of Sudetenland (increasing the numbers of Jews and gypsies resident within areas under the control of the German Reich) and the November 'Kristallnacht' (a night remembered for the destruction of synagogues and widespread violence against Jews). The number of refugees displaced by the German Reich doubled between the beginning of 1938 and the middle of 1939.[74] By this time, the United Kingdom had fixed quotas on the numbers of Jews allowed to settle in Palestine, and the outbreak of war in September 1939 reinforced the general reluctance to receive refugees from Germany. Hitler had originally favoured mass emigration as a means of ridding Germany of its unwanted minority populations, but as receiving countries tightened up their immigration controls the effectiveness of this solution came into question. The Nazi policy of encouraging emigration was eventually super-seded by a policy of institutionalized genocide.

Millions of people were displaced during the war itself, including 100,000 French Alsatians forcibly moved from Alsace-Lorraine to areas under Vichy control following the German invasion of France,[75] and forced transfers of people to labour and concentration camps from other areas falling under German occupation. The Soviet occupation of Eastern Poland in the winter of 1939/40 led to one of a series of collective deportations and population transfers carried out by Stalin as roughly 1.5 million Poles and Jewish refugees were sent to the Soviet interior.[76] This was followed in 1940 with the forced movement of up to 0.5 million Finns,[77] and in 1941/2 with the deportation of about 61,000 Latvians, Lithuanians and Estonians into Soviet Asia and Siberia after the 1941 invasion of the Baltic states,[78] and the movement of over 0.5 million Volga Germans. Huge numbers of civilians were forced to move throughout Europe as they were evacuated or fled areas suffering aerial bombardment. The advance of German forces into France generated one of the greatest upheavals of the war as up to a quarter of the entire French population moved South.[79] One estimate puts the number of people forced to move within Europe during the war at roughly 30 million.[80]

At the end of the war there were approximately 14 million 'displaced persons' who would need to be repatriated or resettled.[81] The aim of the Western Allies was to repatriate as many as possible as quickly as possible – a task to be carried out primarily by the military institutions. Soon after the war had ended, nearly a quarter of the population of the former German Reich was made up of refugees. In 1946 the International Refugee Organization (IRO) was established by the United Nations in response to the problem of the 'last million' refugees who could not be repatriated.[82] The establishment of the IRO marked the beginning of a recognition among governments that the refugee problem was not one that would disappear with the end of the war. In 1949 the United Nations General Assembly adopted a resolution to create the office of the United Nations High Commissioner for Refugees, which was to have a wider mandate than the IRO and, although initially set up with a life-span of only three years, was to become a more permanent fixture. The UNHCR statute was adopted a year later and included a universal definition of the refugee* and the obligation for the UNHCR to seek 'permanent solutions' to refugee problems. In 1951 the United Nations adopted the Convention Relating to the Status of Refugees, which bound signatory states to minimum standards of protection for refugees, including the undertaking not to return refugees to a country where they might suffer persecution. The Convention limited application of the refugee definition to those who acquired such status 'as a result of events occurring before 1 January 1951', and included the optional geographical limitation permitting states to limit their obligations to refugees resulting from events occurring in Europe prior to the critical date.[83] These temporal and geographical restrictions reflected a recognition that new refugee crises were likely to occur in the future and that

---

*A person who is outside his or her country of origin and unable or unwilling to avail him/herself of its protection owing to a well-founded fear of being persecuted on the grounds of his or her race, religion, nationality or political opinion.

these might not be confined to Europe,[84] and constituted an attempt by party states to limit their obligations vis-à-vis future refugees.[85]

Immediately following the war, over 14 million Germans were expelled from Eastern Europe in accordance with a protocol agreed to at Potsdam in 1945. Article 13 of the protocol stated that: 'The Three Governments ... recognise that the transfer to Germany of German populations, or elements thereof, will have to be undertaken'[86] – a resolution introduced partly in response to the expulsions already being carried out by Poland, Czechoslovakia, Romania, Yugoslavia and Bulgaria. As a result of these expulsions, only about 2.5 million ethnic Germans remained in Eastern Europe outside Germany and the Soviet Union. In the same year, an agreement reached at Yalta sanctioned the forced repatriation of Soviet prisoners of war by Britain and the United States. Over 2 million were sent back before the operation was halted as a result of concern within the British Foreign Office over the fate of returnees.[87]

These postwar repatriations did not mark the end of large-scale population movements within Europe; the emerging cold war and the division of Europe started to produce new waves of refugees. Shortly after the war, up to one million Poles and roughly 400,000 Finns fled areas annexed by the Soviet Union, and between 1949 and 1952 over 170,000 ethnic Turks were forced out of Bulgaria. In 1956 at least 200,000 Hungarians fled after the crushing of the Budapest revolution, and in 1968 about the same number of people left Czechoslovakia following the Soviet invasion. The largest flow out of the Eastern bloc during the 1950s was created by the exodus of some 3.5 million Germans from areas under Soviet control into West Germany. This flow represented about 20% of the East German population and began to bring about a serious labour shortage. It was, as Alan Dowty noted, 'easier, and more natural, for [the citizens of Eastern Europe] ... to contemplate crossing a border in response to economic or political pressures, especially in East Germany, bordered as it [was] ... by a state of the same culture and language ... The threat of manpower loss was therefore quite real, and it came at a time when these regimes could least afford it.'[88]

During the 1950s, the communist regimes of Eastern and Central Europe began to implement the kind of emigration controls which had been in place in the Soviet Union since the 1920s. Emigration not only threatened the labour markets of these states, but also constituted a challenge to the ideological foundations of the new regimes. Emigration came to be seen in several countries as a crime against the state. By introducing measures such as restrictions in the issue of passports and access to foreign currency, exit was made virtually impossible for all but a small minority of the population. Through instituting policies promoting population growth and curtailment of emigration, the communist regimes of Eastern and Central Europe began to resemble those of classical mercantilism.

The East German authorities failed to control the numbers of people leaving, and on 13 August 1961 resorted to sealing the border between East and West Berlin with a barrier that was to become the Berlin Wall. Emigration from the GDR was cut down significantly as a result.* In general, the Eastern bloc countries succeeded in reducing emigration to a trickle of refugees during the 1960s and 1970s.† Just as the economic or strategic value of refugees in the fifteenth century facilitated their reception in countries of refuge, so the political value of refugees from communism ensured a welcome in the West in the cold-war conditions that followed the Second World War. Most were accepted without question and granted what may be termed 'presumptive refugee status', made easier by the limited numbers involved and the fact that 'ancient cultural and ethnic affinities between populations of receiving countries and European refugees made their reception and integration relatively smooth'.[89] In the United States a series of acts were passed after the war which resulted in an American conception of refugees virtually tied to refugees from communism.[90] The USA admitted a total of about 400,000 European refugees over the three decades following the war.

Just as the absolutist monarchs attempted forced assimilation of certain religious minorities or practised periodic expulsions of groups deemed unassimilable, so communist governments of twentieth-century Europe demonstrated a concern to integrate populations at least on ideological grounds and at times allowed the emigration of sizeable numbers of members of certain minority groups, particularly those with a 'homeland' or strong ties elsewhere. For example, in 1970 Poland, having sought the voluntary emigration of ethnic Germans since the expulsions that followed the Second World War, reached an agreement with the Federal Republic of Germany designed to expedite the emigration of the remaining German population. Three years before this, Poland had tried to rid itself of the Jewish community that had remained within its borders since the war. Approximately 25,000 out of a population of 30,000 emigrated, most to Israel and the United States. The most significant emigration from Bulgaria was that of ethnic Turks fleeing

---

*Of the some 840,000 East German migrants lost to the West after 1961, about a quarter left in 1989.
†Except Yugoslavia, which exported labour to Western Europe throughout this period.

Bulgarian policies of forced assimilation. Although the Soviet Union had adhered to strict policies preventing emigration since the 1920s, it did allow the emigration of members of certain minority groups which, because of their strong links with the United States or Germany, were conspicuous in terms of East/West relations: the Russian Jews, ethnic Germans and Armenians.

It was not only refugees that moved overseas following the Second World War; there was a general increase in voluntary transcontinental migration from Western Europe to North America and white-controlled Common-wealth countries. Although the USA reaffirmed quantitive immigration limitations and reduced ethnic selection criteria with the 1952 Walter-McCarren Act, in practice a more liberal attitude to European immigration developed during the 1950s and 1960s. When European immigration re-sumed, it continually exceeded annual quota figures by four times or more (particularly in the case of emigration from South European states). This migration was motivated largely by the initially slow postwar recovery of the West European economies or (in the cases of Ireland, Portugal, Italy and Greece) relative underdevelopment. As postwar reconstruction took off in Europe, however, the pressures to emigrate from Northwestern countries began to wane, declining rapidly during the 1960s. Nevertheless, many continued to migrate to Australia, which was gradually reducing immigration restrictions for all European groups and providing financial assistance for large numbers of Northwest Europeans wishing to migrate.

The dominant pattern of migration which was to emerge after the Second World War linking Western Europe with other continents of the world, was, however, that of migration into, rather than out of, Northwestern Europe. Economic recovery not only reduced the pressure to emigrate, but brought with it a new demand for labour which could not be satisfied by the indigenous labour force, or, in many cases, by the labour forces of contiguous states. The postwar years signalled a new era of labour migration for Western Europe which was to have a fundamental social and political impact on European societies of a sort that was hardly recognized at the time, and which, indeed, is still poorly understood today.

Chapter 4

Immigration Policy in Postwar Europe

The implementation of the postwar Marshall Plan for Europe was followed by rapid economic recovery and over two decades of sustained economic growth in all the most industrialized states of Northwestern Europe. This paved the way for a transformation in the structure of interregional and international migration patterns as these states progressively extended the scope of their labour markets to fuel economic reconstruction and development. The pattern of international labour migration that arose in Europe during the 1950s and 1960s can be seen in some respects as a revival and expansion of pre-First World War labour migration patterns. Yet whereas European labour migration flows of the late-nineteenth and twentieth centuries were largely restricted to localized regions and to movements between neighbouring countries, those of the postwar era took place within increasingly broader zones – from contiguous labour pools on to more distant countries, such as those bordering the Mediterranean and the former colonies.[1]

By the early 1960s all the highly industrialized countries of Northwestern Europe were experiencing sectoral labour shortages and had become labour importers. Although the form, dynamics and rationale of in-migration differed from one receiving country to the next, certain common trends can be identified over the four and a half decades following the war. This period can be roughly divided into three phases according to the general thrust of immigration policies predominating at the time: (1) 1945 to 1973, policies facilitating or encouraging large-scale labour immigration; (2) 1973 into the 1980s, introduction of policies designed to halt all further labour immigration; (3) 1980s and 1990s, strengthening of restrictive immigration policies and increasing preoccupation with illegal immigration and asylum-seekers.

The past decade has also witnessed new efforts to achieve a degree of harmonization in West European immigration policies, as discussed in Chapter 7. Although much of the ensuing discussion is relevant to the majority of Europe's traditional receiving states, reference to national policies is restricted to the three European countries with the greatest number of immigrants in the 1960s and 1970s, comparisons between which illustrate both common trends and points of divergence: France, the Federal Republic of Germany and the United Kingdom.[2]

Open doors? 1945–73   *économie necessarily*

Although the underlying factors generating high levels of immigration were on the whole similar for all Europe's receiving states during the period 1945–73, it was perhaps at this time that the particular policies pursued by each country manifested the greatest diversity. What states shared in common was a demand for manpower, initially connected with the drive for economic recovery in the years immediately following the war, and subsequently linked to sectoral labour shortages caused by rapid economic growth. As the economies of Northwest Europe revived and expanded, employers in certain sectors of heavy industry, in the new and growing service sectors, and – in the cases of France and West Germany – in agriculture, found it increasingly difficult to attract indigenous labour. Explicit recognition of this demand by governments and state authorities in France and in West Germany resulted in state policies designed to facilitate and encourage in-migration of workers from less-developed countries with a surplus of manpower.

Nowhere was the link between economic development and labour needs made so explicit as in France, where the 'population deficit' persisted as a concern of primary national importance. In 1946 the Commissariat Général du Plan de Modernisation et d'Equipement issued a statement to the effect that 'the population problem is the number one problem in the whole of French economic policy'.[3] Government estimates for the levels of immigration needed to stand the country on its feet again ranged from one to five million.[4] Already in 1945 a ministerial order had been issued calling for the creation of the Office National d'Immigration (ONI), charged with organizing and facilitating large-scale immigration.[5] As noted by one writer, 'in the spring of 1946, a vast immigration programme appeared to be on the point of taking place, in a bold national recovery policy in which demographic needs would be happily reconciled with economic necessities'.[6]

The large numbers of displaced persons requiring resettlement in the years immediately following the war was seen by some as a potentially useful labour pool. Indeed, West Germany felt no need to look abroad for labour when faced with the task of settling millions of German refugees and expellees from East and Central Europe.[7] Furthermore, migration from East to West Germany served as a major source of manpower up until the erection of the Berlin Wall in 1961.[8] Although the French government was reluctant to authorize any immigration from Germany,[9] agreements were reached with the International Refugee Organization on resettlement of refugees, and an accord was signed in 1947 with the allies which foresaw the possibility of turning German prisoners of war into free workers.[10] In the same year the UK government passed the 1947 Polish Resettlement Act providing for a coordinated effort to integrate over 100,000 Poles who had served in the Allied Forces.[11] This was followed shortly after by the promotion of European Voluntary Worker schemes, aimed at recruiting displaced persons and prisoners of war from the continent for one-year contracts to work in, for example, hospitals, agriculture, coal mining, textiles and construction where labour shortages were already being felt.[12] Yet for France and the UK, projects of this sort proved relatively unsuccessful, since the numbers of workers that had been hoped for never materialized.

It was also in 1947 that France redefined Algeria's status as a colony with the 'statut organique de l'Algérie' (organic status of Algeria), which conferred French citizenship on all Algerians and confirmed the principle of free movement between Algeria and the metropole. In 1947 roughly 65,000 Algerians migrated to France,[13] and by 1949 the figure had reached 265,000.[14] Although this immigration was doubtless seen to be of economic benefit, the French government, ONI and the Ministry of Population were concerned that policy should be aimed at a large-scale immigration most 'suitable' for cultural 'adaptation' and 'assimilation',[15] favouring, therefore, European immigration over immigration from North Africa. The then director of ONI later stated the aim as having been to avoid 'the formation of colonies that could not be assimilated on the national territory'.[16] France was already looking towards Italy as a potential large-scale supplier of labour, entering into a series of accords with the Italian government designed to facilitate an in-migration of Italian labour and to ensure a degree of state control over the direction of flows and sectoral/geographical distribution of workers.[17] The agreement reached in November 1946 had envisaged the immigration of over 200,000 Italians over the following year. However, only 49,000 were registered by ONI.[18] Disappointed with these figures, the French government sought a new agreement with Germany, which included the establishment of an ONI mission there in July 1950.[19] A further accord was signed with Italy in March 1951, followed three years later by a recruitment agreement with Greece.[20]

Britain, having traditionally favoured free movement of capital and labour within the empire, and being anxious to maintain close links with the 'Old' and expanding 'New' Commonwealth (note Britain's withdrawal from India in 1947), passed a Nationality Act in 1948 which reaffirmed the principle of free movement within the Empire and Commonwealth by stating that all colonial and Commonwealth citizens were British subjects. As such, they were free to hold a British passport and could enter Britain to find work, to settle and to bring families without being subject to immigration controls. Once here, Commonwealth immigrants could exercise full citizenship rights, including the right to vote. Although the primary rationale behind the Nationality Act was one of foreign policy (maintaining influence in the Empire and the Commonwealth) rather than labour market considerations, the same year saw the government's establishment of a working party on Employment in the United Kingdom of Surplus Colonial Labour, which was charged with investigating the 'possibilities of employing in the United Kingdom surplus manpower of certain colonial territories in order to assist the manpower situation in this country and to relieve unemployment in these colonial territories'.[21] In fact the working party concluded that, in view of the probable discrimination which would be directed towards 'coloured' workers, large-scale immigration from the colonies should be discouraged.[22] The following year the Royal Commission on Population published a report which stated that: 'A systematic immigration policy could only be welcomed without reserve if the migrants were of good human stock and not prevented by religion or race from intermarrying with the host population and becoming merged with it.'[23]

Despite these misgivings, colonial immigration was already underway with the first arrivals from the West Indies in 1948.[24] Although Britain never formulated an explicit labour recruitment policy, labour shortages did appear over the next decade, particularly in regions with expanding industries and in sectors where working conditions were unattractive to the indigenous labour force.[25] These labour demands were not being met by Irish immigration, and, since no other European labour pool was easily accessible by Britain,[26] significant flows from the colonies and the Commonwealth soon developed which were fuelled by 'push' factors in the sending regions (relative poverty, unemployment, etc.) as well as by the 'pull' of labour demand in Britain. This flow was also certainly accelerated by a drop in West Indian migration to the United States following the passage of the US 1952 Walter-McCarren Act, which restricted Caribbean migration to the USA to a hundred per year. As noted by Stuart Hall, 'this piece of legislation diverted interest back to the United Kingdom which, in addition to being the head of the Commonwealth, was also the only major industrial country to which large-scale migration from the Caribbean was possible'.[27] The latter was manifested most clearly when certain state employers (e.g. London Transport[28] and the National Health Service) began to recruit directly from the West Indies. Flows from the Caribbean were soon followed by high levels of immigration from the Indian sub-continent and – to a lesser extent – from Africa, Malaysia and Hong Kong. Between the census years of 1951 and 1961, the enumerated population of West Indian origin in Britain had increased from 15,300 to 171,800, that of Indian origin from 30,800 to 81,400, and that of Pakistani origin from 5,000 to 24,900.[29]

Whereas immigration flows into the UK developed outside any system of state control because no such system had been implemented, immigration into France took on an increasingly anarchic character because the state structures established to regulate flows proved too rigid to respond to the growing demand for labour.[30] Moreover, as in Britain, colonial immigration did not fall within the mandate of state regulatory institutions. Immigration into France was at that time dominated by flows from Italy and – subsequently – from the Iberian peninsula (and, in the north, from Belgium), much of which was seasonal, serving manpower needs in agriculture brought about by large-scale rural to urban migration of the French population. Whether migration was temporary or more permanent, it suited employers and migrants to by-pass the heavily bureaucratic state mechanisms which had been designed to regulate and channel flows. In this respect, economic necessity began to take precedence over demographic concerns, resulting in an increasing perception of migrants as an economic commodity and a progressive abandonment of the original aim to ensure 'permanent settlement and integration of foreigners into French society'.[31]

West Germany only began to experience labour shortages in the mid- to late 1950s. Following consultations among the Federal government, the Federal Employment Agency, employers and labour unions, the Federal Republic reached a bilateral labour recruitment agreement with Italy in 1955.

This was to serve as a precedent for a series of later agreements reached during the 1960s with less-developed states in Europe and further afield. In 1960 similar agreements were reached with Greece and Spain. The impetus for large-scale labour recruitment strengthened after the erection of the Berlin Wall in 1961 and the resulting loss of access to East German labour. By 1968 Germany had established extensive labour recruitment programmes not only with Italy, Spain and Greece, but also with Morocco, Turkey, Portugal, Tunisia and Yugoslavia.[32] The recruitment arrangements established by Germany did not amount only to formal legal arrangements between the contracting states, but extended to comprehensive programmes which included the setting up of German recruitment commissions within the territory of the sending states concerned. The intention was to regulate flows in such a way that would benefit employers at the same time as protecting the German labour market: German employers notified the nearest Employment Office of their manpower needs, and the Employment Office, having checked that no German workers were available to fill the vacancies, informed the Federal Labour Office of the demand, which in turn contacted the recruitment commission offices set up in the sending states.

Constrained neither by the kinds of foreign policy concerns impinging on France and Britain as a result of their imperial history, nor by the demographic considerations which had troubled France for so long, the Federal Republic was free to practise a 'qualified' immigration policy, indeed a labour recruitment policy deemed explicitly not to be an immigration policy at all. Throughout the 1960s, the economic primacy of Germany's 'immigration' policies was never questioned. The Aliens Act of 1965[33] intended immigrant labour to be 'a manoeuvrable resource ... for solving ... economic problems'.[34] The system of residence and work permits established by the 1965 Act was based on the intention to create a 'rotation' of workers. Workers in this *Gastarbeiter* or 'guestworker' category should stay in the Federal Republic for a limited period for the purposes of employment and then return to be replaced by new recruits according to need, thereby ensuring a match in supply and demand in the labour market. Residence permits were valid for periods ranging from two to five years and were granted on the basis of possession of a work permit, which in turn was dependent on employment guarantees. Underlying the development of this policy was a consensus among both sending and receiving states that all would benefit economically – the migrants because of the earnings and training that would accrue during the period spent in Germany, the Federal Republic because of labour supply, and the sending state because of the potential for unemployment relief, capital transfers and the eventual return of skilled workers.

Yet, just as the state structures set up in France to regulate immigration proved too rigid to cope with employer demands, so Germany's 'rotation' model proved inefficient in its attempt to balance the manpower needs of employers, despite the fact that the bulk of Germany's immigrants did enter through the official channels. The basic flaw in the German recruitment policies was the notion that temporary workers should fill what were essentially permanent jobs. Rotation of workers conflicted with employers' concern for continuity in a trained workforce. Under pressure from the business and industrial sectors, the system of rotation effectively gave way to one of permanent immigration. A large number of immigrants themselves, often not wanting to return after only a few years, were able to renew residence and work permits with the backing of their employers. Gradually it became clear that most of Germany's foreign workers would not leave. During the recession of 1967, lower numbers than might have been expected returned to the country of origin, despite unemployment within immigrant communities.[35] The pattern of Italian migration, characterized by relatively high levels of return migration when conditions in Italy began to improve,[36] hints at the fact that the migrants' decision to stay or return depended (and depends today) as much on perceptions of conditions in the country of origin as on conditions in the host country.

The series of agreements with sending countries sought by the French government during the early 1960s proved even less successful in regulating migration flows than those instituted by Germany. As noted above, the French authorities had begun to lose control over immigration soon after the regulatory institutions had been put in place. This trend continued into the mid- to late 1960s as immigration rates accelerated and migration sources diversified. Towards the end of the decade most migration to France was spontaneous, and the role of the Office National d'Immigration had been reduced to one of *a posteriori* regularization of immigrants who had already entered and established themselves.[37] Declining Italian immigration was being replaced by Spanish, then Portuguese, and, from the early 1960s, Tunisian, Moroccan, Yugoslav and a resurgence of Algerian immigration.[38] As observed by one writer, 'it is a question of an immigration that is for the most part uncontrolled, characterized by the great variety of countries of origin and the legal (or illegal) routes through which they entered the country

– unorganized, lacking in any sense of security, deprived of political rights, poorly integrated into workers' organizations, and mainly apolitical'.[39]

The agreements reached with the sending countries (Morocco, Tunisia and Portugal in 1963, and Yugoslavia and Turkey in 1965) constituted an attempt to fill the institutional and juridical vacuum alluded to above. The French government's new desire to rationalize and streamline immigration was evident in the fact that the Evian Accords, signed between France and Algeria in 1962[40] guaranteeing freedom of movement between the two countries, were followed only two years later by an agreement designed to limit Algerian immigration according to the needs of the labour market.[41] This attempt was not successful, and two further Franco-Algerian accords were signed, in 1968 and in 1971, aimed at restricting Algerian immigration to an annual contingent of 35,000 and 25,000 respectively (with only temporary rights of entry).[42] These agreements, together with the establishment of a new governmental office, La Direction de la Population et des Migrations, in 1966, reflected the growing recognition of the need for a new and coherent immigration policy. Nevertheless, the Minister for Social Affairs still felt justified in stating in 1966 that 'illegal immigration itself is not pointless, for if we were to stick to the strict application of the international rules and accords, we would perhaps end up with a shortage of manpower'.[43]

By the early 1970s, the situations in which France, Germany and Britain, and indeed all the labour-importing countries of Northwestern Europe, found themselves vis-à-vis immigration were very similar despite having implemented different immigration policies over the preceding two decades. All had experienced large-scale migration inflows over which direct government control had been limited. All were having to face up to the fact that the majority of immigrants – particularly those from outside Europe – were not destined to return to their countries of origin when and if demand for their labour declined. In this respect (whether it had been intended or not) postwar immigration had not been a temporary economic phenomenon, but was, as Wihtol de Wenden observed, permanent, structural, and socially and politically significant.

Closing doors? The 1970s and 1980s

The oil crisis of 1973 marked a turning-point in postwar immigration policies in Europe. As economic recession set in, European labour-importing states one by one[44] introduced measures designed to close their doors to any further influx of workers from outside their regional economic groupings (European

Economic Community, European Free Trade Association). By this time, foreigners constituted at least 16% of the total population of Switzerland, 5% in the Federal Republic, 6.5% in France, 7.5% in Britain (foreign-born including Irish), 7% in Belgium and 2% in the Netherlands.[45] In every case a significant proportion of these foreign populations had migrated from outside Europe.

Although the economic recession was – and still is – given by governments and many observers as the reason or justification behind the immigration 'stop' of 1973/4, there are clear signs that concern over the social and political costs associated with these large immigrant populations had been growing for several years before the clamp-down, and that this anxiety might have had more than a little to do with decisions to suspend any further labour immigration. In a special report published by the Organization for Economic Cooperation and Development (OECD), prompted by the halt on immigration, correspondents noted the social tensions in countries apparently 'saturated' with migrants, but argued that there was very little competition between indigenous and immigrant labour in the job market and therefore that nationals of the host countries would not substitute for foreign workers. In a further report the following year it was suggested that decisions taken by governments to restrict immigration levels should be seen as 'the result of essentially political considerations', since 'the social and political drawbacks of immigration now seem to have become greater than the economic advantages'.[46]

Indeed, in the United Kingdom it would have been difficult to claim that restrictive measures had been introduced for any other than social and political reasons. Having never couched immigration policy in terms of economic necessity, British leaders had tended to be rather reticent on the subject of immigrants' economic contribution to the country,* and discussion on immigration had been dominated by anxiety about the social repercussions of 'coloured' immigration since the first arrivals from the colonies.[47] Preoccupation with the social and political costs of Commonwealth immigration led to comparatively early moves towards the introduction of legislative immigration controls. The first of these was enacted in 1962 with the Commonwealth Immigrants Act, which aimed to regulate migration flows through a system of employment vouchers.[48] These were granted liberally

---

*Note that economic growth during the 1950s and 1960s had been slower in Britain than in other Northwest European states.

until the 1964 general election in which immigration figured as an issue of central concern. In a review of the post-electoral situation in Britain, Enoch Powell, the Conservative Party Spokesman on Defence, stated that 'immigration was, and is, an issue. In my constituency it has for years been question number one, into which discussion of every other political topic – housing, health, benefits, employment – promptly turns ... Only if substantial further addition to our population is now prevented will it be possible to assimilate the immigrants already here, which in turn is the only way to avoid the evils of a colour question.'[49] Although Enoch Powell was marginalized in British politics for his extreme views,[50] this very point was to be repeated continually by policy-makers over the following two decades, not only in Britain, but in every European state that was host to immigrant populations, and was to form one of the bases for immigration control policies from the early 1970s onwards. At the time of the introduction of Britain's second Commonwealth Immigrants Act (1968) the then Prime Minister, Harold Wilson, stated that: 'We shall remain subject to ... risks of continuing tensions and stimulation of prejudice unless we amend the law so that the public in this country is confident that immigration is being effectively controlled. Only in such an atmosphere can good race relations be fostered'.[51] The British government enacted its first race relations legislation in 1965.[52]

Whereas other countries were able to implement a halt on labour recruitment as a measure to restrict immigration, in Britain immigrants were on the whole British subjects exercising their citizenship rights, and thus, if immigration was to be controlled, the government was bound to introduce legislation involving a redefinition of these rights. The question of citizenship and the right to enter the United Kingdom was raised most graphically in 1967 when the Kenyan government announced its intention to expel the Kenyan Asian population, most of whom had opted for UK and colonies rather than Kenyan citizenship when offered the choice after independence in 1962.[53] During the two months before the 1968 Commonwealth Immigrants Act came into force, 12,823 Asians entered the United Kingdom. By restricting right of entry into Britain to passport holders who could claim a close connection with the UK, the Act effectively extended immigration controls both to this group[54] and to all non-patrial UK passport holders. This legislation came in for criticism on the grounds that it favoured immigration from the 'Old' Commonwealth and was designed to limit 'coloured' immigration from the New Commonwealth. Both the 1962 and 1968 Acts were succeeded in 1971 by the Immigration Act,[55] which replaced all previous immigration legislation with a single statute introducing provisions for control of admission and stay of Commonwealth citizens and foreign nationals. Free movement for Irish nationals and the 1968 distinction between patrials and non-patrials were preserved. Provisions were also included for the introduction of visa requirements for nationals of particular foreign or Commonwealth countries as might be required.

It was not until the late 1960s that concern over the social impacts of immigration began to figure prominently in French political discourse. By the early 1970s, however, the question of integration of foreigners was coming to the fore. Anxiety began to be expressed over a range of issues including immigrants' housing and working conditions, the risks of xenophobic reactions among host communities, and the possibility that immigrants were a drain on public spending, hindering modernization of industrial structures and damaging general working conditions. This heightened concern over the social implications of immigration was reflected in the so-called 'Marcellin-Fontanet' circulars of 1972, issued by the Ministers of the Interior and of Employment. These called for restrictions on regularization of immigrants, confining the granting of residence permits to those who could produce evidence of employment and adequate accommodation.[56] Two subsequent circulars were issued the same year designed to limit regularization of illegal immigrants by stipulating that regularizations would be restricted to those who had entered France before a specific date.[57] The summer of 1973 witnessed an explosion of racial tension in Marseille directed primarily against Algerian immigrants, prompting the Algerian government to announce its intention to suspend all further emigration to France. President Georges Pompidou responded to the trouble in Marseille with an official condemnation of racism. During the months leading up to the 1974 election, the immigration debate had become public and politicized, and although consensus on the issue was limited, it was in the early summer of that year, following the election of Valéry Giscard d'Estaing to the presidency, that the decision was taken to halt all further immigration.[58] A new office of Secretary of State for Immigrant Workers was created. This post was filled by André Paul Dijoud, who issued a circular on 5 July suspending worker immigration, followed by a second on 19 July implementing a stop on 'secondary' family immigration.

Concern over the social aspects of immigration and a reordering of priorities in favour of integration of foreigners and away from recruitment was also evident in West Germany at the very beginning of the 1970s. By

1971, the German Federal government had already begun restricting entry of workers to those processed by the German Commissions stationed in the sending countries, and in June 1973 the government published a new 'Action Programme on Employment of Foreigners' which indicated a new awareness of the integration problem (and of rising unemployment, particularly within immigrant groups). Anxious to cut down foreign worker inflows, but not wanting to abrogate the agreements entered into with the sending countries, the government introduced domestic measures designed to discourage employers from seeking to take on any more foreigners, including stricter supervision of housing supplied by employers, higher fees to be paid for each recruited worker, and penalties for employment of illegal immigrants. Mandatory rotation was deemed unacceptable, in line with the government's new intention to ensure successful integration of all foreigners who did not wish to return voluntarily. Only a few months after announcing this policy, the government decided that it was necessary to implement a complete stop on all further recruitment activities from non-EC states.[59] The reorientation of policy towards integration of 'foreigners' (cf. 'immigrants') amounted to a tacit recognition that (although it had not been intended) the Federal Republic had become an immigration country. However, despite continued immigration ever since the time of the first recruitment agreements, this has never been acknowledged officially, as reflected in a recent government document: 'The fact that aliens stay here for a long time or permanently does not mean that the Federal Republic of Germany has become an "immigration country".'[60]

In the interests of achieving the integration of foreigners, and in accordance with various international legal instruments dealing with human rights,[61] the 1973 stop on immigration throughout Northwestern Europe generally did not extend to family members and dependants of immigrants already resident in the host countries. Many might have agreed with Enoch Powell when he stated that 'It can be no part of any policy that existing families should be kept divided, but there are two directions in which families can be reunited, and if our former and present immigration laws have brought about the division of families ... we ought to be prepared to arrange for them to be reunited in their countries of origin.' Yet no European democracy would have been prepared to embark on a programme of comprehensive forced repatriations, and although there were early signs of hesitation on the part of governments over the extent to which family reunification should be facilitated,[62] by the late 1970s immigration had resumed relatively high levels in all the prior labour-importing countries as more and more immigrants resident before 1973/4 began bringing in their families.* The emphasis remained, nevertheless, on restriction and control. In July 1978 the British Home Secretary observed that 'subject to commitments to United Kingdom passport holders under the special voucher scheme ... and to those arising out of the Immigration Act 1971 and from our membership of the EEC, "there will be no further major primary immigration in the foreseeable future"'. In respect of family reunification he stated that 'The great majority of those who qualify for settlement now do so by virtue of their family relationship with someone already settled here ... subject to the requirement ... that the sponsor ... must be able to support and accommodate them without recourse to public funds ... the Government acknowledges a clear commitment to them.'[63] Most countries attached conditions to the entry of family members, most notably, as mentioned here, proof of adequate funds and accommodation on the part of the sponsor.[64]

Despite continuing family immigration, migration inflows during the 1970s and into the 1980s did not lead to a marked increase in total stocks of foreign population in Europe's main receiving countries, in-migration being balanced by voluntary return migration, particularly to the European sending states. The changes that took place over the decade after 1973 were more structural than numerical. Thus, although the total legally resident alien population of Germany increased by only 5.7% between 1974 and 1984,[65] the proportion of immigrants of non-European origin was increasing while that of southern Europeans was declining. As noted in the 1985 OECD report, 'the OECD immigrant populations are changing in favour of populations from increasingly physically and culturally distant lands'.[66] This shift was accompanied by a significant feminization of immigrant populations as well as a decrease in the average age.[67] These changes created the impression that immigration levels were increasing at a much higher rate than they actually were.[68]

The 1970s and 1980s witnessed an overall convergence in the immigration policies of West European states, following the rather disparate approaches of the preceding two decades,† all professing a commitment to strict controls on primary immigration from outside the EC (/EFTA) and regulated

---

*Family immigration had been increasing as immigrant communities became more settled, but it was not until after the labour immigration stop of the early 1970s that family immigration came to dominate immigration flows.

†Note that Italy, Spain, Portugal and Greece began introducing immigration policies in line with those of states farther north as they started experiencing significant immigration flows from the mid-1980s onwards.

family (secondary) immigration in the interests of the integration of foreign populations. Indeed, as noted below, even the traditional sending states of Southern Europe had, by the late 1980s, introduced immigration legislation comparable to that operating elsewhere in Western Europe, since there was not only declining emigration and increasing return migration to these countries, but also a significant increase in immigration, much of which derived from countries outside Europe which had previously dominated migration to the major receiving states of the 1960s and 1970s. This convergence in European policies was reflected at the international level, where tentative moves had been made towards international cooperation and harmonization on the issue of immigration. In October 1974, Paul Dijoud (French Secretary of State for Immigrant Workers) stated that 'Europe ... must strive to reach a common definition of objectives and to organize a model of cooperation with the countries, in which immigration will find its true place'.[69]

Prior international instruments dealing with migrant workers included: the 1949 International Labour Organization (ILO) Convention concerning Migration for Employment (Revised), setting out modest provisions for recruitment, conditions of work, etc.; the accompanying Migration for Employment Recommendation (Revised), which recommended a general duty to facilitate movement of manpower from areas of labour surplus to those of labour deficiency (about which few states had many reservations at the time); the 1955 European Convention on Establishment, which was to regulate nearly all legal questions affecting aliens permanently resident in a European state but which attracted very few ratifications; and the European Social Charter, signed in 1961, which dealt with the rights of migrant workers and their families, but only applied to nationals of Contracting States. Two further instruments were established in the mid-1970s which reflected both the desire to create a cohesive international or European 'migration regime' and the highly restrictive climate which prevailed at the time. The ILO Migrant Workers (Supplementary Provisions) Convention of 1975, which dealt with 'migrations in abusive conditions and the promotion of equality of opportunity and treatment of migrant workers', began with a preamble stating the 'need to avoid excessive and uncontrolled or unassisted increase of migratory movements'.[70] The European Convention on the Legal Status of Migrant Workers included provisions for equal treatment of migrants, but was very limited in its scope, extending minimal protection only to nationals of signatory states in situations of permanent paid employment. As noted by Richard Plender, the fact that 'only five States have ratified this Convention, which imposes such modest obligations, illustrates with pellucid clarity the reserve with which most West European States have treated migration for employment since the date when it was opened for signature'.[71]

By the late 1970s, the preoccupation of receiving states with finding solutions to the 'immigration problem' was extending beyond simple immigration control to an increasing interest in positive encouragement of return migration. In June 1977, France introduced a programme of financial incentives to induce immigrants to leave. Over the following year, roughly 45,000 immigrants returned to their country of origin – nowhere near the officially declared target of 200,000.[72] Furthermore, it seems that most returns were largely autonomous, being as a result of individual decisions based on an evaluation of opportunities in the country of origin, rather than being related to the government programme. This was evident in the fact that most of those making use of the assistance were Spaniards and Portuguese – groups that the authorities might have been most willing to keep. In September 1980 France entered into an agreement to encourage the resettlement of Algerian workers that involved financial assistance from France and help in housing and employment from Algeria (reflecting a shift towards seeking cooperation with countries of origin).[73] In Germany, the aim of encouraging returns was made clear in February 1982 in the government's consolidation of the basic tenets of its policy on aliens (restriction, encouragement of repatriation, integration), and in July decisions were taken that translated this objective into a clear policy, including financial incentives for returns and measures taken in the field of development. These decisions were reaffirmed the following year in an Act of 28 November 1983 to Promote the Preparedness of Foreign Workers to Return.[74] No return policies introduced during the late 1970s and early 1980s had any significant impact on migration trends.

Aware that efforts to return migrants would not provide a solution to the immigration problem, receiving states continued to focus attention on immigration control. In Germany, recommendations were issued by the Federal government in December 1981 on 'urgent measures dictated by social responsibility to control subsequent immigration of dependants (in particular, lowering the maximum age of children who immigrate subsequently to 16 years and limitation of subsequent immigration of spouses joining aliens of the second generation)'. In December of the following year, visa requirements were introduced for aliens from non-EC member states intending to stay longer than three months on German territory.[75] In France, controls had been progressively strengthened over the three years leading up to the 1981 elections, the most notable policy developments being ever more stringent entry conditions (for all non-EC immigrants), improved expulsion powers introduced by Lionel Stoleru (Secretary of State for Manual Labour) and beginning in 1977, and the 'Loi Bonnet' of spring 1979, based on the measures implemented by Stoleru but designed to introduce a degree of clarity and coherence into what had become 'un véritable labyrinthe administratif'.[76] In Britain, 1981 saw the passing of the British Nationality Act, which further defined different categories of British citizenship and connected rights, reflecting a 'wish to divest itself of remaining obligations to the imperial status of British subjects'.[77]

Both as a concomitant of the restrictive climate which prevailed at the time, and as a partial consequence of the restrictive policies in place (policies which closed off many channels for legal immigration), illegal immigration and the growth in arrivals of asylum-seekers, as discussed in Chapter 2, began to emerge as the primary policy concerns for the 1980s. In France, 'la lutte contre l'immigration clandestine' (the fight against illegal imigration) was a phrase quoted over and over again in policy statements from the beginning of that decade. The two central tenets of the new, more liberal, approach to immigration adopted in France after the socialist victory in the presidential and legislative elections of 1981 were expressed as (1) the restriction of any new immigration and the fight against illegal immigration, and (2) the improvement of the living and working conditions of those already resident in France. A circular was issued in August of that year which stipulated that all foreigners in France in an irregular situation could be regularized if able to prove that they were in France before 1 January 1981;[78] employers could regularize their position before 1 January 1982. It was stated that thereafter no regularizations would take place, and that control of borders and sanctioning of employers of illegal immigrants would be strictly applied.[79]

Illegal immigration has never proved to be as significant a factor for Britain as for other countries in Western Europe. Nevertheless, the Home Secretary affirmed in 1978 the government's determination 'to take firm action to prevent evasion and abuse of the immigration control', noting that 'the prevention and detection of attempted evasion and abuse of the control ... is one of the main features of the Government's immigration policy ... The system is open to abuse at four points: at the entry clearance stage, or at the port of entry (on the basis of false documents or statements), or by clandestine illegal immigration, or by overstaying in this country by people originally properly admitted on a temporary basis.'[80] The methods of illegal or clandestine entry listed here would apply to all receiving states, although in the case of Britain overstaying accounts for the bulk of illegal immigration (difficult to monitor in a country which relies on checks on entry rather than post-entry internal controls).[81]

Germany also became increasingly concerned about illegal immigration during the 1980s, as reflected in the adoption of a range of new laws, policies and procedures beginning with the Act to Control Illegal Employment, passed in January 1982, and followed in 1985 by the Recruitment Promotion Act, and in 1990 by the Act Amending the Aliens Law. Together, these Acts contain regulations on the imprisonment, fining or expulsion of illegal immigrants, employer sanctions, and sanctions imposed on transport companies caught transporting foreigners not in possession of the requisite documentation[82] – the kind of measures in place or considered throughout Western Europe during the 1980s and early 1990s.

By the late 1980s, the new immigration states of Southern Europe were also becoming seriously concerned about rising levels of unwanted immigration. Italy, for example, passed its first immigration legislation in December 1986 (law no. 943), which included a legalization programme for clandestine workers and set out general principles for the regulation of the conditions of non-EC workers. This was followed in 1989/90 by the so-called 'Martelli Law' (law no. 39), which allowed for a second wave of regularizations, established annual quotas for the number of immigrants to be admitted, introduced severe sanctions for employers and traffickers encouraging illegal immigration, and introduced new powers for the expulsion of immigrants violating immigration laws.[83] On balance, however, such measures have not had any great success. Despite the regularizations and strengthened efforts to prevent illegal immigration, an estimated 25% of Italy's one million-plus immigrants are present illegally; of these, an estimated 60% have been resident in Italy for less than four years.[84] Law no. 39 also embodied Italy's first comprehensive legislation for dealing with asylum applications. This included, importantly, the abolition of the geographical limitation which had previously precluded refugees from outside Europe applying for asylum in Italy – a limitation which had almost certainly resulted in large numbers of would-be asylum-seekers entering Italy as illegal immigrants.

The three main areas of concern of the early 1980s – illegal immigration, asylum inflows and immigrant and minority integration – largely remain those of the early 1990s, and although a new urgency has entered the policy debate in more recent years, the primary reliance on the direct control measures that emerged after the brake was put on immigration in 1973/4 has remained intact. For over a decade, the main problem areas as identified by the OECD's Continuous Reporting System on Migration in 1984 – 'problems of insertion into the social fabric, of education of young people, of the harmonisation of different cultural traditions, of naturalisation ... illegal immigration in its many aspects, the growth in the number of asylum-seekers, and, more generally, the results of a migratory pressure ... originating in the less-developed countries' – have remained essentially the same. The policy questions raised by these issues are returned to in Chapter 6, which considers the development of policies affecting immigrant settlement and integration, and Chapter 7, which looks at the harmonization of migration policy in Western Europe in the 1980s and early 1990s.

Chapter 5

The Sending Countries

Traditionally, as Papademetriou points out, labour-surplus countries have seen 'the opportunity for emigration of their un- and underemployed workers as an unqualified blessing ... The coincidence of interests between labour-scarce and labour-surplus societies gave rise to a buoyant, almost reckless enthusiasm for both organised and spontaneous migratory flows.'[1] But the economic benefits of emigration are by no means certain. Indeed, according to the ILO, the effects may be negative in the aggregate: 'The worst but not the most unlikely effect is that emigration breeds the emigrating subproletariat of tomorrow. Clearly, the sending countries do not profit as much from emigration ... [as] the receiving countries.'[2]

When looking at questions of policy in international migration, there has been a tendency for observers to focus on the role of receiving states and thus fail to take full notice of the importance of sending countries' emigration policies. This bias has been attributed to the assumption that the international labour market is largely controlled by labour-receiving countries.[3] The result has been an implicit neglect of the part played by sending countries in influencing, and to a varying extent controlling, migration flows. The building of the Berlin Wall in 1961, and the subsequent separation of the East and West European labour markets, provides perhaps the most graphic example of the influence of sending countries (or potential sending countries) over international labour flows. Although the no-exit policies pursued by the Eastern bloc countries were exceptional, a number of postwar sending states did develop emigration policies which reflected domestic labour market or national development interests, and all, to a greater or lesser extent, exerted influence over migration flows.

The huge variation in causes, impacts and responses to migration in different sending countries and regions means that generalization is extremely difficult.[4] Nevertheless, certain central questions relating to migrant-sending countries have been raised repeatedly over the past three decades. Attention has focused particularly on the macroeconomic impact of emigration on these countries. Although a full consideration of this issue falls well beyond the scope of this discussion, it is hoped that by looking at policies pursued by certain sending states since the early 1960s some indication can be given of the most important questions raised in this context. This chapter centres on the main postwar labour-sending countries which are still significant in the context of current (and future) migration flows into Western Europe. The discussion is therefore limited to the non-European sending states of the Mediterranean basin (Turkey and the North African states).*

Promotion of emigration

As noted in Chapter 4, the postwar economic boom in Northwestern Europe was accompanied by a progressive expansion of labour markets in the industrialized states to incorporate workers not only from less-developed European countries (Italy, Spain, Portugal, Ireland, etc.), but also from non-European countries, including the colonies and former colonies. According to some observers, this development marked the start of 'the progressive disappearance of national boundaries for labour and [the] transformation [of labour] into a structural component of the international political economy'.[5] For the sending countries, it signified their 'penetration by, and incorporation into, the world economy',[6] an incorporation based on ties of dependency between the less-developed and the more-developed economies of the world.[7] However, although their position in relation to the industrialized migrant-receiving countries was undoubtedly unequal, a number of existing or potential sending countries looked very positively on the idea of emigration. Labour export appeared to be a solution to many ills, particularly employment and balance-of-payments problems which – although in some cases linked directly to national development programmes – were seen to be hampering further economic progress. Encouraged by the high demand for labour in Northwestern Europe, a number of countries began implementing policies aimed specifically at encouraging the emigration of workers.

In Turkey, for example, development planning during the 1960s and

*Excepting the former Yugoslavia which, while obviously of primary importance in current migration flows, is now giving rise to flows of an entirely different nature. Note also that the countries listed were not the major postwar labour-sending countries for the UK.

1970s stressed rapid industrialization on the basis of large-scale capital-intensive industries. This programme was not expected to lead to extensive job-creation (at least in the short term), and it implied a reliance on other countries for the import of raw materials, semi-manufactured goods and technology. Emigration of workers was seen as an instant solution to Turkey's growing unemployment problem and worsening balance-of-payments position. Promotion of emigration was stated as an explicit policy objective in Turkey's first three five-year plans. Throughout the 1960s and early 1970s, 'the emphasis was on maximising the outflow of individuals and the consequent inflow of hard currency – little else had such high priority'.[8]

Turkey entered into bilateral labour recruitment agreements with the Federal Republic of Germany in 1961, with Austria, Belgium and the Netherlands in 1964, with France in 1965, and with Sweden in 1967.[9] These agreements, although covering a range of issues, such as workers' pensions, health, identity cards, etc., were primarily concerned with matching labour supply in Turkey with demand in the recruiting country. The 1965 Franco-Turkish accord, for example, began as follows:

> The French government and the Turkish government, being desirous of organizing in their mutual interest the recruitment of Turkish workers, have hereby agreed as follows:
> *Art. 1*: The French government will periodically inform the Turkish government about any of its manpower needs that would be suitable for Turkish workers. This information will, in particular, provide exact details of requirements regarding age, specializations, professional aptitudes and health. The Turkish government will provide the French government with as precise details as possible on the number, age and qualifications of Turkish workers desirous of working in France.[10]

The recruitment of workers required a high degree of cooperation between Turkey and the recruiting country. Although the recruiting government and employers had the final say in selection, the Turkish Employment Service (TES) played an active role and maintained a monopoly over the registration of potential migrants throughout the recruitment period. By 1974 there were close to one million Turkish workers resident in Northwestern Europe, of whom roughly 800,000 had migrated through the TES.[11]

The North African sending states also came to support emigration, reaching a whole series of bilateral labour-exchange agreements with the

European labour recruiters during the course of the 1960s. Both Tunisia and Morocco signed agreements with France in 1963, and although that between Tunisia and France was not implemented until 1969, both Tunisia and Morocco were soon actively promoting emigration through their national development plans in an effort to reduce the growing pressures of un- and underemployment. The Office of Professional Training and Employment[12] in Tunisia performed a similar role to Turkey's TES, being responsible for finding new markets for Tunisian emigrant labour, and for selecting candidates; by 1972, at least 75% of Tunisian departures passed through official channels.[13] Morocco similarly created a Central Emigration Service so as to introduce more effective coordination of emigration. However, beyond policy statements supporting labour export, the Moroccan authorities achieved little more than the negotiation of labour agreements with the European receiving countries. The Moroccan position was thus largely one of *laissez-faire*.

The Algerian government's attitude towards emigration, at least during the second half of the 1960s, mirrored that of Turkey. Algerian support for emigration was, in fact, hesitant during the first few years after independence, but the overthrow of Ben Bella, the Algerian Republic's first president, by Colonel Houari Boumédienne in 1965 ushered in a new phase of development which favoured the rapid expansion of high-technology, capital-intensive, heavy industries. This programme implied a neglect of agricultural development and the creation of relatively few jobs in relation to the capital invested. Labour export was seen as a 'vital safety valve'[14] to relieve the social and economic pressures of unemployment and underemployment.

However, Algeria was in a rather different position from Turkey and the other North African states in terms of its negotiating position. The primary destination for Algerian migrants was, of course, France – as it was for Tunisia and Morocco. However, in the case of Algeria (in contrast to Tunisia and Morocco), labour migration to France dated back to the First World War, when Algerians were recruited to work in French munitions factories, mines and armed services, and by 1962 migration had become 'a massive, structural, permanent feature' of both the Algerian and the French economies.[15] By virtue of its oil and gas resources and close integration with the French economy, Algeria, as compared with other sending states, was in a peculiarly strong position to negotiate labour export agreements with the French government. Although the labour agreements reached between the two countries after 1962 seemed to reflect French interests more than those of Algeria,[16] the latter's negotiating position can be seen to have strengthened during this period such that, by 1973, Algeria was able to impose a unilateral freeze on all further labour emigration before France introduced immigration restrictions. The reasons for this action were almost certainly political, reflecting, among other things, Algeria's concern to sever all obvious links with its colonial past in the lead up to the Algiers 'non-aligned' summit. The decision to stop emigration was facilitated, however, by Algeria's improved economic position following the nationalization of the oil industry in 1971. Algeria was no longer so reliant on remittances from labour export,[17] and, it was argued, was in a better position to create employment at home. This view was reflected in the 1976 National Charter, which stated that: 'Because of the development of the country, workers no longer need to emigrate to find a job. Moreover ... the Revolution has created for each Algerian the obligation [to make] his contribution to the common task of national reconstruction.'[18]

Nevertheless, on balance, the sending countries were disadvantaged in the bilateral recruitment negotiations of the 1960s because the volume, composition and timing of migration flows were determined more by labour demand than by supply. This was observed by Adler in the context of the 1964 Franco-Algerian 'Nekhache–Grandval' Agreement (named after the negotiatiors). He noted that although in principle labour migration was to be regulated according to availability of labour in Algeria as well as to demand in France, Algerian labour supply was in effect 'infinitely elastic', and thus France could decide more or less unilaterally how many Algerian workers to admit.[19]

The weaker position of the labour-sending countries became more obvious with the halt on recruitment in 1973/4. The unilateral decision by the receiving countries to discontinue recruitment not only removed labour export promotion from the sending countries' choice of policy options (at least as regards export to Europe), but also faced the sending countries with the prospect of a sudden flood of returning migrants. This was a scenario for which they were ill-prepared and over which they would have little control. In fact the massive returns that some had feared never materialized, indicating, among other things, an inherent weakness in the receiving countries' position vis-à-vis control of immigrant labour. None the less, the policy changes introduced by the receiving states in the early 1970s, and the resulting fluctuations in migration flows, caused sufficient concern among sending countries to prompt the ILO to call for a Programme of Action encouraging agreements which would make 'migration movements, remittances and returns ... a predictable and continuous part of sending-country development programmes'.[20]

Since the sending countries were no longer in a position to negotiate labour transfers with the European receiving states after 1973, their attention shifted to the questions of return migration, of the status and treatment of migrants and their families in the receiving countries, and of remittances.

From labour emigration to return migration and family migration
The fact that two recessions (in 1966/7 and that following the 1973 oil crisis) and the recruitment stop had not resulted in a wholesale return of migrants was a cause of considerable concern in Western Europe, and led to a growing interest in proposals to encourage (or force) return migration in the mid- to late 1970s. The policies subsequently introduced were motivated by the domestic political interests of the receiving states concerned (France and West Germany). This development was not entirely divorced from the concerns of the sending states, however.

An interest in return migration after 1973 might appear to be a departure by the sending states from the labour export policies of the 1960s and early 1970s. However, because the sending states hoped to benefit from a constant and continuing inflow of migrants' remittances and soon the return of skilled and motivated emigrants, their primary interest was in 'temporary but long-term' migration[21] rather than permanent emigration (cf. receiving-country interest in temporary but short-term migration). Despite the widely held belief that labour emigration would provide a cheap mechanism for training workers, concern about the potential skill-drain effect of emigration was apparent within the sending countries even before any labour agreements had been signed. In Tunisia, for example – a country which had no tradition of emigration before independence in 1956 – emigration was initially discouraged so as to protect against the loss of skilled workers, and it was only when unemployment began to present itself as a serious problem that the position of the Tunisian government shifted to a positive encouragement of emigration.[22] The attitudes of the sending countries varied a great deal during the 1960s, but all were concerned to safeguard domestic labour markets while reaping maximum benefit from emigration. The 1973/4 recruitment halt forced a reordering of priorities in sending states' migration policies, but did not result in a total break from the interests pursued during the period of labour recruitment.

During the 1960s and early 1970s, the concern of sending countries to protect and/or improve skill levels within the domestic labour market was commonly reflected in policies and procedures designed explicitly to manipulate the composition of migration flows. As already noted, the TES in

Turkey, the OFPE/OTTEEFP in Tunisia, and the Office National Algérien de Main-d'Oeuvre (National Algerian Manpower Office) were all directly involved in the recruitment process, and all at one stage or another introduced selection procedures which favoured the emigration of certain groups over others. The Turkish government, for example, introduced restrictions on the emigration of coal miners following production losses resulting from the emigration of skilled workers from the Zonguldak mining area;[23] by the late 1960s, the TES was favouring unskilled applicants from the less-developed areas of Turkey.[24]

In Algeria, administered and controlled departure of emigrants was emphasized from the very beginning, reflecting in part an ambivalence towards policies which implied dependence on France. As early as 1964, Algeria was attempting to regulate emigration through the operation of a work permit scheme (ONAMO permits), which enabled the authorities to encourage emigration from particular areas and thus diversify the sources of migration. This, it was hoped, would ensure that returning migrants would settle in areas in which their new skills would be needed. It is also possible that this policy was motivated by a concern to reduce the proportion of migrants from the (Berber) Kabylia region. The Algerian government was not unaware of the potential political dangers associated with a predominantly Berber expatriate community in France. By the early 1970s, the emphasis of Algerian emigration policy had shifted away from a concern with overall numbers (note the contingency negotiations of the 1960s) towards an interest in the qualitative nature of migration flows. Adler notes that, although numbers of emigrants dominated the Franco-Algerian negotiations in 1964, attention had turned more to questions of training by 1968, and by 1973 'qualitative questions completely overshadowed quantitative ones'. The nationalization of the oil industry in 1971 not only reduced Algeria's reliance on emigration, but also enabled the government to plan a programme of rapid industrialization. This threw Algeria's shortage of skilled workers into sharp relief, and planners began to think more seriously about the possibility of using the pool of skilled Algerian labour currently in France.

The Algerian government maintained stricter control over emigration than the governments of either Morocco or Tunisia.[25] The efforts made by the OTTEEFP in Tunisia to control the composition of emigrant flows came rather late in the day and had very little impact. In as far as Morocco had an emigration policy,[26] it was designed more to remove barriers to emigration than to regulate it. The 1968–72 Moroccan Development Plan recommended the reorganization of the Central Emigration Service (SCE) to ensure more effective coordination, but emigration continued to follow patterns which had developed independently of government control.[27] Even in Turkey, despite the stated policy aims, control over worker emigration was limited. According to Rinus Penninx, the priority to be accorded to candidates from underdeveloped regions of the country remained a gesture rather than an influential policy line, reflecting a 'general negligence of the phenomenon of uneven regional development' in Turkish state planning.[28]

The degree of skill-drain experienced by the sending states during the 1960s and early 1970s, and the implications of this for the economies of those countries, varied considerably. The fact that the loss of skilled workers was often sectorally and/or geographically very localized meant that the overall impact on one particular country was (and is) difficult to gauge. However, it is clear that, in general, emigration did not result in any significant return of skilled and motivated workers to the sending regions, and in fact often resulted in substantial skill losses. For example, of the 800,000 emigrants who left Turkey through the TES, approximately one-third were skilled or qualified. Roughly 17% of Turkey's population of men aged between 20 and 35, up to 40% of all carpenters, masons and miners, and between 5% and 10% of Turkish plumbers and electricians departed during the peak years of labour emigration between 1967 and 1973.[29] Most Turkish emigrants, including those who migrated with skills, were employed in unskilled positions in Germany. Thus, in terms of occupation, emigration resulted in downward mobility for many, and little or no upward mobility for the majority. It is likely that those who received training and/or occupied skilled or qualified positions in Europe were (and are) less likely to return to Turkey than those who remained in unskilled jobs.[30]

As already noted, sending countries' interest in promoting return migration was founded on an interest in the reinsertion of skilled and enterprising emigrants. By 1974, Turkey, Tunisia and Algeria had all formulated policies to encourage workers to return.[31] In Algeria, the emphasis was on skilled industrial workers; in Tunisia, it was on migrants who might establish themselves as small merchants or businessmen; and in Turkey, on a combination of these. Priorities reflected broader development interests in each country. Moroccan policy during the early 1970s was unique in that labour export continued to be promoted in official development plans (including the 1973–7 National Plan). The 1978–80 Three Year Plan, while not encouraging labour emigration, made no provision for return migration.[32]

Algeria's first comprehensive return policy was introduced in 1977 with the establishment of the *Service de Réinsertion* (at the same time as the French government introduced a programme of financial incentives to encourage migrants to return). The Algerian government also put pressure on France to improve training facilities for Algerian immigrants, and the *Amicale des Algériens en Europe** actively encouraged the *Sociétés Nationales* in Algeria to recruit from the emigrant community in France. Despite these efforts, and the 1974–7 Four Year Development Plan which stressed job-creation, relatively few skilled emigrants were attracted back. Labour market conditions in Algeria in the late 1970s were not sufficiently attractive to encourage the reinsertion of substantial numbers of emigrants.† In 1980, Algeria entered into an agreement with France to cooperate in a three-year programme to encourage migrant resettlement. The provisions included repatriation allowances, training opportunities and enterprise loans for returning migrants. Again, the response was very limited.[33] Despite high levels of unemployment and underemployment, Algeria continued to suffer skill shortages, and eventually resorted to importing skilled workers from advanced industrial economies (including France) and from Asia (the Philippines and Indonesia).

The varied impact of the skill-drain on sending countries is reflected in the fact that, despite a high level of skill emigration and low rates of return migration, Turkey did not seem to suffer from the kinds of skill shortages experienced in Algeria. Suzanne Paine wrote in 1974 that the Turkish economy had 'certainly lost some scarce skilled manpower, but this does not as yet seem to have been accompanied by serious output losses'.[34] According to Adler, this may be explained by the increasing use of sophisticated and modern technology in Turkish factories, which led to a decline in the demand for the traditional artisan skills lost through emigration (carpenters, masons, etc.).[35] The Turkish government was none the less keen to promote return migration, particularly of emigrants returning with savings to set up small and medium-sized enterprises, since it was hoped that this would stimulate job-creation and development in the areas to which they returned. In 1962 the Turkish government established a Village Development Cooperatives scheme (VDC) to promote rural development. The TES gave priority to VDC members in selecting emigrants in the hope that these migrants would channel resources into the cooperatives and eventually return with knowledge and

---

*The government-backed organization set up to promote the interests of Algerian migrants.
†Although there was some success in certain areas experiencing labour shortages, e.g. Oran.

skills to expand the cooperatives' activities.[36] In 1972, Turkey reached an agreement with West Germany under which German funds would be made available to returning migrants wishing to set up small businesses in Turkey (on the condition that the migrants participated in training programmes in both Germany and Turkey[37]). However, according to Werner and König, this programme proved too costly and complicated to work effectively.[38] In no sending country did efforts to encourage return migration prove particularly successful.[39]

The 1973 halt on recruitment in Europe marked the beginning of a declining trend in return migration to all the non-European sending states. Indeed in some areas the recruitment stop signalled a sudden upsurge in emigration as migrants hurried to bring their families to Europe before any further restrictions were imposed. The restrictions on family immigration introduced by the French and West German governments during the 1970s and early 1980s posed a dilemma for the sending countries. All had turned their attention to the treatment of their nationals in the recruitment countries, and were concerned to see an improvement in migrants' living and working conditions. It is worth noting, for example, that the Algerian government's stated reason for suspending emigration in 1973 was the failure of the French government to protect Algerians from racist attacks.[40] Restricting family reunion conflicted with the sending countries' concern for the social and economic rights of migrants in the receiving countries. On the other hand, support for family migration conflicted with the sending countries' primary interest in maximizing remittance flows (and promoting return migration). Family migration implied two developments which were considered to have a direct bearing on remittances: (1) it suggested permanent settlement and thus a shift in migrants' orientation away from the country of origin; and (2) it indicated an increase in the amount of migrants' earnings being spent in the receiving country (family consumption) and thus less being sent back in the form of remittances. Adler notes, for example, that the Algerian authorities were undecided on the issue of family migration: on the one hand, they were annoyed by French efforts to restrict family immigration, but on the other, they were concerned about the dangers associated with family migration. The slowdown in Algerian family migration which took place in the late 1960s can be partly attributed to restrictions imposed by the Algerian government.[41] It is likely that much louder protest would have been voiced by the sending states over receiving states' restriction of family migration had it not been for the overarching concern to protect remittance flows.

A number of governments attempted to compensate for the effects of family migration by introducing or strengthening indirect measures to 'maintain the umbilical cord between motherland and emigrants'.[42] Some governments have been more successful in this regard than others. The *Amicale des Algériens en Europe* dates back to the Ben Bella government in Algeria, and from the beginning it actively tried to shape migrants' social, cultural and political life outside Algeria.[43] Yugoslav cultural associations performed a similar function. Turkey, on the other hand, never succeeded in institutionalizing state interests within emigrant communities.[44]

Remittances

Writing about Turkey in 1982, Rinus Penninx observed that 'the effort of the national government is mainly directed to one aim: to attract as much hard currency from Turkish migrants in Europe as possible'.[45] In 1973, remittances from migrant workers represented 64% of Turkish exported goods and services.[46] Although this proportion has fallen since that time (to 27% in 1982 and 17% in 1989[47]), the total sums involved have increased.* Remittances returned through official channels† totalled over US$2 billion in 1980 and over US$3 billion in 1990.[48] Workers' remittances in 1989 (just over US$3 billion) offset roughly 75% of Turkey's visible trade deficit.[49] Comparable figures apply in the cases of Algeria, Morocco, Tunisia and Yugoslavia. It should be noted, however, that remittances tend to fluctuate from year to year, and in the case of countries that have not succeeded in exporting labour to the Middle East oil producers (e.g. Algeria, Morocco, Tunisia), their value has tended to decline over the past decade.

In terms of their actual value, the overall sums involved in remittance transfers may be somewhat misleading. One reason for this is that government control over how remittances are used, for example whether the money is invested (e.g. in state bank accounts) or channelled into immediate consumption, is usually limited. As observed by Penninx, 'migration on the national level seems to be a fortune, but it is paid in small change and it seems to yield little profit'.[50] There has been a long-standing debate over the overall benefits of remittances and their impact on economic development. Although remittances have often been seen as the litmus test of a successful emigration policy, considerable costs associated with their inflow have also been identified. It has been argued, for example, that (1) dependence on remit-

*Owing in part to the export of labour to the Middle East.
†A considerable proportion of migrants' savings tend to be remitted through unofficial channels, since exchange rates are often (usually) more favourable. Thus actual figures can be assumed to be significantly higher than those quoted from official sources.

tances is self-reinforcing and increases dependency on labour importers; (2) remittances are unreliable and susceptible to sudden swings; and (3) they distort and sometimes damage the development process by increasing income differentials or – since they tend to be channelled into consumption rather than productive investment – by generating or reinforcing inflation.[51] Ismail Serageldin et al. come to this conclusion in their 1983 study of manpower and international migration in the Middle East and North Africa,

> Remittances are the most tangible benefit from labor migration, yet evaluating their effect on the economy is difficult ... They are not by any means unambiguously beneficial or, on the contrary, deleterious in their impact. Remittances appear to cause demand-led inflation [and there] ... is evidence of changes in consumption patterns [which are] ... to the detriment of indigenous agriculture and domestic industries. This is a perfect example of the difficulty of evaluating the impact of migration on economic development and the impact of remittances in particular on these capital-poor economies. Overall, migration for employment ... cannot be seen as having accelerated economic growth among the labor-supplying countries as a whole.[52]

Nevertheless, remittances have proved an essential source of foreign currency for most sending countries, as is reflected in the range of policies introduced to encourage migrants to send back their savings. In Turkey, for example, preferential exchange rates for remittances were introduced in the early 1960s. In the face of strong inflation and the constant devaluation of the Turkish lira, this measure failed to make an appreciable impact on remittance flows, and new measures were introduced after 1973 when remittances began to decline. These included a foreign exchange deposit programme, whereby migrants were allowed to open foreign currency accounts in Turkey. Paying premium interest rates,[53] these accounts attracted some US$4 billion between 1979 and 1988.[54] As well as trying to maximize remittance flows, the Turkish government also sought to channel foreign currency into productive investment. Thus, for example, migrants returning with cars, trucks and professional equipment, or those wishing to secure loans for homes, farms and businesses, were required to open foreign currency savings accounts with the Turkish Central Bank. However, Turkey has not succeeded in developing an effective policy on the investment of migrant transfers, and non-productive personal investment continues to dominate over the productive investment of remittances. The same can be said of remittance transfers to the North African sending states.

Redirection of emigration flows?

Despite a growing recognition of the costs associated with large-scale emigration, labour export still constituted an important element of the development programmes in many sending states when the European receiving countries closed their labour markets in the early 1970s. In this respect, the 1973 recruitment halt resulted in an 'emigration crisis'[55] for a number of sending countries. Emigration to Europe had failed to have a significant or lasting impact on un- or underemployment in any of the non-European sending states, and thus problems of labour surplus were as, if not more, critical in the early 1970s as they had been a decade before. All sending states turned to domestic development strategies to substitute for labour export (Algeria particularly), but some also looked to redirecting migration flows to new destinations (Tunisia, Morocco and Turkey, and also Portugal and Yugoslavia). The rapid expansion of the economies of the Middle East oil-producing states after 1973, and the resulting acute labour shortages, raised hopes in a number of sending countries of a new market for labour exports.

By the late 1960s Tunisia had already diversified emigrant destinations to include Libya. Although migration to Libya proved very vulnerable to fluctuating political relations between the two countries,[56] by 1974 Tunisian workers migrating to Libya outnumbered those leaving for France. Morocco also sought to redirect migrant flows after 1973, but migration to Libya was prevented by poor political relations between the two states after Colonel Muammar Qadhafi came to power in 1969. By contrast, relations between Libya and Turkey were good during the 1970s, and in 1975 an agreement was signed for the transfer to Libya of 10,000 skilled Turkish workers.[57] According to one estimate, there were some 84,000 Turks resident there by 1982.[58]

By the mid- to late 1970s, acute labour shortages had appeared in the oil-rich Gulf states. In 1976, Morocco signed an agreement with Saudi Arabia for the transfer of 50–100,000 Moroccan workers, and, in the same year, some 300 Tunisian workers left for Saudi Arabia under direct contract. However, this did not mark the beginnings of a substantial transfer of labour between North Africa and the Gulf; by 1981 there were no more than 700 Tunisians working in Saudi Arabia, and only 650 North Africans were living in Kuwait.

Turkey has been far more successful in exporting labour to the Middle East than either Morocco or Tunisia, thanks largely to the success of Turkish companies in winning construction contracts in the region. Turkish migration to the Middle East accelerated so rapidly during the first half of the 1980s that by 1985 movement to Arab countries accounted for over 90% of all departures recorded by the Turkish Labour Office,[59] and the number of Turkish workers living in Libya and Saudi Arabia exceeded the figures for Turks working in France, the Netherlands, Belgium and Switzerland (roughly 177,000 and 135,400 respectively).[60]

However, even in the case of Turkey, the Middle East oil-producing countries have not provided a replacement market for labour previously directed towards Western Europe. Although the foreign currency receipts from contracts in the Middle East are enormous, the numbers of workers involved in emigration to the oil-producing countries do not compare with the figures for migration to West Germany and other European receiving states two decades earlier. Moreover, this new migration is qualitatively very different from previous flows. Migrants to the Middle East are predominantly skilled men drawn from the less-developed areas of Turkey (carpenters, builders, mechanics, engineers, etc.), who are recruited for specific contracts. They are attracted by the opportunity of saving relatively large amounts of money over a short duration; and they generally migrate without their families and return at the end of the contract or on completion of a particular project (usually one to three years). The incentive to remain abroad for long periods is weaker than that in Europe in the past, since living and working conditions experienced on project sites are usually very harsh.

For Turkey, migration to the Middle East has proved financially advantageous, but it has not been on a scale sufficient to provide a solution to long-term employment problems. For Morocco and Tunisia, prospects for substantial labour transfers to the Gulf remain very slim. Even if major new labour export opportunities were to present themselves in the future, the experiences of the 1960s and early 1970s indicate that resumed large-scale emigration of workers would not have a significant impact on the deeper structural economic problems currently faced by these countries. Indeed, changes in the international labour market over the past decade are such that future demand for migrant workers is likely to be increasingly for skilled and qualified workers whom the sending countries can ill-afford to lose.[61]

Because official access to external labour markets is now extremely limited for the sending countries of the Mediterranean basin, debates over the advantages and disadvantages of emigration have become less and less relevant for policy-makers in the labour-sending countries. To some extent, however, the migration policies of both sending and receiving countries defy the facts, for, despite an official clamp-down on immigration throughout Western Europe, migration from these countries – particularly from North Africa – continues at substantial levels. Although the actual numbers are unknown, estimates of the size of foreign populations in the new immigration countries of Southern Europe (Italy, Spain, Portugal and Greece) provide some indication of the scale. In 1990, the total foreign population in these four countries was estimated to be around 3 million.[62] Illegal immigrants probably account for some 50% of this figure. Although these populations are very mixed, North Africans appear to be the dominant group, particularly in Italy. In view of the rapid intensification of migration pressures – measured in terms of un- and underemployment, relative poverty and population growth (in North Africa in particular)[63] – it is quite possible that the rate of migration out of the Maghreb will increase significantly between now and the end of the decade.

New questions have emerged over recent years which are connected to the upsurge in irregular migration into Western Europe. The central issue is no longer that of how emigration might be promoted to benefit the economies of the sending countries, but rather how to tackle fundamental economic and demographic problems in sending countries which give rise to uncontrolled migration into Western Europe. As argued by Bimal Ghosh,

> In the light of contemporary economic realities it is not difficult to agree that migration is no short-cut to enduring development. The very magnitude of the problem of development, or the absence of it, measured in terms, for example, of unemployment, underemployment and absolute poverty in the labour-sending developing countries, should drive home the point. When they are juxtaposed against the relevant migration statistics such as the annual outflow of migrants from developing countries (roughly 0.4 per cent of the labour force) ... the absurdity of looking to migration as a short-cut to effective development becomes even more clear.[64]

Emphasis is thus now increasingly placed on development to prevent migration, rather than migration to spur development. The relationship between migration and development, however, is complex in the extreme, and understanding of it still wholly inadequate for the planning of policy measures which could possibly have any substantial short-term impact on migration trends. In the meantime, there appears to be a widening gap opening up between the reality of migration trends and the rationale of receiving states' policies which are founded almost entirely on concepts of prevention, restriction and control. There is, in this context, a growing need for policy-makers on both sides of the Mediterranean to incorporate the existence and persistence of migration into their respective migration policies, since without an explicit recognition of the reality, little can be done towards minimizing the disruptive effects or maximizing the potential benefits of migration for both sending and receiving countries. If policies were to develop in this way, many of the arguments which guided those of the Mediterranean sending states during the period of labour recruitment might once again resurface, for planners might begin to approach migration (as before) as an instrument and not merely as an object of policy. This should not, however, be seen as an instrument capable of solving all the problems of underdevelopment in today's sending countries, but rather one which could be factored positively into the development process. As argued recently by Reginald Appleyard,

> Maintaining the *status quo* is the best way to invite the next wave of international migration into the OECD countries which, in turn, would further stimulate extreme political reactions. What is needed is an *active* policy with respect to international migration and not just passive *ad hoc* reaction to events as they materialise. A comprehensive development strategy in which international migration is assigned a specific role, represents the most promising direction.[65]

Chapter 6

Immigrant and Ethnic Minorities in Europe Today

A recognition of the potential social and political impacts of postwar immigration, and its expression as a central policy issue in European immigration states, appeared in the main as a reaction to a process that had been underway for two decades or more and which was to a large extent irreversible. Labour immigration of the 1950s and 1960s had given rise to the *de facto* permanent settlement of large foreign populations. These were often distinctive in terms of culture, language, religion and/or ethnic group. They posed a new, and in many respects unprecedented, challenge to the idea of the European nation-state based on a common cultural, racial and linguistic identity. By the early 1970s, all governments were turning their attention towards the question of integration: those immigrants who could not be expected or persuaded to return to their country of origin would have to be inserted into the fabric of the host society in such a way that would cause least social and political disruption. The only alternative to integration was segregation (cf. segregation policies pursued by the Gulf states). However, the notion of a permanent and institutionalized segregation of immigrant groups ran counter to the ideological basis of the new welfare democracies and raised troubling questions relating to the future social stability of the receiving countries. Segregation could not be contemplated, so 'the integration of immigrants into the social system ... had become inevitable'.[1]

Despite a common concern over the integration of immigrants, diverse approaches to the problem have been adopted by the various host countries (and by different institutions and interest groups within countries). These reflect the different socio-political structures of the receiving states (e.g. degree of centralization and state intervention in social affairs), contrasting immigration experiences, and differing interpretations or expectations of processes of integration. 'Integration' is a rather vague term which can be used to denote a varying range of processes across the spectrum from social and cultural assimilation of minorities to the preservation of distinct minority identities. Some countries have leant towards broadly assimilationist programmes (such as France and the FRG), while others have opted for policies promoting multiculturalism or supporting recognition of a 'multiracial society' (the Netherlands, Sweden[2] and Britain). Attitudes and policies adopted towards immigrant minorities have also differed according to identities of the groups concerned (e.g. European versus African, Christian versus Muslim), and have varied over time and according to the 'maturity' of different immigration flows and the particular aspects of the immigration history (e.g. permanent colonial immigration versus 'temporary' recruited labour). The picture is complicated further by the fact that integration – to the extent that it is accomplished – is never a straightforward one-way process, but one based on the dynamic interactive relationships which develop between immigrants and the state, and between immigrant and receiving communities. Not only have receiving states and communities responded to immigrant populations in different ways, but immigrant groups themselves have adopted a great variety of strategies and demonstrated widely contrasting responses to their situation as minorities, in turn influencing the reactions and responses of the indigenous society. The nature of the integration process varies not only from country to country and from group to group, but from one region, town or locality to another, and from one sub-group, family or individual to another. For this reason, any effort to generalize on the subject of integration is extremely difficult.

Considerable variation is also apparent in the vocabulary used to describe minorities of immigrant origin, indicative of the specific socio-political, historical and legal background to the immigration phenomenon in each receiving country. The terminology is significant inasmuch as it reflects much about attitudes which have shaped the reception and integration of immigrant groups and the bases of immigrant minority status in receiving countries. This issue takes on a particular salience in relation to the position of the descendants of immigrants who have spent all or most of their lives in the host country. As observed by Czarina Wilpert, 'in the UK, the descendants of immigrants are black and Asian ethnic minorities; in France, they are young foreigners or French of foreign origin ... in Belgium, the Federal Republic of Germany and Switzerland, they are the offspring of migrant workers or young foreigners'.[3] The term 'second-generation immigrants' is also commonly used in a number of countries (e.g. FRG, France, Switzerland, Belgium) but may be considered inappropriate in others (Britain[4]). To some extent these terms reflect objective differences in the nationality/citizenship laws,[5] but they are perhaps more indicative of the degree to which immigrant minorities are 'identified as a class apart'.[6] For the purposes of this discussion, I shall in general use the term 'immigrant minorities' or 'immigrant groups' to denote minorities of immigrant origin – a loose category which should be taken to include descendants of immigrants[7] as well as immigrants themselves.

The first section of this chapter is devoted to a brief quantification and breakdown of the different immigrant minorities in Western Europe, focusing on France, the Federal Republic of Germany, the United Kingdom (the countries with the largest immigrant minorities) and Italy (as an example of Europe's 'new' receiving states). More detailed information on the size and distribution of immigrant groups is provided in Table 6.1. The subsequent three sections will deal with some of the issues alluded to above, the first looking at integration as a policy issue, the second at immigrant settlement as a substantive issue, and the third considering the place of immigrant minorities in Western Europe in terms of their citizenship status. Consideration of immigrant integration in Italy will be limited, since this country has only very recently had to face up to large-scale foreign immigration as a policy issue.

Europe's immigrant minority population

Statistical data on immigration, emigration and stocks of foreign population are generally very unsatisfactory. Not only are statistics frequently defective, with illegal immigrants excluded, but different countries depend on different methods of data collection, use different defining categories, and carry out censuses and other surveys at different times.[8] This makes cross-country comparison and data compilation extremely difficult. Furthermore, data from separate sources within one country often disagree. For example, estimates of the numbers of foreigners in France issued by different ministries can vary by as much as one million.[9] The situation is further complicated by the fact that distinctions between nationals and 'foreigners' are blurred because different citizenship and nationality laws operate in different countries. Especially in Britain, but also in France and the Netherlands, substantial proportions of immigrant or immigrant-origin ethnic populations are not classified as foreigners by virtue of having entered as citizens of the host

Table 6.1: Stocks of foreign population by nationality: major recruitment countries and major immigrant groups in the early 1980s and 1990 (in thousands)

Nationality	Belgium 1981	Belgium 1990	France 1982	France 1990	Germany 1980	Germany 1990	Netherlands 1980	Netherlands 1990	UK 1984	UK 1990	Switzerland 1980	Switzerland 1990
Italy	277	241	340	254	618	548	21	17	83	75	421	379
Ireland	1	2	—	—	—	—	—	—	491	638	—	—
Spain	58	52	327	216	180	135	23	17	25	24	97	116
Portugal	11	17	767	646	112	85	9	8	10[a]	21	11	86
Greece	21	21	—	—	298	315	4	5	—	—	9	8
Turkey	66	85	122	202	1462	1675	139	204	—	—	38	64
former Yugoslavia	6	6	63	52	632	653	14	14	—	—	44	141
Algeria	11	11	805	620	5[b]	7	—	—	—	—	—	—
Morocco	110	142	441	585	36	66	83	157	—	—	—	—
Tunisia	7	6	191	208	23	26	2	3	—	—	—	—
Poland	—	—	65	46	88[c]	241	—	—	—	—	—	5
New C'wealth & E/W Africa	—	—	—	—	—	—	—	—	442	394	—	—
Other countries	318	322	593	780	999	1491	226	267	550	723	273	301
Total	886	905	3714	3609	4453	5242	521	692	1601	1875	893	1100
of which EEC	594	550	1595	1309	1494[d]	1325[e]	171	168	701[f]	889	701	760

[a]Less than 10,000; [b]Figure for 1982; [c]Figure for 1983; [d]Figure for 1982; [e]Figure for 1989; [f]Figure for 1983

Source: SOPEMI (OECD Continuous Reporting System on Migration), *Trends in International Migration*, OECD, Paris, 1992.

country, having naturalized to host-country citizenship, or having been born within the territory of the host country.[10] On the other hand, virtually all immigrants and descendants of immigrants in Germany are defined as foreigners. To exclude immigrants (and descendants of immigrants) who are nationals of a receiving state from cross-country comparisons means to exclude a large category of people who share many of the defining features of foreign minorities as a group.

Perhaps the most useful cross-country immigration and immigrant population statistics are those compiled by the OECD Continuous Reporting System on Migration (SOPEMI)[11] and those compiled by the Statistical Office of the European Communities (Eurostat)[12] which aim for greatest possible comparative consistency. However, both rely on state-specific official statistical sources and are therefore subject to all the inaccuracies referred to above. According to Eurostat, there are between 13 and 14 million foreigners resident in the twelve EC member states out of a total population of 329 million (excluding additional population of the former GDR). Foreigners (defined as such and legally resident) thus account for about 4% of the total. However, this figure includes EC citizens resident in another country. The population of legally resident third-country nationals who are not citizens of a member state is estimated at close to 9 million, or 2.7% of the total. Over one million non-EC/non-EFTA nationals may be added if account is taken of foreign populations in Switzerland, Sweden, Norway and Austria.[13] Of the 8 million third-country nationals living in the European Community, some 1.8 million come from the Northern industrialized countries (EFTA countries, USA, Canada, Australia, Japan, etc.) and are not seen as 'immigrants' by the general public.[14] Thus the legally resident foreign population of the EC, excluding EC nationals and nationals of other advanced industrialized countries, can be estimated on the basis of these data to amount to some 7 million. These figures, however, exclude members of immigrant-origin ethnic minorities who are EC nationals, creating a particularly distorted picture in the case, for example, of the United Kingdom, where most members of an immigrant-origin ethnic minority are British citizens (total non-EC foreign population of about one million[15] versus an ethnic minority population of about 2.6 million[16]). Similarly in France a very large proportion of immigrants or members of immigrant-origin minorities are naturalized (automatically for those born in France of foreign parents)[17] or, like in Britain, previously migrated with French citizenship. Indeed, in Germany close to a million 'ethnic Germans' have immigrated as German citizens since 1989.

In all cases the figures quoted can be assumed to be below the actual numbers as a result of 'invisible' groups such as illegal immigrants, seasonal workers and those possessing host-country citizenship. There are no reliable estimates for numbers of illegal or clandestine immigrants in Europe. It is reckoned that the largest numbers are in the new receiving countries of the northern Mediterranean: of the collective foreign population of some 2.7 million in Italy, Spain, Portugal and Greece, roughly half are thought to be illegal immigrants (1.3 to 1.5 million[18]). To come up with an estimate for Europe as a whole it would be necessary to add unknown numbers of illegal immigrants from Eastern and Central Europe* (the largest numbers of whom are thought to be in Germany, Switzerland, Austria and France).

The majority of non-EC immigrants and their descendants live in France (over 2 million,[19] excluding those with French citizenship), Germany (over 3.5 million in 1989) and Britain (over one million, excluding those with British citizenship).[20] The origins of immigrant minority populations in France and Germany reflect the fact that the majority of third-country nationals resident in the European Community come from Mediterranean countries,† most notably Turkey (24.4%), Algeria (10.3%), Yugoslavia (8.6%) and Morocco (9.7%).[21] Thus in Germany, Turks form by far the largest contingent (over 1.6 million) followed by Yugoslavs (over 600,000),[22] while in France, Algerians form the largest immigrant group (at least 820,000[23]), and the Moroccan population exceeds 440,000.

Exclusion of EC nationals from the statistics hides the fact that both France and Germany have substantial minority populations originating in Mediterranean countries that are now within the European Community: the second-largest immigrant group in France is that of Portuguese origin, numbering some 650,000, and Spaniards and Italians together account for almost 500,000; Italians constitute the third-largest immigrant group in Germany (over 500,000) followed by roughly 300,000 Greeks.[24] In addition to these groups, both France and Germany contain a variety of smaller – but in many cases growing – minorities from sub-Saharan Africa (France particularly), Eastern and Central Europe (Germany), Asia and the Middle East (both countries).[25] At least in so far as the largest minorities are concerned, the profile of immigrant groups in Germany broadly reflects the recruitment policies of the 1950s and 1960s, while that of France reflects past colonial links and geographical position vis-à-vis the European sending

*Plus, of course, illegal immigrants from Africa, Middle East, Asia, etc. in all European countries.
†Not reflected in the composition of Britain's ethnic minorities, since the majority of non-EC immigrants in the UK came from the New Commonwealth.

states.[26] Overall, non-EC foreigners account for roughly 4.1% and 5.6% of the total populations of France and Germany respectively.[27]

The profile of the ethnic minority population of immigrant origin in the United Kingdom is very different from those of continental European receiving states, since it is dominated by minorities of New Commonwealth origin.[28] As noted above, the most appropriate quantification of immigrant-origin minority groups in the UK is by ethnic identity rather than by nationality. Of the some 2.6 million persons identifying themselves as belonging to an ethnic minority (approximately 4.7% of the British population),[29] just over half are of Indian (31%), Pakistani (17%) or Bangladeshi descent (3%); roughly 19% are of West Indian origin;[30] the remainder includes those of mixed ethnic origin (11%), and the smaller categories of Chinese, African or Arab descent (each around 3–4%).[31] It should also be noted that the substantial population of Irish immigrants resident in Britain represents an important group (about 650,000 were born in the Irish Republic). Ethnic minorities in Britain reflect past colonial ties more clearly than in any other receiving country.

Although in Italy the presence of large immigrant groups is a very recent phenomenon, its postwar immigration history does none the less date back at least to the early 1960s. This history is reflected in a very complex immigrant or immigrant-origin population. The longer-established immigrant groups in Italy include Eritreans who first began entering at the beginning of the 1960s, often as domestics accompanying Italian families returning from the former colony – a flow which took on a more political and spontaneous character as it continued through the 1970s. Somali immigration also dates back to the early post-independence years; however, all migration from sub-Saharan Africa was generally very limited until the 1980s, when increasing numbers of (predominantly) single men began migrating from a number of African countries. The pattern of this immigration stream has been highly disorganized.[32] Other immigrant groups dating back to the 1970s or early 1980s include Filipinos and Sinhalese (predominantly female domestic workers*), South Americans (many of whom entered as refugees or exiles, some of Italian descent), Chinese (dating back to the interwar period) and Tamils (refugees fleeing violence in Sri Lanka). Italy is also host to large numbers of immigrants from Lebanon, Iran, Iraq, India and Poland. North Africans (Algerian, Moroccan, Tunisian, plus Egyptians[33]), however, constitute the

*Many of whom have been in Italy for ten years or more and can be considered 'immigrants'.

largest immigrant contingent in Italy. Although dating back to the early 1970s, this group has taken on significant dimensions only over the past few years. In a recent survey, almost 60% of immigrants interviewed had been in Italy for no more than three years, and over 30% had arrived in the twelve months prior to March 1990.[34] Although traditionally a sending country, Italy is now an immigration country. Net migration of Italians has largely stabilized, with emigration of Italians in 1989 (estimated at 49,400) balancing numbers returning (49,100).[35] Recent estimates put the number of foreigners resident in Italy at roughly one million[36] (just under 2% of the total population). This is almost double the number registered by the Ministry of the Interior and about three times the number recorded in the municipal records offices.

Demographic trends
As noted in Chapter 5, the clamp-down on immigration in the early 1970s had the general effect of stabilizing and consolidating immigrant populations in all the main postwar receiving states, although the impact of the new immigration controls and changes in the economic climate differed from one immigrant group to another. In Germany, for example, the Italian, Greek, Spanish, Portuguese and Yugoslav populations decreased in the decade after 1973, while the Turkish immigrant population increased by roughly 150%.[37] The overall percentage of foreigners in the total population of Germany increased by only about 1% during the same period. With worker immigration suspended, family migration accounted almost entirely for immigration flows after 1973, indicative of the fact that immigrants who remained in Germany had settled more or less permanently. France also experienced an increase in non-European immigrants in relation to numbers of European immigrants, although this pattern was not entirely clear-cut: the number of Italian and Spanish immigrants in France declined significantly between 1975 and 1982, while the Portuguese immigrant population increased slightly.[38]

In Britain, the West Indian population was already well established by the early 1970s, the stream having started earlier and having included a high proportion of women and children from the very beginning. Immigration during the 1970s was dominated by family migration from the Indian subcontinent, since flows from India, Pakistan and Bangladesh had initially been characterized by inflows of men migrating individually. Thus, whereas the population of West Indian ethnic origin increased by only 9% between

1971 and 1976 (and subsequently decreased by 6% between 1981 and 1988*), the Pakistani/Bangladeshi and Indian ethnic group populations increased by 44% and 27% respectively. This trend continued into the 1980s, particularly in the case of the Pakistani minority, which expanded by 144% between 1981 and 1988 (from 284,000 to 479,000).[39] The entry of some 100,000 East African Asians during the 1970s further boosted Britain's Asian population.

Of course, the growth in immigrant populations in all the receiving states since the early 1970s is due not only to continuing immigration, but also to a natural increase within these populations. As a consequence of family reunion, immigrant populations became progressively balanced in terms of age and sex. This resulted in a substantial rise in fertility rates and thus a growth in the so-called 'second generation' of immigrant groups. The fertility component as a factor in the development of the size of immigrant minorities has become more and more significant relative to immigration rates over the past decade. Whereas fertility rates among most European host populations have declined to near or below the replacement threshold (2.1),[40] those within immigrant populations tend to be significantly higher (e.g. 6.19 for Tunisian women who arrived in France after 1975).[41] For this reason, and because of the overall younger age profiles of immigrant populations,[†] immigrant minority populations have become particularly important in the lowest age-groups. For example, 17% of all children born in the Federal Republic in 1974 had foreign parents.[42]

Fertility rates, however, vary considerably from one nationality group to another, and within nationality groups from one country to another,[43] reflecting a range of factors such as fertility rates in the country of origin, length of settlement in the receiving country and rates of female participation in the labour force. For example, the fertility rate among the Italian immigrant population in France was 1.74 (below the replacement threshold) in 1982, whereas that of the Moroccan community was 5.23.[44] The overall trend among immigrant groups is one of declining fertility over time, often converging with or even dropping below the fertility rate of the population as a whole.[45] As noted in a recent OECD report, 'the arrival of more fertile population groups ... has not ... led to an explosion in foreign births that some segments of public opinion allege or fear ... In fact ... foreign natality as a

*Owing primarily to an excess of births over deaths.
†At least during the first few decades of settlement, owing to low numbers of persons falling into the older age-group categories, as well as being due to higher numbers of children.

proportion of total births has remained quite moderate in most countries and is even tending to decline.'[46]

According to Eurostat, the total population of the European Community rose by 1.647 million in 1989, and by 2 million in 1990, half to two-thirds of which was attributable to net migration and one-third to a half due to a surplus of births over deaths.[47] A 1990 Eurostat report observes that net migration into the Community 'was higher than ever before, and for the first time, too, net migration was the main component of population growth', but that 'this exceptional situation results from the upheavals in eastern Europe in 1989'.[48] The overall increase for the Community as a whole therefore masks considerable differences between member states. The Federal Republic of Germany experienced an inflow of approximately one million immigrants in 1989, predominantly from Eastern and Central Europe and including some 344,000 *Ubersiedler* (Germans from the former GDR) and 377,000 *Aussiedler* (persons of German ethnic origin from outside the Federal Republic or the former GDR),[49] and thus immigration accounted for a much greater part of the country's population growth than did natural increase. On the other hand, the predominant factor accounting for population growth in France during the same year was natural increase rather than immigration. Population grew in the Federal Republic by 984,000 or 1.58% in 1989; by 287,000 or 0.51% in France (of which 50,000 attributed to net migration); by 183,000 or 0.32% in the UK (of which 64,000 as a result of net migration); and by 65,800 or 1.1% in Italy (of which 36,000 as a result of net migration). The populations of Spain and the Republic of Ireland declined by an estimated 13,600 and 42,500 respectively.[50] It is worth noting that net migration was negative for Britain during most of the 1980s despite inflows of foreign population (e.g. a net loss through migration of 21,000 in 1988). This is indicative of the downward trend in net immigration rates for all the postwar receiving states during the mid-1980s – a trend that has reversed only over the past few years. Although it may be assumed that net migration was in fact considerably higher for all countries than is indicated by these figures (which exclude undocumented migrants, such as seasonal workers and illegal immigrants), it can be concluded that the major European receiving states generally succeeded in stabilizing the growth of immigrant populations after 1973 – at least up until the late 1980s.[51] Indeed, it may be suggested that considerably more was achieved in the field of immigration control[52] than was accomplished in efforts to ensure the successful integration of immigrant groups.

Integration as a policy issue

By the mid-1970s, all of Europe's receiving states had introduced policies geared towards the integration of immigrant minorities. Until then there had been surprisingly little open recognition of the potential social and political impacts of immigration, and virtually nothing in the way of long-term planning for the integration of immigrants. Indeed, even after the importance of integration had gained explicit recognition, the tendency was for policies to be adopted in a largely piecemeal and reactive way, responding to specific problems as they arose, rather than through the formulation of comprehensive and far-sighted strategies. This was particularly apparent in the 'guestworker' countries (West Germany, Switzerland and, to a lesser extent, the Nether-lands), where the emphasis on return of workers and *de facto* institutionalized segregation of foreign workers during the 1950s and 1960s meant that recognition of a need for full integration of immigrants was slow to develop. Those countries which had experienced more permanent immigration, or, rather, those countries that had not developed policies of labour rotation (including the United Kingdom and France), demonstrated a concern for integration or responded to integration-related issues rather earlier.

As noted in Chapter 5, the social implications of large-scale New Commonwealth immigration had been a subject of national debate in Britain ever since the first arrivals of West Indian immigrants in the late 1940s and 1950s. Nevertheless, the fact that immigrants migrated independently with full civic and political rights meant that it was over a decade before special measures on behalf of immigrant minorities were considered necessary or appropriate. The first race relations legislation passed in Britain (the 1965 Race Relations Act) was limited in scope (outlawing discrimination in public places) and could not have been expected to have a substantial impact on the position of immigrants in British society.[53] Similarly in France, the assumption prevailed for a long time that immigrants' welfare could be sufficiently protected through the formal guarantee of legal rights deriving from the Constitution and the operation of state institutions applicable to French society as a whole. State action on behalf of immigrants was initially restricted to attempts to tackle the problem of immigrant housing, and then only in connection with efforts to eliminate the infamous immigrant *bidonvilles* (slum shanty towns)[54] that had grown up around Paris and other large French cities during the 1950s. The differences in approaches to integration that were manifest between states in the 1960s were also apparent during the 1970s despite the new and universal expressions of concern over the issue which arose in conjunction with the immigration clamp-down of 1973/4.

The United Kingdom

In Britain the term 'integration', when used, came to be defined 'not as a flattening process of assimilation but as equal opportunity, accompanied by cultural diversity, in an atmosphere of mutual tolerance'.[55] All the main political parties have consistently expressed a commitment to the elimination of racial disadvantage in a multiracial society, but, fearing a backlash from the white population (particularly the white working class), policy-makers have been wary of instituting any programmes aimed openly and directly at improving the social and economic status of immigrants. The emphasis at national level has therefore been on the promotion of equal opportunities through enforceable anti-discrimination legislation rather than on the creation of positive programmes to benefit ethnic minorities.[56] This was expressed by the Home Secretary when he introduced the second reading of the 1968 Race Relations Bill: 'The Bill is concerned with equal rights, equal responsibilities and equal opportunities and it is therefore a Bill for the whole nation and not just minority groups ... Its purpose is to protect society as a whole against actions which will lead to social disruption and to prevent the emergence of a class of second-class citizens.'[57] Where housing and employment conditions and education of minorities have been the specific objects of policy, this has tended to have been at the local authority level; indeed, it is hardly possible to speak of a national policy on these issues. Where central government has addressed these matters, it has generally been in terms that avoid the singling-out of ethnic minorities (e.g. general 'urban renewal' or 'youth opportunity' programmes).

By the mid-1970s it was apparent that discrimination against ethnic minorities was still widespread, particularly in the fields of housing and employment, and that it could not be combated effectively on the basis of the two existing race relations acts. In 1976 a new bill was passed which outlawed indirect as well as direct discrimination in all areas of public life, and which established the Commission for Racial Equality (CRE) as the institution responsible for ensuring its enforcement (replacing the Race Relations Board and Community Relations Commission). The 1976 Race Relations Act and the CRE remain as the backbone of British policy aimed at promoting the integration of ethnic minorities. The CRE has far greater powers of investigation and enforcement than its predecessors had,[58] and is charged with working towards the elimination of discrimination and working to promote equality of opportunity and good relations between persons of different racial groups. Although it has had some degree of success, the CRE has generally failed to live up to expectations. A survey carried out in 1984/5 revealed that over 30% of employers discriminate directly against black job applicants, indicating 'a level of discrimination on racial grounds that is widespread, serious and persistent over time'.[59] In a recent annual report of the CRE, it is noted that 'the prejudices and hostility which showed in crude outbursts and exclusive practices may now hide behind less inelegant expression and more covert behaviour ... and it is too complacent to comfort ourselves that we have seen off the most blatant forms of racism when we witness the scale of harassment on housing estates and in schools or the neo-fascist desecration of Jewish cemeteries'.[60]

France

The French and West German approaches to integration contrast signifi-cantly with Britain's stress on anti-discrimination and recognition of a multiracial society. On the basis of an extensive study of the position of immigrants in Lyon in the 1970s, one writer observed that 'since the French Revolution the problem of how to handle *étrangeté* ... has been a significant one in the development of a French social order', and he goes on to suggest that 'Britain allows more room for, and pays greater attention to, independent immigrant representation, just as it allows more room for cultural autonomy ... the French state is engaged in a much closer monitoring and control of its citizens than we like to believe occurs in Britain ... There is a contrast here between two traditions of nation and state that tempers the way in which each country handles its constituent minorities.'[61] In fact, as discussed in Chapter 4, the French state had little control over the immigration process during the first two decades of immigration, and although the assimilation of immigrants was expressed as an ultimate goal it was assumed or hoped that this would come about automatically if immigrants were forced to address existing traditional French institutions. Until the late 1960s the only effective organi-zations set up to deal with immigrant issues were those created informally on a local and voluntary basis.

The state only started to involve itself directly with immigrants' welfare in the 1960s with the creation of institutional housing specifically for immigrants – *cités de transit* and *foyers-hôtels* – and the resettlement of certain groups in normal social housing. However, in the years leading up to the stop on immigration of 1974, worries began to be expressed at state level over a whole range of immigrant issues (employment conditions, inter-ethnic relations, etc.), and with the creation of the new office of Secretary of State for Immigrant Workers in 1974, a machinery was set in motion to place all immigrant affairs – welfare, housing, employment, education, training, cultural expression – under the control of the state. Rather than relying on general measures to ensure equal opportunity, the French state embarked on a programme of direct insertion of immigrants into French society. Yet, in the very restrictive climate of the 1970s, this was pursued in tandem with the somewhat contradictory aim of encouraging immigrants to return to their countries of origin, an objective which could only be carried out by maintaining a sense of insecurity among immigrant groups. Those groups that were deemed least assimilable – North Africans (particularly Algerians) and to some extent Portuguese – suffered the brunt of a state policy that was based largely on the notion of 'assimilate or return'. Speaking at a meeting in Lyon in 1975, Paul Dijoud (Secretary of State for Immigrant Workers) stated that there must be 'justice, assimilation, integration, living together', but although half of the some 4 million immigrants in France rarely posed problems, if nothing were done about the other half, 'we might have an *îlot de blocage social*, which might lead to the same situation as with the blacks in the United States'.[62]

On coming to power in 1981, the new socialist government promised to replace the discriminatory and segregationist/assimilationist policies of the previous decade with policies promoting cultural pluralism and more liberal and egalitarian integration programmes, emphasizing the right to live and work in France without having to assimilate and without discrimination in employment and housing.[63] The policies of return and arbitrary expulsion of immigrants were done away with in the interests of creating a feeling of security within immigrant communities – such security being seen as a prerequisite for successful integration. As in the past, the government has seen the integration of immigrants as the direct responsibility of the state, which is reflected in a plethora of state institutions created to deal with the immigrant issue. In 1989 and 1990 alone, measures taken at state level included the setting up of an Interministerial Committee for Integration,[64] the reinstatement of the National Council for Immigrant Populations, the creation of a Council for Reflection on Islam in France, and the issuing of countless ministerial circulars on the subject of social integration (housing, urban development, education, etc.). The state also assumes a directive and coordinating role in respect of regional or local integration programmes, as expressed in a circular of 24 April 1990, which sets out the basis for negotiation between the state and local communities. The priorities identified include: 'the strengthening of social action linked to accommodation to immigrant families finding themselves in difficulties, activities preparing them for work, and promoting the expression of views by foreign residents on decisions affecting them, and everything relating to their reception, information, schools and community life'.[65] No anti-discrimination machinery has been introduced comparable to that operating in Britain.[66]

The Federal Republic of Germany
The French authorities had been forced to consider the issue of immigrants' welfare relatively early on because of problems that arose in connection with housing shortages. West Germany was also faced with a considerable housing shortage in the decades following the Second World War, but this was not a problem which initially affected immigrants because employers in Germany were bound to provide accommodation for all foreign workers. Immigrants were housed in workers' hostels or barracks, often on-site, and were effectively segregated from the general population and from the German housing market. This, coupled with the notion that foreign workers would eventually return, meant that for the first two decades of immigration there was no pressure or incentive for the state to consider questions of integration. It was only with the increase in family immigration towards the end of the 1960s, which resulted in a progressive movement of immigrants into the general housing markets and which raised questions related to the status of workers' families, that German policy-makers began to concern themselves with the social aspects of immigration.

The first official attempts to develop a policy framework geared towards integration appeared in the form of the 1973 Action Programme for the Employment of Immigrant Labour, aimed primarily at housing and education for immigrants, and in the creation in 1975 of a committee responsible for formulating guidelines for an immigration policy. This committee issued a report which called for priority to be given to the social over the economic aspects of immigration, while at the same time demanding stronger promotion of return migration.[67] The stress was less one of 'assimilate or return' than one of 'temporary integration and return', reflecting a reluctance to accept that a large proportion of immigrants were here for good.[68] As in France, the interest to preserve an element of mobility (and therefore preparedness to return) within immigrant groups was translated into policies which kept immigrants in 'a state of dependence and insecurity'.[69] The 1965 Aliens Act did not include a right of residence, even for those who had been in the Federal Republic for over ten years, but instead stated that 'a residence permit may be granted if it does not harm the interests of the German Federal Republic'.[70] The Act also stated that 'foreigners enjoy all basic rights, except the basic rights of freedom of assembly, freedom of association, freedom of movement and free choice of occupation, place of work and place of education, and protection from extradition abroad'.[71] The law linked residence permits to work permits, and allowed considerable administrative discretion in their issue and renewal. In accordance with a decree issued in 1973, foreign workers' family members were to be issued residence permits without work permits, although this was rescinded in 1979.

The first official report representing an attempt to come to terms fully with the presence of immigrant minorities in the Federal Republic was that published in 1979 by Heinz Kuhn, the federal ombudsman for foreign workers and their families. Kuhn stated that 'future policy towards foreign employees and their families living in the FRG must be based on the assumption that a development has taken place which can no longer be reversed and that the majority of those concerned are no longer guestworkers but immigrants, for whom return to their countries of origin is for various reasons no longer a viable option'.[72] He recommended a series of measures designed to ensure a more secure legal status and greater opportunities for foreigners, including the restriction of arbitrary powers in the policing of foreigners and the introduction of the right of foreigners to vote in local elections after eight to ten years' residence. The same year, a list of guidelines were drawn up by the Coordination Committee on Foreign Workers, which stressed in particular the need to concentrate on the social integration of the second and third generations, a recommendation which implied a writing-off of the first immigrant generation and which persists in many respects today.[73] The generally progressive tone of these two reports, however, was not reproduced in government policy for over a decade. As in France, the restrictive climate in respect of immigrants intensified in the lead-up to the 1982 national elections with politicians talking more and more in terms of 'assimilate or return'[74] – sentiments that were directed primarily at Turkish immigrants (cf. North Africans in France) and which were reaffirmed in 1983 with the Act to Promote the Preparedness of Foreign Workers to Return.[75]

The 'foreigners problem' had come to be seen predominantly as a 'Turkish problem'.

The 1980s witnessed a growing recognition of immigrants as a permanent and structural feature of German society and an increasing concern for the integration of immigrant minorities, particularly those of the second and third generations who had been born or spent most of their lives in the Federal Republic. A recent report issued by the Federal Minister of the Interior states that 'approximately 60 percent of aliens staying in the Federal Republic of Germany have been living here for ten years or more ... More than two-thirds of foreign children and juveniles were born in the Federal Republic of Germany ... The Federal Government assumes that most of them will stay for a considerable period of time or that some of them will even stay for ever ... For these persons there is no convincing alternative to integration.'[76] A new Foreigners Act was passed in January 1991 which states as its primary objective the improvement of conditions for the integration of immigrants, and includes for the first time a 'right to reside' for foreigners who have held a residence permit for eight years or more. However, this is dependent on the applicants' ability to prove that they can finance their living costs.[77] There is little reference to the notion of 'multiculturalism' in official circles, and the broadly assimilationist attitudes prevalent at the beginning of the 1980s are echoed in this Act, which states that 'integration as a process of adaptation to German conditions ... requires some participation of the aliens who have to accustom themselves above all to the values, norms and ways of living prevailing here ... Respect for our culture ... the acquisition of some knowledge of the German language, abandonment of excessive national-religious behaviours and integration into school and professional life ... are the prerequisites which have to be fulfilled.' Nevertheless immigrants have generally enjoyed considerable cultural autonomy in Germany, not by virtue of a policy commitment to multiculturalism, but as a result of policies which stressed the maintenance of a return-orientation among immigrant groups. Support of immigrants' links with their countries of origin and the socialization of children into the culture of the country of origin was seen as a way to facilitate and encourage return migration. However, the degree to which policy has stressed segregation or integration of immigrants has varied from one region or city to another, because – unlike France and more like Britain – central state control over integration policies is limited compared to that assumed by the regional (Länder) and local authorities, especially in relation to housing and education.

Italy

As in the case of Europe's traditional receiving states, Italy has adopted the dual policy of restricting immigration while at the same time promoting the integration of those who have already settled within its borders. Italian immigration policy has developed only very recently, however, as a response to the new escalation in immigrant inflows and in an effort to bring its immigration control and treatment of immigrants more in line with that of other EC member states. Italy's first major policy response to immigration was Law no. 943, passed in December 1986. This was followed in February 1990 by Law no. 39, commonly referred to as the 'Martelli Law'. Perhaps the most significant integration measures to arise out of these laws were the amnesties providing for large-scale regularization of 'irregular' or 'illegal' immigrants, comparable with the regularization carried out by the French authorities in 1981/2. According to one estimate, roughly 80% of North African immigrants were in Italy on an irregular basis before 1986.[78] Law 943 came into effect in January 1987 with an amnesty initially to last for a period of three months, but extended by successive amendments up to September 1988. Law 39 introduced the second amnesty, which provided for the registration of illegal immigrants who were present in Italy on 31 December 1989 and who came forward to register before 29 June 1990. It was hoped that these regularizations would not only benefit the state by introducing a greater degree of control over the immigration phenomenon, but that the immigrants themselves would benefit by virtue of the general social and economic rights associated with legal residency status. However neither amnesty proved particularly successful: only about 10% of irregular immigrants came forward under the first amnesty,[79] and it is estimated that up to 50% of immigrants currently in Italy are present and/or working on an irregular basis.[80] A number of reasons are put forward for why the regularization rate was so low, perhaps the most important being that most immigrants saw more disadvantages than advantages in registering.[81]

A comprehensive framework of integration policies which could substantially affect the living and working conditions of immigrants is only at an early stage of development in Italy. Law 39 is concerned primarily with immigration control, and thus, apart from the 1981 law ratifying the 1975 ILO Migrant Workers Convention[82] (ratified in the context of Italian emigration), Law 943 still stands as the primary piece of Italian legislation dealing with integration. While appearing relatively far-reaching in its intention to guarantee 'all non-Community workers ... and ... their families equality of treatment and full equality of rights to the use of social and health services ... to the maintenance of cultural identity, to schooling and to the availability of housing',[83] this legislation has not been backed up by an effective enforcement machinery. In practice, it places considerable responsibility with local authorities and on the voluntary sector, but does not provide clear guidelines on what policies should be implemented. According to a recent survey, the 'variegated world of voluntary associations performs a vital task in helping immigrants with social, bureaucratic and work-related problems', but 'analysis of local policies ... shows the fragmentary and incoherent nature of most interventions ... [which] range from a total abandoning of responsibility and buck-passing to (rarely) full integration ... What is needed is a coherent policy which promotes immigrants in both job-related and cultural fields and which seeks to construct a forum for the dignified exchange of views.'[84] In connection with a National Conference on Immigration held in Rome in 1990,[85] the Bocconi University was commissioned to carry out an analysis of the immigration and integration policies of France, Germany, the Netherlands and Great Britain so as to provide information on the main types and forms of immigration policies that could potentially be applied in Italy. The conclusions presented at the conference included 'the necessity of ... an integration which neither produces ghettos nor is complete assimilation ... of structures which ... would monitor the various aspects of integration ... [and] a promotion of greater understanding and respect between ethnic groups'.[86]

Immigrant settlement and integration: substantive issues
Despite the varying orientations of different states towards the question of integration, the basic position of postwar immigrants in all European receiving states is very similar. Whatever the policies introduced, states have generally failed to achieve the secure integration of immigrant groups. This is particularly so in respect of groups that have been the primary focus of concern: those of non-European origin. Every state has expressed greater anxiety over certain immigrant groups than others. Indeed, it is generally possible to speak of a hierarchy of preference for immigrants of different origins. In France, Italians have been preferred over Portuguese, Portuguese over Tunisians, Tunisians over Algerians. In Germany, it is the Turks who have traditionally been seen as presenting the most serious integration problems. To some extent this is translated into a social and economic status hierarchy, the most marginalized groups being those that are perceived as culturally or ethnically most 'distant'. Thus it is difficult to compare the

position of Italian immigrants in France or Germany with that of Algerians or Turks, or the position of Irish immigrants in Britain with that of Bangladeshis.

Of course, the status of different immigrant groups vis-à-vis the dominant society is not only determined by the degree to which one group is favoured over another, but by a range of factors such as the timing of immigration, the sectors of housing and employment into which groups originally entered, and the levels of unemployment in the areas of high immigrant concentration. Nevertheless, it is probably fair to state that in all receiving countries, immigrant minorities of non-European origin are the least integrated in terms of housing, employment and educational opportunities, and to a large extent, their position in any one of these three sectors is dependent on their position in another. This is illustrated by the well-documented process of geographical concentration of immigrant groups in the inner-city areas of Britain's largest conurbations,[87] a process which is in many respects common to the main cities of all the postwar receiving countries. To what extent this concentration has been as a result of 'exclusion, attraction or retention'[88] is debatable, and would anyway have varied from group to group. In the case of Britain, the process may be very generally – if somewhat crudely – explained in terms of immigrants' original location in the housing and labour markets. The majority of immigrants initially filled unskilled or manual jobs in industries that were located in the cities. However, British society was at that time undergoing a major process of economic and social decentralization. Economic and technological developments were already underway which were favouring shifts in the industrial sector to cheaper out-of-city locations, from heavy to light industry, and from a reliance on cheap unskilled labour to a demand for skilled workers. This process was accompanied by a growth in real income among the white population and a significant population movement out of the inner cities to more preferable housing in the suburbs or smaller towns. Unable to compete equally in the housing markets (owing to discrimination and low income), and initially excluded from local authority housing, immigrants were generally forced into the cheapest and most marginal privately rented* or owner-occupied accommodation† in the declining inner cities. Because these types of accommodation tended to be concen-

---

*West Indian immigrants particularly, followed later by movement into council housing. Immigrants were initially excluded from local authority housing because eligibility depended on a certain period of residence in the area, and housing was generally allocated to those who had been waiting the longest.
†Particularly Asian immigrants.

trated in certain areas, and because immigrants tended to create and maintain distinct communities, the outcome was a significant spatial segregation. It is often when areas are looked at ward by ward (the most local level of government) that the concentration of ethnic groups is most striking, the proportion of households headed by a person of New Commonwealth and/or Pakistani (NCWP) origin sometimes exceeding 50%.[89] The disadvantaged position of immigrants in the labour market has therefore to be explained not only in terms of discrimination, but also in terms of a combination of sectoral and spatial segregation: from the very beginning, immigrants became concentrated in sectors of the economy and in geographical areas that have been marked by a progressive decline in demand for labour and, eventually, by high levels of unemployment.

In France the process was somewhat different, explained as much by the state's direct involvement in immigrant housing after the destruction of the *bidonvilles* as by processes of discrimination in the general housing market and by inner-city decay. Three 'solutions' to the immigrant housing problem were adopted in the 1960s: normal social housing rented from one of the regional social housing organizations ('*Habitat à Loyer Modéré*' or HLM), *cités de transit* and *foyers-hôtels*.[90] The *cités de transit* were government-financed, purpose-built, low-standard housing designed specifically for immigrant families moved out of the *bidonvilles*. They were intended to provide temporary housing for those groups that were not deemed 'ready' to move into normal social housing since they were considered too culturally or socially different to be moved into housing markets shared with the French population as a whole. The *cités* were therefore filled primarily by North African immigrants who would receive education during their stay 'in preparation' for a move to HLM housing. The move into social housing was very difficult for many families because of the restrictions the HLM put on numbers of immigrants and family size accepted, so for many the *cités* turned out to be not provisional staging-posts, but areas of permanent settlement and *de facto* segregation.[91] A similar segregation was applied to single North African men, many of whom were housed in barrack-like conditions in the *foyers-hôtels* – hostels for single workers. These are still in use, and although conditions were improved somewhat after protests mounted by residents in the early to mid-1970s,[92] they still represent one of the most marginal categories of housing available to immigrants. Movement of North African immigrants into social housing and privately rented or owned property has generally been accompanied by a process of concentration similar to that which developed in Britain. This has not been so apparent in the case of European immigrant groups, as noted by Paul White in his survey of immigrant housing in Paris: 'Those real community neighbourhoods that do exist and have significance in Paris concern the more ethnically differentiated populations who are ... the least liked by the French.'[93]

The concentration of immigrant groups in Germany associated with the move out of employer accommodation has largely come about through a combination of 'exclusion' (discrimination and low income) and 'attraction' (development and maintenance of community networks). Alarmed by what it saw as a progressive 'ghettoization' among immigrant groups, the Federal government introduced foreign residence quotas for urban regions in 1975, whereby local authorities could declare themselves overburdened and stop any further settlement of immigrants if the foreign population rose above 12%. In fact the authorities could not effectively control immigrants' settlement patterns and the measure was discontinued in 1977. Similar dispersal policies tried on occasion in Britain also met with failure.[94] They were nevertheless significant, since they reflected a concern common to all receiving states over the social implications of immigrant concentration.[95] The worry was as much about the capacity problems of social infrastructures in areas of high immigrant population as about the longer-term implications for the integration of immigrants. They represented an attempt to solve these problems through a direct manipulation of residence rather than through the elimination of disadvantage and discrimination.[96]

It is interesting to note that such policies have come into use again more recently in Germany as a result of efforts to cope with the now substantial inflow of asylum-seekers. In this context, concerns have focused more on the problem of sharing the asylum burden among different Länder and local authorities than on an interest in promoting the social and economic integration of asylum-seekers. Indeed, in many respects this policy may be seen as anti-integration, since large numbers of asylum-seekers have found themselves in areas with no other established immigrant communities (particularly in Eastern Germany), where they are forced to live in segregated housing if only for protection against attacks from increasingly hostile indigenous communities. There is a strong argument to support the view that the isolation of asylum-seekers in areas of Germany already experiencing severe social and economic tension will fuel the now fast-growing anti-immigrant movement in a way that will have a negative impact on the integration not only of new arrivals, but of all immigrants and so-called 'foreigners' in Germany.

More sophisticated approaches to the integration of immigrants and immigrant-origin minorities have, however, been developed over the past decade. An issue which has attracted particular attention is that of the integration of the so-called 'second' and 'third' generations, since it has become increasingly apparent that the marginal position of immigrants in housing, employment and all areas of public life has tended to be perpetuated in the case of their children and their children's offspring. Indeed, unemployment levels among descendants of immigrants are frequently higher than among their parents. For example, in 1985, foreign youths in West Germany were two to three times more likely to be registered as unemployed than their German peers.[97] Furthermore, of those who were working, nearly 90% were employed as manual labourers, and only 20% of those as skilled workers.[98] Anxious to prevent the formation of a permanent 'minority under-class', governments have developed policies aimed at improving opportunities for the younger age-groups through education and training. However, in all the postwar receiving countries, children of immigrants or ethnic minority children continue to be overrepresented in the slowest tracks of the education system and underrepresented at the higher levels of secondary and tertiary education (although the extent of underachievement varies considerably from group to group[99]). In all countries, certain groups have been targeted for special language classes (particularly the lowest age-groups[100]), since language has been seen as one of the most important factors contributing to their problems at school.[101] However, the significance of the language factor must decline as more and more children are born into an environment in which the host-country language is dominant. This points to the importance of connecting education with broader integration programmes, for it is becoming increasingly apparent that the entire basis of minority disadvantage must be tackled if significant progress is to be made in any one area.

Other efforts to improve employment opportunities for ethnic minority labour-market entrants have included programmes of vocational training (e.g. Youth Opportunities and Youth Training Programmes in Britain). However, these have failed to have any significant impact because training cannot guarantee jobs, particularly in areas of high unemployment. Furthermore, the ethnic minorities are frequently overrepresented in programmes that offer little or no opportunity for skilled or more qualified occupations.[102] Aware that disadvantage among minority groups as a whole is often connected with economic stagnation in areas with high immigrant populations, most governments have also instituted programmes of urban renewal and rejuvenation. These have generally not led to a substantial improvement in the position of immigrant groups. Indeed, a common pattern is the displacement of immigrant groups from areas that have undergone redevelopment[103] – a trend often associated with a process of 'gentrification', particularly in the inner cities.

Immigrants and immigrant minorities: a 'class apart'?

Despite the *de facto* marginalization of many immigrants and immigrant groups in the social and economic spheres of society in Western Europe, most immigrants and descendants of immigrants in Europe now enjoy a relatively secure legal status that allows for permanent settlement and *de jure* equal treatment in areas such as housing, employment, education and welfare benefits. Thus most enjoy, at least formally, full civic and social rights, and – as indicated in the previous section – much of the effort made by governments and other authorities to secure the integration of immigrant groups is devoted to promoting and protecting immigrants' and minorities' access to and enjoyment of these rights. However, even if these groups were to enjoy full substantive equality in these areas, the extent of their member-ship of the wider society in which they live might still be questioned. An important factor militating against the full integration of immigrant minority groups is the legal definition and wider perceptions of immigrants and their offspring as 'outsiders' in many countries. As observed by Czarina Wilpert in a study of Turkish immigrant groups in Berlin, 'there exists, for all second-generation Turks, a tension between their lack of a legitimate future and membership of German society (institutional marginality) and the *de facto* experience of a legitimate claim to belongingness through a life lived [in the Federal Republic] ... [This] conflict is enhanced by the ascriptive experiences of discrimination, denigration and youths' concomitant identification with their family and culture of origin.'[104]

One key to this tension can be found in the concepts of citizenship that apply in Western Europe today. Both in formal terms (membership of a state) and in substantive meaning (possession of a number of rights and duties in that state),[105] it is citizenship which may ultimately define who are 'insiders' and who are 'outsiders' in the modern West European state, and – in the case of many immigrant minorities in Western Europe today – who are neither one nor the other. As Tomas Hammar observes, and as is hinted at by Czarina Wilpert in the quote above, the majority of immigrants and immigrant minorities in Western Europe could be considered to be both insiders and outsiders, members and non-members of the societies in which they live, and therefore can be seen as forming a 'class apart' within these societies. Hammar thus identifies three categories of person in Western Europe according to citizenship status: foreigners (those with no rights associated with citizenship, e.g. short-stay visitors), citizens and 'denizens'. He estimates that over half of all non-nationals resident in Western Europe (excluding the UK) fall into the third category. As he observes:

> Many foreign citizens have ... gained a secure residence status [in Western Europe]. Even if they are not citizens of the country, they can for example only be deported in extreme emergency situations. They may have lived such a long period in the host country ... [or] their family ties may be so strong ... that they in fact constitute a new category of foreign citizens whose residence status is fully guaranteed or almost so. Those who belong to this category have also in several countries been entitled to equal treatment in all spheres of life, with full access to the labour market, business, education, social welfare, even to employment in branches of the public service, etc. A new status group has emerged, and members of this group are not regular and plain foreign citizens any more, but also not naturalized citizens of the receiving country.[106]

Because members of this group usually enjoy full social and economic rights (at least formally), their status is substantively different from that of citizens principally by their exclusion from participation in most areas of the formal political process. Thus, although in general all states allow immigrants to express themselves politically (to form associations, to take part in union activities, to demonstrate and strike, and to join political parties), immigrants are usually excluded from participation in national elections, and it is only in recent years that a number of states have introduced the right to vote for certain (usually restricted) categories of foreign nationals in municipal or regional elections.[107] As a result, a substantial proportion of immigrants and immigrant minorities (and thus a substantial proportion of the population of Western Europe) are not represented politically, at least at the regional and national levels. This not only raises questions as to the health of representative democracy in Western Europe, but also may be seen to constitute a significant challenge to the substantive integration of many immigrant minority groups. There are two main reasons for this. First, because the promotion of immigrants' interests through formal political channels has to take place on the basis of an often weak and distorting filter-through process (or outside such channels altogether), the potential for immigrants to have any meaningful say in the policies developed to promote their integration is likely to be limited. Second, and perhaps more importantly, with no political voice, there exists little incentive or, indeed, little potential for such groups to develop any significant sense of political citizenship.[108] This implies a danger of alienation, disaffection, and a persistent orientation to the country of origin among many immigrants, an orientation which may be not only political but also social and cultural in nature, and which is likely in turn to work against the processes of social and economic integration which the host governments are so keen to promote. Czarina Wilpert observed in Berlin, for example, the persistence of a return-orientation (or 'myth of return') not only among first-generation migrants, but also among their children, a situation which she ascribed in part to their status as 'outsiders' or 'denizens'.[109]

In this context, however, generalization is extremely problematic. Just as approaches to the social and economic integration of immigrants differ from country to country and group to group, so do policies affecting the residence and citizenship status of immigrant minority communities. Immigration policy in the United Kingdom is the most obvious exception: the majority of immigrants who arrived in the UK during the postwar period did so as British subjects with full citizenship (and thus full political) rights; naturalization and dual citizenship are relatively easy to attain; most offspring of immigrants born in the country are accorded British citizenship; and all Commonwealth citizens migrating today gain the right to vote in national elections after one year's residence in the UK. In France, the situation differs in that most immigrants did not enter with citizenship rights. Nevertheless, all offspring of immigrants born in France are automatically granted French citizenship. In Germany, on the other hand, not only most first-generation immigrants but also the second- and third-generation offspring of immigrants born in Germany remain unnaturalized, and thus remain foreigners in the juridical sense – foreigners with all the attributes of denizens as described above.

Such variation can be partly explained in terms of differing concepts of citizenship, which in turn derive from the historical development of nation-states in Western Europe, a process specific to each country in question. Thus, as Uri Ra'anan observes, the relative openness of both Britain and France to the acceptance of foreigners as nationals or citizens could be traced back in part to the fact that centralization and bureaucratic statehood as they developed in these countries assisted the processes of creating the modern French and British *nations*. As a consequence, residence, allegiance to the state and submission to its jurisdiction became the hallmarks of citizenship, and thus territorial concepts – place of birth (according to the principle of *jus soli*) and place of residence – came largely to determine nationality in these countries.[110] Such concepts lent themselves to conceiving of the populations of these states' empires as attached juridically to the centre as subjects or citizens. In Germany, in contrast, the centralized nation-state developed much later, and in such a way that suggested a case of the nation creating the state, rather than the state creating the nation. Consequently, the criteria determining German nationality came to be derived from *jus sanguinis* rather than *jus soli*. As Ra'anan describes, 'it is not *where* an individual resides and which state has jurisdiction over him that determines his nationality, but rather *who* he is – his cultural, religious and historic identity, i.e. his ethnicity, a heritage received from his ancestors and carried with him, in mind and body, irrespective of his current place of domicile'.[111] In the case of Germany, this meant membership of the German *Volk*. Thus, recently, large numbers of so-called 'ethnic Germans' or '*Aussiedler*' have been able to migrate to Germany as full citizens, whereas at the same time the majority of foreign immigrants and those born of foreign immigrant parentage in Germany remain foreigners and thus non-citizens.

The language used to denote immigrant minority communities in these countries is indicative of these differing models. Whereas in Germany all immigrants and descendants of immigrants continue to be referred to as 'foreigners' or 'aliens',[112] in Britain such groups are referred to as 'ethnic minorities'. In France, the term 'minorities' runs counter to the French insistence on a unitary state, thus 'immigrants' and 'populations of immigrant origin' are the most widely used terms. It is interesting to note that both 'ethnic minorities' and 'immigrants' denote groups with a specific status within the socio-legal structure of the nation-state, whereas the term 'foreigners' clearly places immigrant communities outside the structure of state membership.

In substantive terms, however, the significance of this variation should probably not be over-emphasized. The problems that France has experienced since the 1950s in accepting immigrants of different cultures, and the United Kingdom's difficulties in coming to terms with the new multicultural and multi-racial nature of its society, demonstrate the limits to the territorial or 'civil' basis of membership and citizenship of these states. Indeed, in Britain, the experience of black and Asian immigration during the postwar period resulted quite directly in the decline in the importance of territorial principles as the foundation of British citizenship. The distinction made between 'patrial' and 'non-patrial' citizens introduced in the 1970s – criticized so much at the time because it was seen to discriminate against potential migrants from the so-called New Commonwealth countries (non-white) – demonstrated a growing emphasis on the principle of *jus sanguinis* in the operation of British citizenship laws, and thus a retreat from policies which had allowed the entry, settlement and exercise of citizenship rights to substantial numbers of non-white and non-Christian immigrants.

Some observers have suggested that the colonial experience of France and Britain implied a greater acceptance of foreign immigration. As argued in a recent Council of Europe report, 'countries with a colonial past, the United Kingdom, France, the Netherlands and Portugal in particular, have more historical familiarity with people from overseas' and thus 'have been more open than others to the possibility of permanent immigration'. The colonial experience, however, was likely to have strengthened ideas of racial or cultural superiority over colonized populations rather than fostered cultural or racial tolerance. The French insistence on cultural assimilation in the past, and, more recently, the Salman Rushdie affair in Britain, the controversy over the wearing of headscarves in French schools, and the resurgence in extreme anti-immigrant sentiment as a mainstream political force in France, are testimony to the limits of tolerance on French or British soil.

Thus, to the extent that particular immigrant minority populations throughout Western Europe are singled out as groups that are excluded from certain rights because of their legal status as outsiders, or as groups that are deprived of equal access to those and other rights (economic, social and political) because of their perceived status as outsiders, many do remain a 'class apart', whether it be in their own eyes or in the eyes of indigenous populations. All nation-states in Western Europe were built in the absence of large racially, culturally, or religiously distinct immigrant communities, and thus in all states ideas of 'belongingness' became tied to those of cultural, linguistic, ethnic and/or religious identity – an identity which, to varying extents, defined the community not only in terms of itself, but also in terms of its relations with outsiders. In all states, those who have least easily conformed to this identity have tended to be those who have remained the most marginalized (e.g. Bangladeshis as compared with the Irish in Britain, or Moroccans and sub-Saharan Africans compared with the Italians in France).

As discussed in Chapter 7, immigrant and minority integration remains as one of the central tenets of migration policy in Western Europe today. The recent upsurge in racism and xenophobia throughout Western Europe may be forcing a number of governments to shy away from instituting the most progressive forms of integration policy. The Netherlands, for example, now seems to be retreating from the explicitly multicultural policies which it has pursued in recent years. However, at the same time, the rise in extreme anti-immigrant sentiment is resulting in governments placing greater and greater stress on the need to integrate existing immigrant and minority populations. As in the 1970s, it is argued that immigrant integration can be achieved only if all further immigration is kept to a minimum. It is therefore old anxieties about the socially disruptive effects of the presence of foreign immigrant populations that continue to force the pace. Thus, it would seem, the driving force behind current efforts to secure the integration of immigrant minority groups in Western Europe today is the same force as that which has underpinned the development of every nation-state in Western Europe, that being the desire to secure a fully integrated population which is unified in its membership of, identification with and allegiance to the state. Unfortunately, it is those very same desires which, if founded too firmly on ideas of a shared cultural, religious, linguistic or racial identity, might result in the failure of those efforts.

Chapter 7

Europe's Receiving States in the 1990s: Towards a Harmonization of Policy?

The *de facto* immigration which took place during the 1950s to 1970s gave rise to a number of problems for Europe's receiving states which have persisted right up to the present day, the most notable of which has been the integration of immigrant groups. Although such concerns were originally limited to Europe's major receivers, new pressures emerged during the 1980s that made immigration a salient issue for almost all states in Western Europe. In addition to continuing family immigration, other immigration channels began expanding during the 1980s which increasingly impacted on previously unaffected countries, including those that had hitherto been the sending states of Southern Europe (Italy and Spain in particular). This development coincided with an acceleration in moves towards closer economic, and subsequently political, integration in Western Europe – limited initially to the European Community, but with the potential for extension to EFTA states and further afield. As an upshot of both developments, the harmonization of migration policies – an issue which had been on the table ever since the clamp-down on immigration of 1973/4 – took on a particular urgency in the second half of the 1980s. Indeed, the pressure for harmonization has been so great over recent years that any discussion of the current and future development of migration policy in Western Europe cannot help but be pulled into a consideration of the harmonization question.

This chapter looks at the current direction of migration policy in Western Europe through the lens of the harmonization process. Although all the elements would seem to be in place for an extensive harmonization in this area, a closer look at a number of issues in question reveals that the road to common policies is unlikely to be a smooth one. Nevertheless, just a cursory glance at those issues touched on by the harmonization process indicates that the basic thrust of migration policy in Western Europe has not undergone any drastic changes since the early 1970s. Thus, although a number of specific problems may emerge as harmonization is accelerated, none of the basic tenets of migration policy in Western Europe seem, as yet, to be being challenged in any substantial way.

Institutional developments

During the 1970s and 1980s, immigration came to be viewed by Europe's receiving states as more and more of a problem. As detailed in previous chapters, attention turned progressively towards issues such as family immigration, return migration, illegal and clandestine immigration, integration and – somewhat later – rising levels of spontaneous arrivals of asylum-seekers. The emphasis was on control. To what extent could family immigration be limited or regulated? How could foreign workers be persuaded to return home? How could those destined to stay be integrated? How could illegal immigration be prevented? What could be done about rising numbers of spontaneous asylum applications? Increasingly, these problems came to be seen as problems shared among all Europe's major receiving states.

Early moves towards international harmonization of immigration and refugee policies revealed a growing recognition of the commonality of such problems, but also reflected the highly restrictive climate which emerged after the postwar recruitment period. For example, a number of international instruments formulated within the framework of the Council of Europe failed to live up to expectations because they sought an extension of and/or a confirmation of states' obligations towards migrants at a time when the primary interest of those states was in restriction and control. Most notable among these instruments was the 1977 European Convention on the Legal Status of Migrant Workers, which, at the time, was ratified by only five states of which three were migrant-senders rather than receivers.[1] In general, the late 1970s and early 1980s witnessed an overall convergence in receiving states' domestic immigration policies but little in the way of formal international policy integration. Although those states which had become members of the European Community had for a long time been cooperating with regard to the intra-Community movement of EC nationals, policy affecting the immigration and residence of so-called third-country nationals remained essentially the subject of national control – constituting, in point of fact, a fundamental expression of state sovereignty.

Although there was still little in the way of formal harmonization, dialogue between ministers and officials from different countries did however increase. This resulted in a process of informal harmonization which still continues today as a mechanism of considerable importance, as reflected in the institutionalization of dialogue in the form of bodies such as the Intergovernmental Consultations on Asylum and Refugee Policies in Europe and North America, and the Council of Europe Conferences of European Ministers Responsible for Migration Affairs. Not only can particular policy developments be attributed to this process, such as the proliferation of legislation on carrier sanctions through many countries in Western Europe during the second half of the 1980s, but so too, to some extent, can the growth in recognition or perception of 'common' problems. It is likely, for instance, that increased consultation resulted not only in a sharing of information and indirect policy harmonization, but also in a sharing of perceptions and prejudices, such that – for example – Germany's particular asylum problems, or Italy's unique problems with illegal immigration, came to be seen as problems shared by all states in Western Europe.

Two developments in the mid-1980s paved the way for more formal and accelerated consultation. First, in June 1985 the Benelux states (Belgium, the Netherlands and Luxembourg) plus France and the Federal Republic of Germany signed what is known as the Schengen Agreement, undertaking to create a frontier-free space for the movement of goods, services and persons, and to harmonize a wide range of policies, including controls on immigration from third countries. The Schengen Agreement was to be implemented ahead of, and in anticipation of, free movement within the European Community as a whole, as set out in the Single European Act of 1986. When ratified in 1987, the Single European Act introduced a new article into the EEC Treaty of Rome which stipulated that 'the Community shall adopt measures with the aim of establishing the internal market over a period expiring on 31 December 1992' comprising 'an area without internal frontiers in which the free movement of goods, persons, services and capital is ensured'.[2] As a concomitant of the abolition of internal borders, the external borders of each Community member state would effectively become external borders for the whole Community. Both agreements thus provided a new impetus for policy harmonization. The aim was no longer harmonization for its own sake and for the sake of migrants, but was now harmonization for the sake of the new Europe and for the member states of the respective groupings. As expressed in a recent European Commission communication:

The inauguration within the European Community of the free movement of persons on 31 December 1992 and the abolition of internal
frontiers ... could entail a risk that the absence of checks at internal
borders will render any control of immigration impossible ... This has
led the Member States to recognise the need for a common approach
by the Twelve and to discuss ways in which they can cooperate. The
interdependence of various national situations, taken together with the
permeability of borders, requires joint action, if only on the grounds
of efficiency.[3]

Yet, given the paucity of prior formal cooperation among member states,
'joint action' could not proceed automatically. There was first a need to reach
closer consensus and consistency among member states through a harmonization of what was still – despite general convergence – a very disparate
assortment of migration policies operating in the different states. As a
reflection of both this variation and the pressure to reach a degree of
consistency, a plethora of different institutional bodies emerged after the
signing of the Single European Act which were, and in most cases still are,
connected directly or indirectly with the harmonization process. The development of these institutions depended on the expansion of two distinct but
interconnected mechanisms of consultation and cooperation: intergovernmental consultations, and formal harmonization through conventions and the
processes of the European Community.

Intergovernmental cooperation continued to proceed on a somewhat ad-
hoc basis, as reflected in the establishment in 1986 of the aptly named Ad Hoc
Group on Immigration. This body grew out of the Trevi Group, set up in
1975, which brings together officials responsible for law enforcement –
European Justice and Interior Ministers and senior civil servants – and which
itself extended its area of interest in the late 1980s to include the examination
of questions connected with illegal and clandestine immigration and asylum
inflows. The Ad Hoc Group was charged more directly with examining issues
connected with migration, looking into matters such as stronger checks at
external frontiers, internal checks, coordination of visa policies, cooperation
to avoid the abuse of passports, and common policies to eliminate abuse of
the right of asylum. Since 1988, the Ad Hoc Group has worked in tandem with
a third body, following the decision of the European Council at Rhodes in
December 1988 to set up a group of coordinators consisting of senior officials
of the member states and representatives of the European Commission which

was to be responsible for supervising activities associated with the implementation of free movement. In addition, there were the mechanisms of the Schengen Group to be considered, the membership of which was (and is) made up entirely of EC member states, but which – despite an expansion in 1990 and 1991 to include Italy, Spain and Portugal – does not include the participation of all the Twelve.[4]

To some extent, the processes of informal consultation which had taken place prior to the establishment of these institutions continued within the framework of the new, more formal intergovernmental bodies. Thus, for example, the late 1980s and early 1990s saw the proliferation of visa requirements and an accelerated convergence in immigration policies of member states (e.g. new immigration legislation introduced in Italy, Spain and Portugal) which were not enshrined in any formal international agreements. Formal conventions did also emerge, however, one of which arose out of the consultations of the Schengen Group, and two of which were drawn up by the Ad Hoc Group on the basis of the 1989 recommendations of the Group of Coordinators (the Palma document).

The Convention on the Application of the Schengen Agreement, signed in June 1990 and covering a wide range of issues connected with cross-border movements (including the entry of asylum-seekers and control of illegal immigration), provided a model for the Draft Convention on the Crossing of External Borders drawn up by the Ad Hoc Group – reflecting, among other things, the high degree of inter-group influence and consultation that has characterized the intergovernmental process. However, this level of consultation has not been matched by dialogue with national parliaments or non-governmental bodies, and, as a result, the Ad Hoc, Schengen and Trevi Groups have come under severe criticism for the secrecy with which negotiations have been carried out.[5] The Draft Convention on the Crossing of External Borders (not yet signed)[6] is one of the two principal EC12 instruments connected with the creation of an internal market which explicitly address migration policy. The second is the Convention Determining the State Responsible for Examining Applications for Asylum (the so-called Dublin Convention), now signed (but not ratified) by all twelve member states,[7] which lays down provisions designed to prevent (1) multiple or successive applications being submitted by an asylum-seeker in more than one state; and (2) the problem of 'refugees in orbit' caused by no state accepting responsibility for particular asylum-seekers.

Both the Border Convention and the Dublin Convention are based on an open recognition that member states' immigration policies have not yet been harmonized,[8] but both are formulated in such a way that their effect would seem to be improved if they were. The statement accompanying the signing of the latter, for instance, emphasises that 'the aim ... is not to amend the rules for examining applications for asylum and refugee status, which continue to be covered by the national law of each of the states ... [but is] solely intended to regulate relations between the member states by laying down their mutual obligations'.[9] However, by establishing rules according to which one member state might consent to having an application lodged with it being processed by another member state, the Convention implicitly presupposes that member states have confidence in one another's asylum policies.[10] In this case, 'harmonization of basic asylum policy is ... merely a logical step towards giving this confidence more substance'.[11]

The Borders Convention sets out conditions for crossing external frontiers and for issuing and using visas. It covers a range of policy areas, including provisions for (1) the mutual recognition of national visas by other member states; and (2) the abolition of visa requirements for non-EC nationals legally resident in one member state when entering another member state for a period of less than three months.[12] Although third-country nationals issued with a visa by, or legally resident in, one member state will not have the right to stay for extended periods in another member state, they can move through, and some may in fact stay for some time in a second state. The Convention therefore provides an inducement, among other things, for a common visa policy among the Twelve.[13]

However, these instruments reflect the fact that the implementation of the Single European Act calls only indirectly for the harmonization of immigration policies and procedures, and only to the extent necessary to achieve the abolition of internal frontiers. The Treaty on European Union signed at Maastricht in December 1991 goes considerably further.[14] Migration policy is touched by each of the three 'pillars' of the Treaty. Within the first pillar (Community matters), a new article is inserted into the Treaty of Rome (Article 100c), stating that the Council of the European Community 'shall determine the third countries whose nationals must be in possession of a visa when crossing the external borders of the member states', and, before 1 January 1996, 'shall adopt the measures related to uniform format for visas'. The first article of the third pillar (intergovernmental cooperation in Justice and Home Affairs) is more wide-ranging, listing areas which member states 'shall regard ... as matters of common interest' which include: (1) asylum policy, (2) rules governing the crossing of external borders, and (3) immigration policy and policy regarding nationals of third countries, in particular conditions of entry and movement, residence, family reunion and access to employment of third-country nationals, and unauthorized immigration. The second pillar (foreign and security policy) – while not explicitly related to migration questions – can be seen as having a potentially important bearing on migration policy owing to the fact that the movement of persons has become increasingly intertwined with wider political and security issues, as evidenced in recent concerns surrounding population movements caused by continuing conflict in the former Yugoslavia.

Shifting priorities or more of the same?
The international movement of population has become so prominent an issue over recent years that the harmonization of migration policies can no longer be seen as an incidental by-product of moves towards greater economic and political integration in Europe. Statements from politicians and government and Community officials increasingly cite joint migration policy as a reason for – rather than a necessary step towards – European union. At an informal meeting of EC foreign ministers held in Britain in September 1992, for example, the British Foreign Secretary, Douglas Hurd, pinpointed migration as 'one of the most serious, perhaps the most serious problem' for Europe,[15] and later asserted in the same connection that 'events, not a treaty, have forced the pace'.[16] Receiving-state interest still underpins moves towards the harmonization of migration policy, but the interest is no longer simply one of creating a single market, as expressed in the Single European Act, but now also one of averting what is seen by many as an impending immigration crisis.

The emergence of widespread worry over a looming migration crisis in Western Europe can be traced back principally to the dramatic events which took place in Europe in 1989. Within the space of just a few months, over a million people surged across the borders from East to West, signalling the collapse of the Eastern bloc, and, with it, the collapse of the barrier which had separated the populations of Eastern and Western Europe for over three decades. This exodus gave rise to a sense of vulnerability to uncontrolled population movements not felt in Western Europe since the Second World War. The entire European geopolitical and economic map had undergone a sudden transformation, and in the wake of this transformation emerged the prospect of a massive influx of migrants fuelled by extreme economic and political instability in the East. America would not provide the safety-valve that it had earlier in the century, and in this respect the new migration from East to West was to be a European problem requiring European responses.

This anxiety seemed not only to strengthen calls for policy harmonization, but also to bring about a partial reappraisal of migration policy in Western Europe. Although hardly a new idea, 'action to address the root-causes' quickly became a central phrase in the European political vocabulary as traditional forms of immigration control, such as border controls and visa regimes, suddenly appeared insufficient to cope with the perceived crisis ahead. At a conference of ministers on the movement of persons from Central and East European countries, convened by the Council of Europe in January 1991, participating states (which included former Eastern bloc countries) were called upon to 'concert their efforts and enter into dialogue with a view to making national policies on migration flows more compatible with one another'. Recommendations for joint action included 'active collaboration to promote those development policies and measures which would help prevent disorderly migration'.[17] Similarly, the conclusions and resolutions adopted at the Fourth Conference of European Ministers Responsible for Migration Affairs held later in the same year included the agreement that 'bilateral and multilateral cooperation should be developed and strengthened in order to reach a better economic balance between countries of origin and host countries', 'programmes of productive investment in the emigration regions should be encouraged', and 'the possibilities of the Social Development Fund of the Council of Europe' be used 'to promote job creation in the disadvantaged regions of European countries.'[18] Adopted within the framework of the Council of Europe, this resolution envisaged cooperation extending beyond the confines of the European Community, not only to include other receiving states in Western Europe, but also the new sending – and, in some cases, receiving – countries of the former Eastern bloc.[19]

Concern has not been restricted to developments on the European continent, however. The same resolution notes the 'continuing pressure for migration into European countries' as a result of 'massive economic, social and demographic imbalances between different parts of the world' – an issue which was already causing considerable concern by the mid-1980s, but which took on a new urgency after 1989. This concern is echoed both in a recent European Commission communication, and in a report issued by the Ad Hoc Group on Immigration in December 1991, which observes the 'substantial intensification of migratory pressure now exerted on almost all Member States' from a variety of sources, including Africa, Asia 'and other parts of the world'.[20] All three statements call for coordinated efforts to tackle external migration pressures both in Europe and farther afield. As expressed in the Ad Hoc Group's document:

> The conviction that, confronted with these developments, a strictly national policy could not provide an adequate response has been consistently gaining ground ... [and on] that basis, it would appear advisable to define a common answer to the question of how this immigration pressure can be accommodated. This will require an extended form of co-operation among Member States.

Concern surrounding the build-up of migration pressures in regions outside Western Europe has been intensified by a real increase in immigration levels which has taken place since the mid-1980s. As observed by the European Commission, a growing unease was being felt, deriving from 'the paradox that characterises immigration: despite the move in the majority of Member States in the mid-1970s to halt permanent legal immigration, it still continues. The facts contradict policy statements, which are becoming increasingly out of step with reality. The reality reflects a certain powerlessness in the face of an immigration not fully under control.'

As noted in Chapter 2, the mid-1980s saw a sudden escalation in spontaneous arrivals of asylum-seekers in Western Europe. Most came from the Third World, but after 1989 increasing numbers began arriving from Eastern and Central Europe. The majority of the latter group have been seen as 'economic migrants', making use of asylum procedures in order to evade immigration restrictions. The last decade has also witnessed a significant increase in levels of illegal and clandestine migration into Western Europe, principally from countries in North and sub-Saharan Africa into Southern Europe, where the population of illegal immigrants increased by over one million during the second half of the 1980s. And, of course, family immigration has continued as before, not signalling any kind of crisis in itself, but remaining, nevertheless, an important channel for immigration from areas previously – and in many cases still – linked into Western Europe's labour markets.

The mass influx of economic migrants from the East which many feared during the earliest stages of transition in Eastern and Central Europe – particularly after the relaxation of Soviet emigration law – failed to materialize. Indeed, of all documented movements which took place from East to West between 1989 and 1991, the great majority involved members of particular ethnic groups with strong ties in the West (Jews, ethnic Germans, Greeks, and Armenians) – groups with a history of emigration which substantially pre-dated the revolutions of 1989 and 1990. It was not long, however, before fears of a mass economic migration from the East were subsumed by fears of mass movements caused by political instability in the former Eastern bloc countries. The first politically generated movements which accompanied the collapse of communism did not stir up serious concerns because of the euphoria which dominated reactions of that time, and because the specific conditions which gave rise to this migration were relatively short-lived. However, subsequent refugee movements have arisen, caused by more intractable problems of inter-ethnic and inter-communal tension and conflict – problems of the sort that gave rise to much of the migration which took place in Europe during the first half of this century, but were kept tightly bottled-up throughout the time of the cold war. Of these, the crisis unfolding in the former Yugoslavia has been the most visible, taking place in an area of critical geopolitical importance, and – unlike population movements which took place in the Balkans earlier in the century – giving rise to substantial refugee flows direct into the neighbouring countries of Western Europe (Germany, Austria, Switzerland and Italy).

Accompanying the increase in immigration (although not necessarily linked directly to it) has been a significant upsurge in anti-immigrant and xenophobic attitudes throughout much of Western Europe – an upsurge which has fed on 'alarmist pronouncements about the danger of an "invasion"'.[21] In Germany, asylum-seekers and other immigrants have recently come under vicious attack from elements of a newly emerging extreme right-wing movement. Although, as argued by the German government, xenophobia 'based on racism and fanatic nationalism' exists in only an 'infinitely small proportion of the population',[22] so-called 'reservations'[23] towards foreigners – in Germany and in other countries, including Austria, France, Italy and Belgium[24] – has resulted in growing support for political parties extolling extreme anti-immigrant policies. Failure to integrate existing immigrant communities is considered by many observers to be a simultaneous cause and effect of this development. A report drawn up on behalf of the European Commission in 1990, for example, noted that the failure of integration policies is likely to 'stimulate the reawakening or development of sentiments based on "fear of the foreigner"', but, at the same time, a collective feeling of mistrust towards foreigners 'may ... affect some specific, important elements of the integration of immigrants, such as access to housing or schooling'.[25] Thus, against the background of growing hostility towards immigrant populations, the need to focus energies on the integration of immigrants has become – somewhat ironically – more salient an issue than ever in European politics. The integration question now figures consistently as a principal aim of new coordinated approaches to migration in Western Europe. As argued by the European Commission in 1991,

> Our societies cannot allow themselves to be riven by the fact that part of the population is not integrated in the mechanisms of solidarity set up by the Welfare State ... The time has come to give serious consideration jointly to the various elements of integration, with a view to taking the necessary steps to ensure that the social fabric is not disrupted.[26]

Today's principal concerns regarding migration into Europe thus centre around the three issues of external migration pressure, immigration control and immigrant integration. This is reflected in the recommendations submitted to the Maastricht European Council by the Ad Hoc Group on Immigration in December 1991, which included proposals for a work programme on immigration to be put into action before the entry into force of the Treaty on European Union,[27] and in the three policy prongs presented by the European Commission as the proper and essential bases of future joint approaches to immigration in the European Community: (1) taking action on migration pressure by making migration an integral element of Community external policy; (2) controlling migration flows through harmonized monitoring, measures to combat illegal immigration, a joint approach to asylum, and the approximation of criteria for reuniting families; and (3) strengthening integration policies for the benefit of legal immigrants.[28] Only calls for action to combat external migration pressure, however, represent any significant departure from the policies of the past. As noted in previous chapters, immigration control and immigrant integration have formed the primary pillars of migration policy in Western Europe ever since the immigration clamp-down of the early 1970s. Moreover, although the new emphasis on tackling migration pressure is ever present in the rhetoric, there has as yet emerged almost nothing in the way of clear policy objectives in this area. Thus the primary concerns among European receiving states might have taken on a new urgency in recent years, and this is certainly having an impact on the level of attention being paid to migration policy, both within the framework of the Single Market and in national politics. But, if anything, the new sense of urgency is resulting in greater and greater emphasis on old forms of control and apparently little in the way of new policy initiatives.

There remain, nevertheless, a number of important and interesting questions to be asked in connection with the harmonization process. Migration policy is an extremely complex issue, the significance of which extends in some respects to the very basis of state organization. Western Europe is by no means a single unitary block, and thus beneath the level of broadly shared interests, shared concerns, and shared (and to some extent unchanging) policy objectives among states in the region, lie a multitude of differences which may not be easily overcome in efforts to coordinate and harmonize the policies of different states. Irrespective of whether the Maastricht Treaty survives ratification, the recommendations of the European Commission and the Ad Hoc Group on Immigration are likely to provide an important guide in these efforts. It is thus worth considering some of the specific issues touched on in the reports of the Commission and the Ad Hoc Group, and examining the extent to which recommendations for joint action reflect a concrete convergence in the aims and concerns of Western Europe's principal migrant-receiving states.[29]

Convergence and divergence in the 1990s

At first sight, the process of policy harmonization would appear relatively straightforward. Since 1973, all receiving states in Western Europe have had a primary interest in controlling immigration, whether it be through direct or indirect measures. All have introduced highly restrictive policies on the immigration of labour; all allow a limited degree of family immigration; all are committed to combating illegal immigration and to achieving the integration of legally resident immigrant groups; all profess a commitment to the protection of refugees as laid out in the provisions of the 1951 UN Convention on the Status of Refugees, while at the same time expressing a common concern to prevent the abuse of asylum procedures by 'economic migrants' hoping to bypass stringent immigration laws; and, finally, all claim a commitment to tackling growing migration pressures in existing or potential sending regions, whether they be of an economic, political, demographic or social nature.

These shared principles reflect a number of common problems. For example, whether they are traditionally labour importers or labour exporters, all member states of the European Community, with the exception of Ireland, are now host to substantial and, in many cases, poorly integrated immigrant populations. All of these countries are experiencing continuing and unwanted immigration, whether it be of refugees or of economic migrants, and whether through asylum or through illegal channels. With the persistence of these immigration channels, and with the prospect of an abolition of borders within the European Community and/or the European Economic Area, all expect to be affected to a greater or lesser degree by the intensification of emigration pressures in regions outside Western Europe – both to the South and to the East.

In view of the likely implications of the Single Market, the European Economic Area, and European political and economic union, the need for joint action would appear self-evident. The situation in any one country is likely to have an increasing impact on other states, whether it be directly, through, for example, secondary movements of migrants out of an initial country of immigration, or indirectly, such as through country-specific changes in labour-market conditions caused by varying patterns of immigration. If social and political contact intensifies between wider segments of West European populations, it is possible that social dislocations caused by high levels of immigration or the unsuccessful integration of immigrant groups in any one state will spill over into other countries, such as through an expansion of intra-European networks of extreme right-wing political groupings. At the same time, European-wide contacts between immigrant groups might be expected to strengthen, with the possible implication that developments in the area of minority and immigrant integration in one country will affect action taken by – or on behalf of – immigrants elsewhere.

It seems clear that in a number of areas common action is called for by simple virtue of the nature of the problems to be tackled. In respect of action to alleviate external economic migration pressures, it is evident that – to the extent that the European Community (and/or EFTA) acts as a unitary economic bloc – a degree of Community-wide agreement will be needed regarding the most appropriate economic policies to be pursued vis-à-vis potential or existing sending regions. Indeed, the very magnitude of the many challenges posed in this area are likely to render unilateral efforts somewhat redundant. Similarly, efforts to remove the root causes of current and future refugee flows call for common approaches to questions of human and minority rights and other issues falling within the confines of states' foreign and security policies. The Maastricht Treaty, if it succeeds, will encourage joint approaches in this area, but in many cases the fundamental impetus for common action is likely to be that of finding effective and appropriate strategies which will necessarily depend on a degree of consistency in the responses of different states.

However, as observed by the European Commission, although 'shared principles have led to comparable difficulties, there are nevertheless differences between the situations in which the Member States find themselves'.[30] These differences – some deriving from specific immigration histories of countries, some from more fundamental departures in political and social traditions, and others from variations in current migration pressures – mean that any moves towards harmonization, and, indeed, the eventual functioning of common approaches to migration, are unlikely to be entirely straightforward. Indeed, the report of the Ad Hoc Group on Immigration includes an explicit reservation to the effect that 'immigration policies are a ... complicated issue' within which 'not all areas lend themselves to immediate harmonization'.[31]

As one might expect, particular procedures relating to immigration vary considerably from one state to another. Thus, for example, the nature of specific authorities responsible for taking decisions on questions such as the issuing of visas and residence permits, or the development of integration programmes, differ according to their degree of independence from central government. As noted in Chapter 5, integration policy is considerably more centralized in France than in the United Kingdom or Germany. Similarly, mechanisms for taking decisions on individual cases vary according to the role played by national courts or other administrative bodies. In the area of asylum policy, for example, appeals against negative decisions in the United Kingdom are taken to an independent adjudicator or Immigration Appeals Tribunal, whereas in the Netherlands appeals are submitted to the Minister of Justice.[32] The rules governing the issuing of residence, work and other permits also differ. In France, for instance, a *carte de séjour* (residence permit) is required only by third-country nationals over the age of 18, while in Germany all foreign children with the exception of EC nationals and citizens of Morocco, Turkey, Tunisia and what was Yugoslavia now require a residence authorization, irrespective of age.[33]

In many areas, harmonization of the details of national immigration procedures would not seem to be of great pressing importance. As argued by the Ad Hoc Group on Immigration in relation to asylum law, if 'too much emphasis were put on uniform procedures in the Twelve, the harmonization process could become bogged down quite simply through the complexity of the issue', reflecting as it does 'matters which concern fundamental aspects of a state's organization'.[34] However, harmonization of procedures would seem to be necessary in areas in which they reflect or lead to substantive differences in approaches to migration policy – procedures which affect not only the mechanism, but also the outcome of the policies in place. This is perhaps most evident in connection with efforts to control migration flows and to strengthen integration policies. The European Commission, for example, takes cognizance of differences in policies and procedures applied to family reunification and sanctions applicable to illegal immigrants. In respect of the former, the Commission notes that:

> Given that a family unit living together remains one of the basic pillars of western societies, Member States permit the arrival of other members of the family. However, a number of Member States are challenging the scope of this concept, which is not interpreted in a uniform manner ... the qualifying criteria (age, length of residence, etc.) are not always the same ... [and here] divergences affect practices from one Member State to another. The resultant exponential effects, together with certain abuses, call into question the extent of this traditional principle.

As it happens, policy harmonization may prove more straightforward in the case of family immigration than in other policy areas, owing to the fact that states share a generally restrictive stance on this question which is qualified by the universal principle of protecting family unity (although this is not a principle that has any significant legal content for immigrants)[35] and a common interest in encouraging immigrants' integration – integration which depends on a sense of belonging among immigrants which itself may depend on the security and integrity of the family.[36] However, greater potential or existing divergence can be detected in other areas of admission policy. Illegal immigration, border controls, visas and the reception of asylum-seekers can be identified as particular problem areas. In connection with such issues, it is necessary to look beyond specific procedures to consider some of the wider forces shaping state policy.

Control measures
There is overall agreement among all receiving states in Western Europe that illegal immigration should be controlled through both direct and indirect measures. Direct measures include detection and expulsion at the borders and internal surveillance – the latter being considered particularly important where there are high levels of clandestine immigration, i.e. immigration of

persons who have entered the country legally on tourist and other visas and subsequently overstayed. Indirect measures include carrier and employer sanctions, that is, the penalization of any company or individual caught transporting or employing illegal immigrants. Both approaches raise a number of important implications as regards application, in terms of both capacity and will on the part of the states in question.

For example, those South European states – Italy, Spain, Portugal and Greece – that are now faced with the most momentous task of controlling illegal flows from the African continent are the same countries which up until the 1980s were senders, rather than receivers, of migrants.[37] A sudden growth in immigration during the second half of the 1980s, coupled with the prospect of the Single Market (and the implementation of the Schengen Agreement), has forced all four states to rush to introduce new immigration controls in line with those operating elsewhere in Western Europe. However – considering the speed with which such controls have had to be developed, the fact that these states had no previous tradition of regulating immigration, and the extent of migration pressures currently experienced in the Mediterranean region – the capacity of these states to control immigration to the degree possible elsewhere in the Community must be questioned. Moreover, the labour markets of Southern Europe differ from those of Northwestern Europe in certain ways which can have further important implications for the control of illegal immigration, owing to the close linkages which exist between the 'informal' economy and illegal immigration and employment. According to one estimate, the informal sector comprises 20% of GDP in Italy, as compared with 4% in France.[38] Where there is a strong informal economy, one must question the capacity – and, perhaps, the will – to implement strict indirect control measures such as employer sanctions.

Nevertheless, in none of these states are the basic methods or objectives of migration control challenged to any significant degree. In particular, none have expressed strong reservations in connection with internal surveillance. Indeed, to some extent, these states are somewhat freer than others to exercise strict controls because they have never had large, long-established immigrant populations. In countries with a longer history of immigration, the balance which needs to be struck between immigration control and immigrant integration is somewhat more delicate. Thus, for example, policing authorities in the United Kingdom have been forced to adopt more sensitive approaches in their dealings with ethnic minorities following charges of discrimination against and harassment of members of the more visible ethnic groups. In this context, the introduction of on-the-spot checks at constant intervals to verify the legality of persons appearing to be immigrants would be extremely problematic. However, the situation in the United Kingdom differs from that in countries such as France and Germany. First, a much higher proportion of Britain's immigrant or minority population is enfranchised, with the possible effect that greater account is taken of minority concerns in the formulation of policies which might affect their treatment by the authorities and members of the wider public. Second, and perhaps more important, is the fact that Britain does not have a tradition of internal controls such as those already exercised in most continental European countries. In this respect, policy in the area of illegal immigration touches on another problem issue – that of border controls.

As noted above, the Single European Act signed in 1986 calls for the abolition of internal border controls so as to allow for the free movement of goods, capital and persons within the European Community after January 1993. If a degree of control is to be maintained over the movement of third-country nationals – whether they be legal or illegal immigrants – the logical outcome of such a step must be the strengthening of internal regulation, such as through the use of identity cards and random spot-checks on migrants' documentation. Most member states have for a long time relied on a combination of border controls and internal controls; the latter are used not only to regulate the residence and movements of immigrants, but also to keep a check on a range of nationals' activities. As a function of its unique geography and political traditions,[39] the United Kingdom has, by contrast, relied almost exclusively on border controls, and thus the population – both indigenous and foreign – is subject to relatively little institutionalized scrutiny once within the UK. There is no obligation to carry any form of identification, no established system of identity cards, and, indeed – unlike all other countries in Western Europe – no enforced personal registration system.[40] With no experience of internal surveillance, the prospect of such measures being introduced in Britain is viewed with considerable suspicion among the general public (particularly members of ethnic minorities), and with a high degree of scepticism among immigration authorities.[41] These and other linked reservations have already led to conflict between the British government and the European Commission, with the former wishing to interpret Article 8a of the Single European Act in such a way that allows for continued – albeit relaxed – checks on movements from other member states at the border, and the latter holding that all such controls should be removed and substituted with internal checks to whatever extent is necessary.[42]

Implicit in this debate is Britain's lack of confidence in other member states' ability to prevent illegal immigration, which hints at a potential for wider conflict in the Community after January 1993. Because migration into any one member state could result in secondary migration through the Community, considerable tension can be expected if any one of the Twelve suspects undue laxity on the part of another as regards the policing of external borders. Such concerns also carry the implication that any unique or exceptional immigration measures taken by one state can no longer be isolated from the interests of other member states. As noted by the Ad Hoc Group on Immigration,

> The volume of third-country nationals is at present still completely determined by national admission policies ... If the Twelve wished to grant further rights to third-country nationals it would be necessary to have at least a probable estimate of the size of the group. In other words, Member States will have to have such confidence in each others' policies that the consequences of a gradual extension of rights may be readily evaluated and that an effective integration policy is not constantly undermined by the addition of further groups of third-country nationals.[43]

For example, in the late 1980s/early 1990s both Italy and Spain opted for large-scale legalization or 'amnesty' programmes to deal with the problem of substantial and growing illegal immigrant populations which neither could realistically expect to expel.[44] Although such action was at the time deemed necessary for the maintenance of social stability and cohesion in these states, if repeated in the context of the Single Market, it could spark off protests from other member states. As observed by the European Commission,

> It seems essential that Member States show greater determination [to control illegal immigration] ... Schemes to give legal resident status to illegal residents, as carried out in certain Member States, make this responsibility weigh even heavier inasmuch as this tends to make illegal residence a long-term route to legal immigration. Irrespective of the humanitarian motives behind such steps, it comprises a fundamental problem.[45]

This issue not only concerns states' policies on the admission of third-country nationals; Germany's exceptional admission of up to one million ethnic Germans from other countries of Eastern and Central Europe after the revolutions of 1989/90, Greece's admission of ethnic Greeks from the former Soviet Union, and Portugal's confirmation of citizenship rights to Macao residents, signify the continuing importance of national interest and varying citizenship policies in place in different countries – policies which may at times give rise to inflows of, or extension of citizenship rights to, substantial numbers of immigrants in a way that might conflict with the wider restrictive interests of the Community. Already the relatively easy acquisition of UK citizenship and the fact that the majority of Britain's immigrants of the 1950s and 1960s entered as British subjects contrasts significantly with countries such as Germany, where citizenship is considerably more restricted (as discussed below in connection with rights of free movement in the European Community). This points to what has always been an important overlap between states' immigration policies and wider domestic and foreign policy interests and traditions – an overlap which was reflected, for example, in the importance of former colonies as sources of migration to France, Britain, Belgium and the Netherlands during the recruitment period.

Visa policies

Differing foreign policy concerns within the European Community – albeit with a degree of cooperation as laid out in the second pillar of the Maastricht Treaty – raise some important questions as regards the formulation of a common visa policy among the Twelve. The External Borders Convention obliges signatory states to recognize visas issued by other states for the purposes of allowing third-country nationals to pass through any country in the Community, and calls explicitly for the formulation of a common list of countries from whose nationals visas will be required by all signatory states.[46] This may not prove overly problematic, since an informal core list of countries for which visas are required for entry into all EC states has, in fact, existed for a number of years. However, the Treaty on European Union goes further by stipulating that: 'The Council, acting by unanimity [and by qualified majority after 1 January 1996] on a proposal from the Commission and after consulting the European Parliament, shall determine the third countries whose nationals must be in possession of a visa when crossing the external borders of the Member States.'[47] As it is explicitly designed to pave the way for a common visa policy among the Twelve, such a list is likely to be considerably more binding than both that already in existence and that called for by the External Borders Convention.

The introduction of a visa requirement for nationals of another state can frequently prove a politically significant act. Thus, for example, the 1981 British Nationality Act, the 1988 Immigration Act, and the introduction of visa restrictions on the admission of nationals of certain former colonies in the 1980s signalled, among other things, the UK's progressive dissociation from the countries of its former empire. On the other hand, the fact that many former colonies still enjoy what could be argued to be privileged status as regards UK visa requirements reflects the continuing importance attached to the Commonwealth – an attitude not shared by other member states of the European Community. One could point similarly to the particular relations which exist between France and the countries of North Africa, or between the Netherlands and, for example, Indonesia. And, more recently, one can point to the removal of visa requirements by a number of states in Western Europe as regards nationals of certain Central European countries – a gesture which arises in large part from a concern to avoid being seen to replace the old Iron Curtain with a new barrier erected by those who for so long had advocated the right of free exit.

A number of reservations have recently been expressed by immigrant and other non-governmental interest groups over the predicted outcome of any harmonized visa policy within the European Community or wider grouping. It is feared that with such variation in the interests of different states, the most likely result of harmonization will be the emergence of a more restrictive regime.[48] The report of the Ad Hoc Group on Immigration takes note of such concerns, stating that 'if the harmonization process were initiated without defining basic principles, harmonization might be carried out at the lowest level. Assuming that immigration into Member States must remain limited, it is above all the restrictive opinions which could dominate.'

According to this argument, the special privilege enjoyed by certain third countries in respect of their nationals' access to particular member states could be lost as a result of other member states' reservations. On the other hand, it is possible to envisage a situation in which states continually depart from agreements reached as regards a common visa policy. Indeed, the External Borders Convention includes a reservation to the effect that a member state 'may exceptionally derogate from these common visa arrangements for over-riding reasons of national policy'.[49] However, what is perhaps just as likely is a proliferation of visa requirements, 'many of which are of little operational value to countries which adopt them'.[50] As argued recently in respect of Great Britain, common visa requirements will probably 'add to the number of visa national countries, with consequence particularly for those New Commonwealth countries which have so far escaped a UK visa requirement – in particular, the countries of the Caribbean. Most other EC countries require visas from all the countries of the New Commonwealth and are unlikely to agree to forgo this in any harmonization.'[51]

Asylum policy
In this connection, concerns regarding the harmonization of visa policies link up with concerns over the direction of asylum policy in Western Europe. The most obvious overlap exists in respect of the increasingly common practice of imposing visa requirements on nationals of particular states generating refugees. Britain, for example, introduced visa restrictions for all nationals of Sri Lanka and Turkey in the 1980s following a rise in the numbers of asylum applications by people originating from these countries. Such practice, in conjunction with the wide use of carrier sanctions in the Community, effectively reduces the chances of certain groups of potential asylum-seekers reaching states in which they might wish to lodge an asylum application. For those seeking asylum from countries upon which no visa restrictions have been imposed (e.g. certain countries in Central and Eastern Europe), consideration of cases depends to a high degree on the receiving states' (subjective) view of conditions in the country from which they have come. Since the granting of asylum – like the issuing of visa restrictions – can be perceived as a political statement by either or both the sending or receiving state, foreign policy concerns may impinge on the application of asylum law just as they do on the formulation of visa policy. For this reason, among others, one state's view of which countries should be deemed 'safe' or 'unsafe' for the return of asylum-seekers (i.e. the refusal to grant asylum) may not square with those of others.

The report of the Ad Hoc Group on Immigration takes note of the fact that, despite common ground within the member states of the Community based on their accession to the 1951 Geneva Convention and 1967 New York Protocol, considerable room exists for divergent appraisals of conditions in countries which are giving rise to asylum-seekers. Such divergent assessments may arise not only from varying interests as regards relations with the sending state, but also from differing interpretations of the provisions of the United Nations refugee instruments. The Ad Hoc Group emphasizes the need for greater harmonization of substantive asylum law so that 'the chances of being granted refugee status or admission will be the same everywhere'. Mirroring anxiety surrounding the formulation of a common visa policy, however, a number of concerns have been voiced within certain non-governmental sectors which reflect a suspicion that a more restrictive asylum regime will emerge as a result of harmonization, i.e. the chances of asylum-seekers being granted admission or refugee status will be universally lower, rather than higher, than at present.* This view is vindicated by the generally restrictive thrust of the specific harmonization proposals currently on the table. The Treaty on European Union, for example, states that 'in the event of an emergency situation in a third country posing a threat of a sudden inflow of nationals from that country into the Community, the Council may ... *introduce*' – rather than remove – 'a visa requirement for nationals from the country in question' (emphasis added).[52]

It is not only in terms of foreign policy, but also in other areas of domestic interest that migration policies may reflect divergent concerns among the Twelve. The issue of asylum stands out again in this regard, as do those of citizenship and the control of national labour markets. In connection with the former, it is important to note that the policies and procedures of reception and subsequent treatment of asylum-seekers has differed considerably from one state to another. The Federal Republic of Germany, for example, has, since the Second World War, upheld a far more liberal stance towards asylum-seekers than any other state in Western Europe. This is reflected in the fact that it is one of only a few countries to have the right of asylum written into its Constitution.[53] In all states, the expulsion of claimants deemed to have 'manifestly unfounded cases' has proved an elusive exercise, but in some countries this has been pursued more rigorously than in others. Similarly, the proportions of, and status accorded to, applicants granted provisional asylum on the basis of *de facto* or 'refugee B' categories has varied. As a result, some countries have proved more attractive for asylum-seekers than others. Largely as a result of its traditionally liberal asylum policies, West Germany emerged as by far the most important destination for asylum-seekers in Europe during the 1980s. Indeed, in 1991 and 1992, Germany received over half of all the asylum applications lodged in Western Europe as a whole.

As noted by the European Commission and the Ad Hoc Group on Immigration, harmonization of asylum policy is called for both in the interests

---

* Note, however, that this view is balanced with concern to see that asylum-seekers are treated properly and fairly in all countries.

of streamlining and clarifying the proper basis of procedures which are at present deemed 'inappropriate for dealing with the present huge number of applications',[54] and to prevent asylum flows shifting 'towards those countries where the arrangements are relatively more favourable'.[55] In fact, the past couple of years have seen an overall convergence in the asylum policies of all Western Europe's receiving states, including those of Germany. This convergence is universally restrictive. Thus in Germany, as elsewhere, the detention of asylum-seekers prior to decisions on applications has been expanded; procedures have been introduced to implement 'fast-track' processing of applications from nationals of countries deemed safe; procedures have been stepped up to increase the rate of refusal of entry to and expulsion of those deemed to have 'manifestly unfounded cases'; and carrier sanctions have been imposed which reduce the number of arrivals from countries targeted as refugee-generators.[56] Moreover, 1992 has witnessed growing pressure to have the German Basic Law amended so as to do away with the right of asylum – a development which may be speeded up in response to the growing crisis of attacks on asylum-seekers and other immigrants by extreme anti-immigrant groups. Yet, despite these moves, Germany remains the principal receiving state for asylum-seekers. Recent events in the former Yugoslavia indicate that it may be not only the nature of asylum policies in force in particular countries, but also the geographical position of potential receiving countries, and, in some cases, links between sending and receiving regions which result in one state being faced with considerably larger asylum inflows than others. Indeed, as regards sudden European refugee movements, geographical position might prove the primary factor in shaping the direction of flows, since these larger flows are likely to be little influenced by calculations as regards small variations in conditions of reception in potential countries of destination.

Given that some states are likely to receive disproportionately large numbers of asylum-seekers irrespective of the particular policies in place, the issue of burden-sharing is particularly salient. For the German government, the move towards harmonization of asylum policies is viewed overall as a positive step, since it can provide a justification for the introduction of restrictive measures while simultaneously opening up a possible route to greater burden-sharing with other members of the Community. However, in other states which have hitherto experienced much lower numbers of asylum applications (e.g. Britain), the principle of burden-sharing may not be quite so easy to swallow, implying as it does either a greater financial burden, or the acceptance of greater numbers of asylum-seekers and refugees. It is thus by no means a question upon which there is consensus among the Twelve.

Perhaps owing to the sensitivity of the issue, neither the report of the Ad Hoc Group on Immigration nor the communications issued by the Commission, and neither the External Borders Convention nor the Treaty on European Union, make any mention of the principle of burden-sharing. The Dublin Convention deals with the question of state responsibility for processing asylum claims, but its aim is to reduce the potential for 'refugees in orbit' rather than to tackle the wider question of burden-sharing. Indeed, by stipulating that asylum claims should be processed by the country of first arrival, the Dublin Convention acts implicitly against the principle of burden-sharing.[57] Yet burden-sharing has emerged as the issue of greatest potential disagreement between member states in respect of asylum questions – first signalled in connection with the Albanian exodus to Italy, and then with outflows from former Yugoslavia. At the September meeting of EC foreign ministers, for example, Klaus Kinkel of Germany is quoted as stating that Germany was shouldering a disproportionate burden of refugees and asylum-seekers, and that Germany 'can't do everything alone'. Yet, despite such appeals, Britain – one of the member states expressing greatest reservations over the issue – has remained staunch in its opposition to any hint that refugees might be relocated from areas of high concentration, such as Germany, to areas of the Community with a lighter burden. In the future, this question may prove all the more significant in the context of cooperation – or lack of cooperation – beyond the confines of the European Community, since the next countries to suffer the greatest refugee influxes may be those further east. As noted recently by the US Refugee Policy Group, 'these countries do not have the resources, nor in some cases the political will, to provide humanitarian assistance or longer-term settlement opportunities. A failure to help these countries cope with such movements could well put them at risk of destabilization.'[58]

Free movement of third-country nationals
Although the social and political traditions of different states have some bearing on variations in asylum policies, the implications of such traditions are likely to have far greater implications for the position and rights of immigrant minority populations in the European Community. The work programme formulated by the Ad Hoc Group on Immigration calls for examination of 'the possibility of granting third-country nationals who are

long-term residents in a member state certain rights or possibilities, for example concerning access to the labour market',[59] while the Treaty on European Union lists 'conditions of entry and movement' and 'conditions of residence' by third-country nationals as 'matters of common interest'.[60] The External Borders Convention limits movement of third-country nationals in states other than that in which they are normally resident to short stays of less than three months. The Ad Hoc Group's work programme, however, suggests the possibility of extending full free-movement rights, hitherto reserved for EC nationals, to certain foreign nationals who have been resident for some time in one member state. This is echoed in a communication issued by the European Commission which suggests that 'consideration could be given to ... granting access to employment in another member state ... to certain categories of non-EC nationals already allowed to reside permanently in one of the member states'.[61]

Such proposals, however, beg the question of inequalities in the rights accorded to immigrants and their descendants in the different states. If proposals for free movement of third-country nationals fail to see the light of day, only immigrants – or the offspring of immigrants – possessing citizenship of the country in which they are resident will enjoy free movement in the Community. Therefore, a far higher proportion of immigrants or members of immigrant minority groups resident in some countries will be accorded this right than in countries where citizenship laws discriminate to a greater extent against the naturalization of foreigners and/or their offspring (e.g. Britain as compared with Germany). Such a situation would not only prove anomalous in terms of principle, but might lead to overt tension within and between states as a result of grievances on the part either of immigrants excluded from free-movement rights, or of states whose immigrants are unable to compete equally in other European labour markets – particularly those that might at the same time be receiving immigrants from other member states. To extend free movement to certain classes of third-country nationals may reduce the potential for such tensions, but anomalies will not be totally eradicated. It is worth noting, for example, that immigrants in those states in which permanent residence is granted more liberally might have an unfair advantage over those in which residence is less secure. A number of proposals for harmonization in status of third-country nationals stress the need for common approaches to questions relating to the socio-legal position of immigrants, but, given differing traditions as regards more fundamental questions such as citizenship, common approaches cannot be expected to develop overnight.

Worker immigration

Like the status of third-country nationals, the regulation of national labour markets has traditionally been the sovereign concern of individual states. However, as noted by the Ad Hoc Group on Immigration:

> Full harmonization of admission policy linked to employment presupposes that this policy will cease to be defined exclusively at national level, as it will no longer be possible unilaterally to extend or tighten the national labour market when conditions for admission are determined at European level. It therefore seems necessary to intensify talks in this regard, while endeavouring to achieve harmonization, in order to achieve a European labour migration policy.[62]

Given that all member states have adopted a highly restrictive position as regards labour immigration, concern over efforts to harmonize policy in this respect might seem somewhat unnecessary. However, three points deserve mention which to some extent justify such concerns. First, the past decade has in fact witnessed increasing levels of worker migration into Western Europe. The current legal inflows differ from those of the 1950s to early 1970s in that they are characterized by (usually temporary) movements of highly skilled workers and professionals.[63] Most come from other advanced industrialized countries, but substantial numbers also come from the South – thereby representing what is still a considerable brain drain, or reverse transfer of technology, from the developing world. As argued by John Salt, demand for such workers is likely to increase rather than decrease in the future as a function of advances in technology and of the expansion in the activities of so-called transnational corporations – companies within which the mobility of those occupying the highest rungs is considerable.[64] However, demand may not be the same in every member state of the Community, partly because of variations in levels and rates of economic growth and development. Furthermore, preferences for sources of such migration may differ according to particular links between certain receiving areas and potential sending regions. Thus, for example, Britain is likely to continue favouring the migration of professionals from former colonies of the Indian subcontinent, while Germany may turn increasingly to the countries of Eastern and Central Europe.

Second, inelasticities in receiving labour markets, coupled with declining economically active populations, mean that demand for immigrant labour not only persists in Western Europe (despite high levels of unemployment), but may well increase in the years to come. The French National Institute of Demographic Studies, for example, has predicted a shortfall of workers in France by the end of the 1990s which could support the immigration of over 100,000 workers per year. Since receiving governments no longer see immigration as a solution to such labour shortages, it is highly unlikely that we will witness a return to the recruitment policies of earlier decades. However, if no room is created for such immigration in receiving-state policies, and demand is not eradicated, one can expect an increase in what are already rising levels of illegal immigration into Western Europe. Again, levels and patterns of such migration will differ from one state to another according to the particular characteristics of each labour market.

Third, labour immigration policies may be incorporated increasingly into wider policies designed to reduce emigration pressures in less-developed regions surrounding Western Europe. Germany, for example, has already introduced a programme for 'the training and short-term employment of workers originating from developing countries or countries of Central and Eastern Europe'.[65] According to a representative of the German Ministry for Labour and Social Affairs, this programme will enable those taking part to 'become acquainted with the technology of the Western industrialized countries, increase their knowledge of the language and thus ensure or increase their means of subsistence, improve their chances on the labour market in their country of origin or lay the foundations for setting up on their own'. At the same time, 'the German labour market is ... taking advantage of additional potential in the form of workers who are available immediately and may be placed in a very specific manner, which is also of considerable importance for German industry, particularly those sectors which have a permanent shortage of qualified workers (building industry – assembly work)'.[66] Some more cynical observers have described this programme as a useful way of making use of cheap immigrant labour without implementing an immigration policy, or without repeating the mistakes of the 1960s.* Whether such suspicions are justified or not, this policy is clearly linked in with Germany's specific labour market interests. These are not interests shared by other member states, and, indeed, a row is already brewing as regards the legality of an employment programme which disregards the preference which should, according to Community Law, be given to EC nationals.

*Although the fact that this is exactly what the *Gastarbeiter* policy was designed to do leads one to question whether the current programme will prove any more successful.

Migration policy 'in the broad sense'
Germany's training programme reflects the particular interest in that country for developing programmes which could reduce economic and social migration pressures in areas already generating growing numbers of actual and potential migrants, whether they be legal, illegal, or entering through asylum channels. The tensions that this programme is generating may reflect the fact that, despite a common interest in the ultimate aim, other member states might prefer other methods, and might like to see policy directed in other directions. Thus, for example, it is likely that countries such as France, Italy and Spain will be more interested in policies which tackle migration pressures in North Africa than in those which target Eastern Europe, whereas Germany is likely to favour the latter.

It is, nevertheless, in the area of action to combat external migration pressure that joint approaches within the European Community or wider grouping in Western Europe can be seen as potentially the most important of all proposals currently on the table. Indeed, many of the more particular preoccupations surrounding the issue of harmonization and free movement in the Community or European Economic Area seem almost to pale into insignificance when one takes a step back to consider the larger picture – one which includes such a wide range of fundamental policy questions that the Ad Hoc Group could come up with no more accurate classification than that of 'migration policy in the broad meaning of the term'. Those areas identified as requiring concerted action are listed as 'relevant human rights policies, substantial development aid, global food and environmental policies, and controlling regional conflicts'. The need for action in such areas is obvious, for, despite all efforts to strengthen Western Europe's external frontiers – whether it be on the basis of harmonized or disparate control measures – the migration problem will not disappear unless something is done to address its deeper causes.

However, having taken note of the wider issues to be tackled, the Ad Hoc Group goes little further in its specific recommendations than suggesting the establishment of an information programme and the preparation of training and apprenticeship contracts for nationals of existing or potential sending regions, together with the development of an early warning system to 'register, in good time, any sudden increase in migration from specific countries of origin, so that relevant measures could be taken in order to find and overcome the causes of this sudden migration'.[67] The European Commission goes somewhat further in calling for 'more extensive incorporation of migration into the Community's external policy', including cooperation projects entailing specific measures targeting 'poor rural and suburban regions of large urban centres identified as principal migration sources' and an examination of 'how, in each of the countries concerned, potential migrant populations can be kept in their regions of origin'.[68]

Yet, despite a mass of rhetoric on the need to address the root causes – not only from the Ad Hoc Group and the Commission, but from virtually every government and concerned body in Western Europe – the concrete issues do not as yet seem to have been faced head-on. As reflected in Germany's very limited training programme for workers from Eastern Europe, the upshot so far has been the development of a range of *ad hoc* policies and proposals, of which none appear sufficiently extensive to have any fundamental impact on the pressures they are ostensibly designed to tackle. In this context, the title given to the Ad Hoc Group seems particularly apt. It is worth noting, for example, that while an early warning system could prove a potentially important instrument of future migration and refugee policy in Western Europe, if functioning as described by the Ad Hoc Group, it would seem likely, if anything, to encourage reactive and short-term responses to what are almost certain to be long-term problems requiring long-term solutions.

In fact, so long as action to address root causes remains limited, joint policies in this area should not prove overly difficult to formulate. As in other areas of migration policy, it is only when harmonization questions begin encroaching on wider and/or more fundamental policy issues such as states' foreign and security policies, or when they are sufficiently far-reaching as to impinge on other domestic economic or political interests, that the harmonization process is likely to run into trouble. Obstacles hindering joint action in this area are not only those arising from differences in states' individual interests. True, Germany may wish to focus on Eastern Europe while France may want to concentrate efforts in North Africa, but other impediments include interests which are shared, at least on a broad level, by all states in the Community or Western Europe as a whole. One can point, for example, to the issues of trade policy and debt relief. These are two areas in which positive action by governments in Western Europe could have an important, albeit long-term, pay-off in terms of reducing economic migration pressures in existing and potential sending regions, and yet they are two issues conspicuously absent from the recommendations of the Ad Hoc Group on Immigration and from the communications of the European Commission.

The European Commission is, nevertheless, correct in stressing that effective action to reduce external migration pressure 'begs the question of North–South [and East–West] relationships'.[69] Only if and when common policy to combat external migration pressure begins to challenge these more fundamental relationships is it likely to run up against considerable opposition from particular states or particular sectors of society in Western Europe (e.g. those most affected by trade liberalization measures).

For the existing and future member states of the European Community and the European Economic Area, the process of policy harmonization in the area of migration will prove an important component in the establishment and expansion of the single market and the development of closer economic and political union. The development of migration policies continues to rest on these aims, despite growing concern with the wider aspects of the migration issue. Thus, although there is the potential for the focus of migration policy to be expanded – as reflected in calls to tackle external migration pressure – the thrust of migration policy in Western Europe is still essentially inward looking. The harmonization process is, in essence, one of shifting traditional national control measures to the supranational level to suit a strengthening supranational grouping. In this respect, migration policies in Western Europe have not changed in any substantial way since the migration clamp-down of the early 1970s. The emphasis is still on negative actions such as tighter border controls and stricter visa regimes, and action still tends to be ruled by short-term objectives and short-term concerns. The primary policy areas receiving attention are, as they were twenty years ago, those of strengthening immigration controls and expanding measures to encourage the integration of immigrants. And underlying all policy measures is a largely negative attitude towards immigration which has changed very little over the past two decades. Receiving states in Western Europe continue to see themselves as non-immigration countries despite the fact that some have, by now, been receiving substantial numbers of foreign immigrants for over a century.

Chapter 8

Conclusion

Migration has always played an important part in the economic, political and social development of European society, and it is a process which, on balance, has proved enriching. For countries such as France, the United Kingdom and what was West Germany, the immigration of foreign workers from the 1950s to 1970s constituted a key element in the postwar economic boom, and the migrants contributed in many important and positive ways to the cultural and social life of the countries in which they settled. Indeed, one may reflect that if international migration could not prove a positive economic, social and political force, the Single European Act would have been unlikely to call for the free movement of persons within the European Community after January 1993. This is certainly true from an economic point of view: immigrants have been found to cause an expansion of markets as consumers, to encourage investment, and to contribute to technological progress and entrepreneurial activity. According to a recent study carried out in Germany, the inflow of 3.8 million people to Western Germany between 1988 and 1991 increased the gross national product by 3.5% and created one million additional jobs.[1] Thus, even if migration into Western Europe is to escalate in the years to come, it is not at all clear that the effects will be overwhelmingly damaging for receiving states – particularly given that movements of 'economic' migrants will be affected not only by growing 'push' factors in regions of origin, but also by 'pull', or demand, in receiving countries.

It is, however, also evident that – coming now at a time of very high sensitivity to the issue in Western Europe – any substantial and unmanaged immigration could have complex social and political ramifications which most states would sensibly seek to avoid. In particular, a widespread perception among the public that control over immigration is largely lacking, or has been lost, could certainly contribute to a strengthening of extreme nationalist sentiment in Western Europe – a development which might have serious implications for the social and political stability both of Western receiving states and of countries in the East. Moreover, in the light of what seems to be a growing potential for inter-ethnic and generalized political tension and conflict in the East, it is clear that 'economic' migration is not the only cause of Europe's migration problems; unregulated mass 'minority' movements, and large-scale refugee and 'survival' flows, are – particularly with the emergence of new refugee movements within and out of the Balkans – increasingly pinpointed as the primary migration challenge facing Europe in the 1990s. Caused usually by traumatic political events, such movements are generally highly volatile and disruptive for every state affected, as well as tragic in terms of the human suffering caused.

Nevertheless, the ability of existing or potential receiving states to prevent unwanted immigration should not be underestimated. In the face of what are already extreme pressures mounting up in areas bordering on Western Europe – rapid population growth, high and rising un- and under-employment, falling incomes and political instability in North Africa, growing inter-ethnic tension and economic and political uncertainty in Eastern and Central Europe and the former Soviet Union – what is perhaps surprising is that so few, rather than so many, people are currently moving towards Western Europe. As in the past, the policies pursued by receiving states are likely to have a decisive influence on patterns of international migration in the decades to come.

This said, the potential for massive levels of international migration is probably greater today than ever before, as demonstrated by the unprecedented scale of population growth in the southern Mediterranean region. Despite the difficulty in positing any direct correlation between demographic growth and migration, the fact that the population of the Maghreb region is set to double over the next three decades will almost certainly have a profound impact on the pressure for migration into Western Europe. These pressures may not be exclusively economic in nature. Economic instability, underdevelopment and population growth may compound or create conditions which give rise to refugee flows; thus, at least in the shorter term, migration strains brought about by factors such as rising unemployment in North Africa or Eastern Europe may be felt more through movements resulting from political turmoil than through migration stemming from poverty or population growth.

In the face of such pressures, a number of new challenges are coming to the fore. For migrant-receiving countries, the issue at stake is no longer simply that of immigration control, but that of the entire security landscape of Western Europe and surrounding regions. Whereas the European states of the eighteenth and nineteenth centuries could export dissenters and 'surplus' population to the New World, no such safety-valve is in place for the existing or potential migrant-sending countries of today. As migration pressures build up in regions surrounding Western Europe, they are likely to have an increasingly destabilizing, and, in some cases, catastrophic effect on political and economic conditions in those regions which may in turn pose new security threats for Western Europe which are unrelated to actual or potential levels of immigration. As Curt Gasteyger notes, 'demographic growth and migration, proliferation of weapons and ethnic revolt are hardly new to our political vocabulary ... but as they begin to impact on each other, they acquire a totally new significance and urgency. As such, they are forming an increasing part of our security concerns.'[2] Just as the consequences of today's migration pressures may extend beyond the confines of migration *per se*, so there is an urgent and growing need for states in Western Europe to look beyond traditional concepts of immigration control in the development of migration policies. Barriers against the entry of 'unwanted' migrants may certainly prove effective as a short-term protective measure, but, if implemented in the absence of more positive forward- and outward-looking steps, nothing will be achieved towards averting or reducing the potentially devastating effects of an unchecked build-up in migration pressures, particularly in Eastern Europe and North Africa, but also in other less-developed regions of the world.

Two particular developments in the policy field can be identified which bode well for the emergence of new and more comprehensive approaches to migration policy in Western Europe. First, as noted in the preceding chapter, policy-makers are talking more and more of the need to address the root-causes of 'unwanted' or disruptive migration through greater cooperation with governments of existing or potential sending states, and through policies which target pressures such as unemployment and population growth or, in the case of refugee movements, inter-ethnic tension. The current refugee crisis caused by the conflict in the former Yugoslavia is already forcing policy-makers to link migration with issues which are qualitatively different from those which have traditionally shaped migration and refugee policy, including foreign policy questions touching on minority and human rights, the principle of self-determination, the sanctity of borders, and intervention.

Second, and accompanying this development, international migration has emerged, perhaps for the first time, as a distinct issue of 'high' politics in Western Europe, no longer subsumed in issues such as domestic labour-market regulation, but now identified as a top policy priority in its own right, to be addressed by government and state officials at the very highest levels.

To counter any undue optimism, however, two major reservations ought to be noted. First, as emphasised in Chapter 7, despite signs of more imaginative thinking, very little has as yet emerged by way of clear policy proposals in the area of action to alleviate migration pressures, and most substantive policy measures currently on the table indicate a continuing, and even growing, reliance on old-style approaches to migration control, such as border controls and visa regimes. Indeed, direct parallels could be drawn between statements and measures being introduced today and those of the interwar period when states talked of their 'saturation' with immigrants and refugees and their reluctance or inability to accept any more. The outcome of this response in the late 1930s, and thus the potential outcome of such a response today, needs little elaboration. Even Germany's new training programme for workers from developing countries and Central and Eastern Europe, while ostensibly set up for the benefit of the workers and labour markets of the sending countries involved, reveals elements very similar to the *Gastarbeiter* programme of the 1950s and 1960s.

Second, it is possible to discern something of a contradiction in the isolation of migration as a policy issue. As indicated in earlier chapters, international migration always reflects the broader economic, political and social context within which it takes place. If policies aimed at tackling the root causes of migration are to have any success, there is a need greater than ever before for migration policy to be placed firmly within its appropriate economic and political setting: that is, within the fold of a wide range of broader development, foreign and security policies. In this context, it is worth referring once again to the working paper of the Ad Hoc Group on Immigration, which, in outlining proposals for the development of 'migration policy in the broader sense', places such important policy issues as development aid, global food and environment policies, and controlling regional conflicts under – rather than above – the heading of 'migration policy'. Such an approach could imply a certain defensive narrowing of the policy agenda if undue emphasis on migration were to encourage fire-fighting responses which divert attention from many of the wider problems at issue. If 'unwanted' migration is a symptom of more fundamental problems of underdevelopment, demographic growth and/or political and economic insecurity and instability in the East and South, it is those fundamental problems which need to be tackled in a comprehensive way. This will not be achieved on the basis of short-term measures, nor will it be achieved through policies which place too much emphasis on migration. As stressed at a Conference on International Migration held in Rome in 1991, new economic policies should not leave out migration, but migration policy must be formulated 'against the background of more global and long-term vision of the development of sending countries'.[3]

Yet the primacy of the migration issue in current political discourse should, at the same time, be viewed as an essentially positive development. First, the conceptual isolation of the migration issue may lead to more long-term and imaginative thinking in the development of migration policies – an element which has been sorely lacking in the *ad-hoc* and reactive responses which have dominated up to now. Second, by forcing the states of Western Europe to focus their attention more fully on the problems of underdevelopment in regions such as North Africa, migration as a highly visible issue may ultimately prove a more potent development force than ever previously envisaged by the sending countries of the 1950s and 1960s. Whether impacting directly on Western Europe, through an increase in 'unwanted' immigration, or indirectly, through growing regional economic and political instability in neighbouring areas or a radicalization of existing immigrant groups,* the intensification of migration pressures is already spelling out to Western Europe that it can no longer isolate itself from the troubles of the less-developed world.

If constructive responses to such concerns are to be developed, they will critically depend on all states in Western Europe recognizing both their responsibility and their capacity to act to lessen migration pressures and cope with migration flows. Certain active policies would be within the means of Western Europe's receiving states if there were a political will to implement them. But it would be totally unrealistic to expect any swift remedy for all the problems of transition in the East and underdevelopment and population growth in the South. Calls for action to narrow the North/South divide are hardly new, and, as regards policy directed at Eastern Europe and the former Soviet Union, Western Europe simply lacks the resources to facilitate a

*For example, of Algerian and other North African groups in Europe in connection with a rise in religious fervour in North Africa – itself not unconnected with economic and demographic problems currently being experienced in these states.

smooth and swift economic and political transition in these areas. Moreover, as noted recently by George Joffe, there is, in the end, 'little that the EC or any other European entity can do to minimize the instability generated by xenophobia' in Eastern Europe, 'nor, in effect, is there much more that can be done over neo-nationalism'.[4] However, as he concludes in the context of the more general security threats facing Europe today, European statesman must take steps to mitigate the problems that emerge.[5]

Perhaps a first step would be for receiving states to face up to the fact that they are countries of immigration, and, as such, have a responsibility both to their own populations and to the sending countries to implement positive measures so as to introduce a degree of 'equity and order'[6] into the control of migration flows. Barriers against the entry of 'unwanted' migrants may certainly prove effective as a short-term protective measure, but if implemented in the absence of more positive steps to reduce migration pressures, or to introduce a system of managed (albeit limited) immigration, receiving states are in the end likely to weaken, rather than strengthen, their hold over the migration process. Western Europe's concerns vis-à-vis migration now clearly extend beyond the old and rather straightforward concepts of national or regional immigration control. If only for reasons of self-interest, these states have a responsibility of acting at least to try to help prevent pressures identified as the root causes of migration translating into more intractable problems of conflict and economic collapse in Eastern Europe and the former Soviet Union and in the less-developed countries of the South. The challenges are enormous, but if the countries of Western Europe shrink from them and retreat into what is the rather fragile shell of 'Fortress Europe', they will only grow greater.

Notes

Preface
1   Myron Weiner, 'On International Migration and International Relations', in *Population and Development Review*, vol. 2, no. 3, 1985, pp. 441–55, at p. 441.

Chapter 1
1   Eugene Kulischer, *Europe on the Move. War and Population Changes 1917–1947*, Columbia University Press, New York, 1943, p. 9.

2   Note also a recent increase in indenture-type labour, including an unknown, but certainly significant, number of foreign domestic servants held in virtual bondage in Britain and other industrialized countries in the West.

3   See, for example, definitions of different types of 'worker' migration as set out in the UN Convention on the Protection of the Rights of All Migrant Workers and Members of Their Families, 1990 (reproduced in the United Nations Press Release, Department of Public Information, *Resolutions and Decisions Adopted by the General Assembly During the First Part of Its Forty-Fifth Session: From 18 September to 21 December 1990*, pp. 471–96). The Convention includes definitions of frontier workers, seasonal workers, seafarers, offshore installation workers, project-tied workers, itinerant workers, specified employment workers, professional, technical and professional workers, and self-employed workers.

4   See John Salt, 'Contemporary Trends in International Migration Study', *International Migration*, vol. 25 (1987), no. 3, pp. 241–7. See also Charles W. Stahl, 'Overview: Economic Perspectives', in Reginald Appleyard, ed., *The Impact of International Migration on Developing Countries*, OECD, Paris, 1989, p. 362; and Claudio Stern in R. Appleyard, ed., *International Migration Today* (vol.1), UNESCO, 1988.

5   Jonas Widgren, 'International Migration: New Challenges to Europe', report prepared for the Third Conference of European Ministers Responsible for Migration (Council of Europe), Porto, Portugal, 13–15 May 1987. Reprinted in *Migration News* no. 2, International Catholic Migration Commission, Geneva, 1987. This figure includes legally employed foreign workers and their dependants, undocumented workers, and official and unofficial refugees.

6   Sharon Stanton Russell and Michael S. Teitelbaum, *International Migration and*

International Trade, World Bank Discussion Paper, no. 160; World Bank, Washington DC, 1992, p. 1.

7   Ibid., p. 29. Russell and Teitelbaum note that theirs represents the first, and possibly only, attempt to calculate the total global volume of remittance flows. They draw on IMF balance-of-payments data for 193 countries. A figure of $65.6 billion is quoted in the publication cited, but subsequent calculations by the same analysts suggested the figure of $60.9 billion as more accurate.

8   Louis Emmerij, 'The International Situation, Economic Development and Employment', paper presented at the OECD International Conference on Migration, Rome, March 1991, p. 9.

9   Russell and Teitelbaum, *International Migration and International Trade*, p. 9. All are conservative estimates.

10   Immigrant populations in Europe are difficult to quantify owing in part to the operation of different citizenship and nationality laws in different countries. Both figures should be taken as very provisional. The term 'foreigners' is used here in a very loose sense and includes EC nationals living in another Community state and immigrants in Britain who hold British citizenship.

11   Russell and Teitelbaum, *International Migration and International Trade*; *World Refugee Survey 1992*, US Committee for Refugees and American Council for Nationalities Service, Washington DC, 1992; OECD Continuous Reporting System on Migration (SOPEMI), *Trends in International Migration*, OECD, Paris, 1992; *Demographic Statistics 1992*, Eurostat, Luxembourg, 1991.

12   See also SOPEMI, *Trends in International Migration*, pp. 13–15.

Chapter 2

1   The World Bank, *World Population Projections, 1989-90 Edition: Short- and Long-Term Estimates*, The Johns Hopkins University Press, Baltimore and London, pp. xiv–xvi.

2   Ibid.

3   OECD Continuous Reporting System on Migration (SOPEMI), *Trends in International Migration*, OECD, Paris, 1992, Tables 34 and 36; and Demetrious Papademetriou, 'International Migration in North America: Issues, Policies and Implications', paper prepared for the UNECE/UNFPA Informal Expert Group Meeting on International Migration, Geneva, July 1991, p. 36 (fn.).

4   SOPEMI, *Trends in International Migration*, Tables 2, 3 and 4, pp. 132–3.

5   Ibid., Table 5, p. 133. This figure is based on data provided for Austria, Belgium, France, Germany, Luxembourg, Netherlands, Sweden, Switzerland, United Kingdom.

6   S. Stanton-Russell, K. Jacobsen and W.D. Stanley, *International Migration and Development in Sub-Saharan Africa, Volume I*, World Bank Discussion Papers, Africa Technical Department Series, no. 101, World Bank, Washington DC, 1990, p. 1.

7   Eurostat, *Demographic Statistics 1991*, Eurostat (Statistical Office of the European Communities), Official Publications Office of the European Communities, Luxembourg, 1991, p. 152 (Table H-1). The table provides an aggregate figure for immigrants from African countries, with a breakdown on those from Algeria, Morocco and Tunisia. Subtracting immigrants of North African origin from the total figure for African immigrants leaves roughly 0.5 million. The statistics should be assumed inaccurate.

8   See, for example, Manolo Abella, 'International Migration in the Middle East: Patterns and Implications for Sending Countries', paper prepared for the UNECE/ UNFPA Informal Expert Group Meeting on International Migration, Geneva, July 1992, p. 7; See also J.S. Birks and C.A. Sinclair, *International Migration and Development in the Arab Region*, International Labour Office, Geneva, 1980, p. 77.

9   Abella, 'International Migration in the Middle East', p. 12.

10 Ibid., p. 16; and Asian Regional Programme on International Labour Migration, *Statistical Report 1990: International Labour Migration from Asian Labour-Sending Countries* (UNDP-ILO Asian Regional Programme on International Labour Migration), International Labour Organisation, Regional Office for Asia and the Pacific, Bangkok, Thailand, 1990. This figure is only a rough estimate. It includes those who left to work as seafarers (630,000) and female domestic workers, but excludes undocumented migration.

11 World Bank, *World Development Report 1991: The Challenge of Development*, Oxford University Press for World Bank, Washington DC, 1991, Table 1 (Basic Indicators), p. 204.

12 Abella, 'International Migration in the Middle East', Table 9, p. 37; Lin Lean Lim, 'International Labour Migration in Asia: Patterns, Implications and Policies', paper prepared for the UNECE/UNFPA Informal Expert Group Meeting on International Migration, Geneva, July, 1992, Table 6, p. 64.

13 UNDP/ILO Asian Regional Programme on International Labour Migration, *Statistical Report 1990: International Labour Migration from Asian Labour-Sending Countries*, International Labour Organisation (World Employment Programme), Regional Office for Asia and the Pacific, Bangkok, Thailand, 1990.

14 World Bank, *World Development Report 1991*, Table 26 (Population Growth and Projections), p. 255.

15 See, for example, John Bauer, 'Demographic Change and Asian Labour Markets in the 1990s', in *Population and Development Review*, vol. 16, no. 4, pp. 615–45.

16 Lim, 'International Labour Migration in Asia', pp. 25–6.

17 See, for example, Mr Kayutaba Shigemi, Deputy Director, General Affairs Division of the Immigration Bureau, Ministry of Justice, Tokyo, Japan. Quote taken from a statement to the International Labour Office: 'Recent Changes in Immigration Control Act and Recent Developments in the Immigration of Foreign Workers to Japan' (ILO, Asia Regional Office, Bangkok).

18 Ibid., pp. 5–6.

19 See, for example, E.G. Ravenstein, 'The Laws of Migration', *Journal of the Royal Statistical Society*, no. 52, London, 1889; Arthur W. Lewis, 'Economic Development with Unlimited Supplies of Labour', The Manchester School of Economic and Social Studies, vol. 22, Manchester, 1954; and Michael Todaro, 'A Model of Labor Migration and Urban Unemployment in Less Developed Countries', *American Economic Review*, vol. 59, March 1969.

20 See, for example, John Salt, 'A Comparative Overview of International Trends and Types, 1950–1980', *International Migration Review*, vol. 23, no. 3, 1989.

21 A. Golini, G. Gerano and F. Heins, 'South–North Migration with Special Reference to Europe', *International Migration*, June 1991, p. 253.

22 Myron Weiner, 'On International Migration and International Relations', in *Population and Development Review*, vol. 2, no. 3 (1985), pp. 441–55, at p. 489.

23 Papademetriou, 'International Migration in North America', p. 5.

24 Weiner, 'On International Migration and International Relations', p. 489.

25   I.J. Seccombe, 'International Migration in the Middle East: Historical Trends, Contemporary Patterns and Consequences', in R. Appleyard, ed., *International Migration Today*, vol. 1, UNESCO, 1988, p. 199; and W.A. Shadid, E.J.A.M. Spaan and J.D. Speckman, 'Labour Migration and the Policy of the Gulf States', in F. Eelens, T. Schampers and J.D. Speckmann, eds., *Labour Migration to the Middle East: From Sri Lanka to the Gulf*, Kegan Paul International, London and New York, 1992, p. 72.

26   See, for example, David North, 'Why Democratic Governments Cannot Cope with Illegal Immigration', paper presented at the International Conference on Migration, Rome, March 1991, OECD (OCDE/GD(91)22), Paris, 1991.

27   For example, the USA in 1987/8, France in 1982, Italy in 1987/8 and 1989/90, Spain in 1985 and 1991. Note also Portugal's intention to carry out a legalization programme in 1993.

28   H. Heydon, 'South–North Migration', paper presented at the Ninth IOM Seminar on Migration, Geneva, 1990. See also John Salt, 'Current and Future International Migration Trends Affecting Europe', paper presented at the 4th Conference of European Ministers Responsible for Migration Affairs, Council of Europe, Luxembourg, 1991; and W.R. Bohning, 'Integration and Immigration Pressures in Western Europe', in *International Labour Review*, vol. 4, no. 4, 1991.

29   US Department of Labor, Bureau of International Labor Affairs: Immigration Policy and Research Report 2, *Employer Sanctions and U.S. Labor Markets: First Report* (prepared by the Division of Immigration Policy and Research as part of the Department of Labor's submission to 'The President's First Report on the Implementation and Impact of Employer Sanctions'), Washington DC, July 1991, p. 7.

30   See Papademetriou, 'International Migration in North America'.

31   See, for example, 'Life, Liberty and Try Pursuing a Bit of Tolerance Too', *The Economist*, 5–11 September 1992.

32   See, for example, L. Dinnerstein and D.M. Reimers, *Ethnic Americans: A History of Immigration*, 3rd Edition, Harper and Row, New York, 1988.

33   Observation made at the Aspen Institute/Refugee Policy Group Conference, 'East–West Migration: Addressing the Root-Causes', Berlin, June 1992.

34   The Statute of the United Nations High Commissioner for Refugees (1950); the 1951 United Nations Convention Relating to the Status of Refugees (*United Nations Treaty Series*, vol. 189, no. 2545, p. 137), and its 1967 Protocol (UNTS, vol. 606). Texts of the UNHCR Statute and the 1951 UN Convention are reproduced in Guy Goodwin-Gill, *The Refugee in International Law*, Oxford University Press, 1983. The 1967 Protocol removed the temporal limitation included in the 1951 Convention which limits application to refugees who acquired their status as a result of events occurring before 1 January 1951. Over one hundred states have acceded to the 1951 Convention and 1967 Protocol.

35   UNHCR, 1992.

36   Ibid.

37   See Louise Holborn, *The International Refugee Organisation: A Specialised Agency of the United Nations, Its History and Work, 1946–52*, Oxford University Press, London, 1956.

38   Gil Loescher and John A. Scanlan, *Calculated Kindness: Refugees and America's Half-Open Door, 1945 to the Present*, Free Press and Collier Macmillan, New York and London, 1986.

39 James C. Hathaway, 'Reconceiving Refugee Law as Human Rights Protection', in
    V. Gowland and K. Samson (eds.), *Problems and Prospects of Refugee Law*,
    Graduate Institute of International Studies, Geneva, 1992, pp. 9–30, at p. 11.
40 See Elizabeth Ferris, *The Central American Refugees*, Praeger, New York, 1987.
41 See, for example, Louise Holborn, *Refugees, A Problem of Our Time: The Work of
    the United Nations High Commissioner for Refugees*, 2 vols., Scarecrow Press,
    Metuchen NJ, 1975.
42 The 1969 OAU Convention Governing the Specific Aspects of Refugee Problems
    in Africa, OAU Document CM/267/Rev.1. Reproduced in Goodwin-Gill, *The
    Refugee in International Law*.
43 UNHCR.
44 Sadruddin Aga Khan, Hassan Bin Talal, et al., *Refugees: The Dynamics of
    Displacement; A Report for the Independent Commission on International Hu-
    manitarian Issues*, Zed Books Ltd, London and New Jersey, 1986, p. 38.
45 UNHCR.
46 UNHCR.
47 In connection, for example, with efforts to introduce a new Asylum Bill in the
    United Kingdom in 1991 and 1992. See House of Commons debates (i) 13
    November 1991 (567-617 CD3/2-3/52); (ii) 2 November 1992, issue no. 1598, vol.
    213 (21–120)
48 UNHCR.
49 Ibid.
50 See US Committee for Refugees, *World Refugee Survey 1992*, American Council
    for Nationalities Service, Washington DC, 1992, especially pp. 32–6.
51 Ibid.
52 UNHCR.
53 US Committee for Refugees, *World Refugee Survey 1992*.
54 Jonas Widgren, 'The Management of Mass Migration in a European Context',
    paper delivered at the Royal Institute of International Affairs, London, 12 March
    1991; and J. Widgren, 'Movements of Refugees and Asylum-Seekers: Recent
    Trends in a Comparative Perspective', paper presented at the International
    Conference on Migration (OECD), Rome, 1991.
55 Indeed, a certain schizophrenia can be detected in public opinion since the out-
    break of hostilities in the former Yugoslavia, giving rise to an emergent tension
    between fear of unmanageable asylum inflows from other parts of Europe and the
    world (and thus support for restrictive asylum laws and procedures), and a concern
    to assist refugees and displaced persons from the Balkans. Memories of the
    consequences of preventing the entry of refugees from Germany during the 1930s
    certainly have a part to play in this context.
56 J.-P. Hocké, 'Beyond Humanitarianism', in Gil Loescher and Laila Monahan
    (eds.), *Refugees and International Relations*, Oxford University Press, 1989.
57 Federal Minister of the Interior, *Survey of the Policy and Law Regarding Aliens in
    the Federal Republic of Germany* (V II 1-937 020/15), Bonn, 1991, pp. 61 and 62.
58 UNHCR.
59 US Department of State Bureau for Refugee Programs, *World Refugee Report*,
    Department of State Publication 9998, Bureau for Refugee Affairs, Office of Policy
    and Budget Coordination, Washington DC, 1992.
60 See, for example, *The Guardian*, 3 November 1992.

Chapter 3

1   Eugene Kulischer, *Europe on the Move. War and Population Changes 1917–1947*, Columbia University Press, New York, 1943, p. 8.

2   Ibid., p. 96.

3   The King of Babylonia who ordered the deportation of much of the Jewish population of Southern Judaea after 586 BC. See Sven Tagil, 'From Nebuchadnezzar to Hitler', in Göran Rystad, ed., *The Uprooted: Forced Migration as an International Problem in the Postwar Era*, Lund University Press, Lund, 1990. See also Kulischer, *Jewish Migrations: Past Experiences and Post-War Prospects*, American Jewish Committee, New York, 1943, p. 14.

4   For a full discussion of the emergence of sovereign power in Europe, see F.H. Hinsley, *Sovereignty*, 2nd Edition, Cambridge University Press, 1986.

5   See, for example, Adam Smith, *An Inquiry into the Nature and Causes of the Wealth of Nations*, Whitestone, Dublin, 1776.

6   Alan Dowty, *Closed Borders*, Yale University Press, New Haven and London, 1987, p. 29.

7   Jews, Moriscos, Protestants from France and the Low Countries, German Catholics. Aristide Zolberg, 'Contemporary Transnational Migrations in Historical Perspective: Patterns and Dilemmas', in Mary M. Kritz, ed., *US Immigration and Refugee Policy. Global and Domestic Issues*, USA and Canada, Lexington Books, Lexington MA, 1983, p. 21.

8   Kulischer, *Europe on the Move*, p. 17.

9   Roughly 100,000. Ibid., p. 18.

10 Ibid., p.18.

11 Dowty, *Closed Borders*, p. 33.

12 Estimates for the number of Huguenots who left France at this time vary (ranging between 150,000 and 900,000). See Tagil, 'From Nebuchadnezzar to Hitler', p. 68 and fn. 23. Tagil notes that the difficulty in estimating a figure for this group is compounded by the fact that the Huguenots were accompanied by other French migrants trying to escape famine and social disorder. See also Aristide R. Zolberg, Astri Suhrke and Sergio Aguayo, *Escape from Violence. Conflict and the Refugee Crisis in the Developing World*, Oxford University Press, New York and Oxford, 1989, p. 6.

13 Zolberg, et al., *Escape from Violence*, p. 8.

14 Tagil, 'From Nebuchadnezzar to Hitler', p. 69.

15 Aristide R. Zolberg, 'Patterns in International Migration Policy: a Diachronic Comparison' in C. Fried, ed., *Minorities: Community and Identity*, Life Sciences Research Report Series no. 27, Springer-Verlag, Berlin, 1983, pp. 232–3. Many Europeans left for the New World under some form of bondage. See, for example, H.J.M. Johnston, *British Emigration Policy 1815–1830: Shovelling out Paupers*, Clarendon Press, Oxford, 1972, pp. 6–7. Johnston notes that between 1717 and 1775 as many as 225,000 Ulstermen arrived in America, most as indentured servants. Many of those who left for the New World were religious dissenters escaping a combination of persecution and economic hardship, including high numbers of Huguenots. See also Zolberg, et al., *Escape from Violence*, p. 8.

16 Kingsley Davis, 'The Migrations of Human Populations', *Scientific American*, no. 231, September 1974, p. 96.

17 See Philip D. Curtin, *The Atlantic Slave Trade: A Census*, University of Wisconsin Press, Madison, 1969, pp. 12–13 and 275–82. Curtin notes that estimates of slave

imports into the Americas range between 3.5 and 25 million. He criticizes many estimates as being based on 'insubstantial guesswork'. Curtin's estimate for slave imports into the Americas and Europe is close to 9.6 million for the period 1451–1870; of these, he estimates that about 7.8 million were taken to the New World.

18   Davis, 'The Migrations of Human Populations', p. 97.

19   Quoted by Dowty, *Closed Borders*, p. 43. The French Revolution itself gave rise to a flow of some 129,000 refugees (Zolberg et al., *Escape from Violence*, p. 9), approximately 8,000 of whom arrived in the United Kingdom over the three years after 1789. It is interesting to note that this influx resulted in Britain's first Alien Bill, which was designed to control the entry of French migrants by way of sanctions imposed on transporters not providing customs officers with details of any foreigners transported, etc. This influx took place during a period of deteriorating relations between Britain and France. Within three years, France had introduced similar controls over aliens within its territory. See Richard Plender, *International Migration Law*, Sijthoff, Leiden, 1972, p. 44. In 1797 France adopted a Passports Law, which can be seen as the starting-point for modern aliens registration. See Grahl-Madsen, *The Status of Refugees in International Law*, vol. 1, Sijthoff, Leiden, 1966, p. 11. In 1798 the USA approved its first Bill providing for the control of immigration.

20   For a succinct analysis of the thinking of theorists such as Locke and Smith in the context of free movement of people and the right to emigrate, see F.G. Whelan, 'Citizenship and the Right to Leave', in *American Political Science Review*, no. 75, September 1981.

21   Frank H. Knight, *Risk, Uncertainty and Profit*, Houghton Mifflin, Boston, 1921, p. 77. Quoted in J.R. Stansfield, *The Economic Thought of Karl Polanyi: Lives and Livelihood*, Macmillan, London, 1986, p. 128.

22   Karl Polanyi, *Origins of Our Time: The Great Transformation*, Victor Gollancz, London, 1945, p. 75.

23   Thomas Robert Malthus, *An Essay on the Principle of Population*, edited by Patricia James, Cambridge University Press for the Royal Economic Society, Cambridge and New York, 1989.

24   Smith, *The Wealth of Nations*.

25   Zolberg, 'Contemporary Transnational Migrations in Historical Perspective', pp. 21–2.

26   Dowty, *Closed Borders*, p. 45.

27   The Passenger Act of 1803, introduced largely in reaction to increased voluntary emigration from the Scottish Highlands. The Highlands and areas of Northern Ireland had a history of emigration to the New World dating back at least as far as the mid-18th century. Between 1717 and 1775, roughly 225,000 Ulstermen arrived in America. See H.J.M. Johnston, *Shovelling out Paupers*, Clarendon Press, Oxford, 1972, pp. 1 and 6–7.

28   Ibid.

29   See Plender, *International Migration Law*, p. 46.

30   By 1886, there were over 250,000 Italian workers in France. See Frank Thistlethwaite, 'Migration from Europe Overseas in the Nineteenth and Twentieth Centuries', *Rapports*, vol. 5, 1960, p. 42. Thistlethwaite notes the significance of France as a country of immigration, particularly after the United States began restricting entry of aliens towards the end of the nineteenth century.

31   Thistlethwaite, 'Migration from Europe Overseas', p. 41. See also Brinley Thomas,

Migration and Economic Growth. A Study of Great Britain and the Atlantic Economy, Cambridge University Press, 1954. Thomas examined how nineteenth-century migration was related to rhythms of economic growth in Britain and the United States, and found changes in Britain to be more decisive in determining levels of emigration.

32   Thistlethwaite, 'Migration from Europe Overseas', p. 47.

33   Davis, 'The Migrations of Human Populations', p. 98. Other destinations included South America, Southern Africa, Central Asia and Australia. About 30% of those who left eventually returned. See M. Piore, *Birds of Passage*, Cambridge University Press, 1979, p. 150.

34   Poire, *Birds of Passage*, p. 98.

35   Davis, 'The Migrations of Human Populations', p. 99.

36   Johnston, *British Emigration Policy*, p.165. Kingsley Davis estimated in 1974 that had it not been for emigration up to that date, the population of Ireland would be nearly 12 million instead of 3 million. See Davis, 'The Migrations of Human Populations', p. 99.

37   See Piore, *Birds of Passage*.

38   Thistlethwaite, 'Migration from Europe Overseas', p. 48.

39   Ibid., p. 50, quoting W.D. Forsyth, *The Myth of the Open Spaces: Australian, British and World Trends of Population and Migration*, Melbourne University Press, Melbourne, 1942, pp. 16–17.

40   Tomas Hammar, ed., *European Immigration Policy*, Cambridge University Press, 1985, p. 240.

41   Zolberg, 'Patterns in International Migration Policy', p. 237. Note that Ireland was still part of the United Kingdom.

42   Ernest Gellner, *Muslim Society*, Cambridge University Press, 1981, p. 96.

43   Michael Marrus, *The Unwanted; European Refugees in the Twentieth Century*, Oxford University Press, New York and Oxford, 1985. See also Zolberg, et al., *Escape from Violence*, pp. 10–11.

44   Hannah Arendt, *The Origins of Totalitarianism*, Harvard University Press, Harvard, 1973, p. 269.

45   Marrus, *The Unwanted*, p. 23.

46   Of a total US immigration figure of 27.5 million for same period; see E. Kulischer, *Europe on the Move*, p. 24.

47   Between 1875 and 1914. See Plender, *International Migration Law*, p. 55.

48   See Zolberg, 'Patterns in International Migration Policy'.

49   Mr Justice Gray in *Nishimura Ekiu vs. USA*, quoted in Plender, *International Migration Law*, p. 51.

50   Ibid., p. 55.

51   The Dillingham Report, which also recommended introduction of provisions for deportation of certain aliens. Ibid., pp. 55–6.

52   Including Australia's 1901 Immigration Registration Act, marking the beginnings of the 'White Australia Policy' which prevailed until the 1970s. Ibid., p. 48.

53   Marrus, *The Unwanted*, p. 25.

54   Ibid., p. 37, and Plender, *International Migration Law*, pp. 56–7 and fn. 114. Marrus notes that in practice the new law had limited effect, but that it was significant in that it represented a shift away from the attitude that refugees should have an automatic right to enter Britain.

55   Zolberg et al., *Escape from Violence*, p. 13.

56   Marrus, *The Unwanted*, p. 45.

57   Convention of Adrianople, November 1913. In fact most of those affected by the agreement had already moved.

58   See S.J. Shaw and E.K. Shaw, *History of the Ottoman Empire and Modern Turkey*, vol. 2, Cambridge University Press, 1977, pp. 347–8.

59   Quoted in Marrus, *The Unwanted*, p. 105.

60   Already before Lausanne, Greece had to absorb about 1 million refugees from the Turkish War of Independence, and after 1920 was faced with settling refugees numbering up to one quarter of the total Greek population of the time. See Marrus, pp. 102–3. Armenians were among those groups who fled to Greece, but the majority were Greeks from Thrace and Western Anatolia.

61   Arendt, *The Origins of Totalitarianism*, p. 277.

62   Estimate made by Sir John Hope Simpson, *The Refugee Problem: Report of a Survey*, Oxford University Press for the RIIA, London, 1939, pp. 80–87. Zolberg et al. note that many estimates of the time (e.g. 3 million) were inflated owing to the inclusion of displaced Poles and Germans returning home. They suggest a figure of around one million refugees outside the boundaries of the old empire. See Zolberg, et al., *Escape from Violence*, p. 17.

63   League of Nations Doc. C.277.M.203.1921.III (1921). The provision of the so-called 'Nansen Passports' (named after the High Commissioner) was agreed to in 1922.

64   Zolberg, 'Contemporary Transnational Migrations'.

65   According to one migration expert, 20–25 million Europeans fell within a nationally alien jurisdiction after the peace settlements. See Marrus, *The Unwanted*, p. 70.

66   The League Council was called upon to extend the identity certificate programme to Armenians in September; the other categories listed fell into December 1926 resolution, named explicitly as groups requiring assistance in 1928. League of Nations OJ 967 (1924) and 155 (1927).

67   Zolberg et al., *Escape fromViolence*, p. 18. See also Marrus, *The Unwanted*, p. 51; and Kulischer, *Europe on the Move*, pp. 248–9.

68   The Dillingham Report. Quoted in Plender, *International Migration Law*.

69   See Dowty, *Closed Borders*, p. 90.

70   Ibid., pp. 90–91. Note that France took over as one of the most important countries of immigration as America began restricting inflows. Between 1919 and 1928 about 1.5 million foreigners entered France (many of whom were refugees). See Marrus, *The Unwanted*, p. 114.

71   Hope Simpson, *The Refugee Problem*, pp. 515–16. See also Marrus, *The Unwanted*, p. 138. Of these at least 100,000 had emigrated overseas, including at least 45,000 who left for Palestine (Marrus, p. 132).

72   The right-wing regimes of these countries were becoming increasingly hostile to their Jewish populations which numbered about 3 million in Poland, 445,000 in Hungary and 757,000 in Romania. See Marrus, *The Unwanted*, p. 142. Sir John Hope Simpson estimated the total population of Jews east of Germany, excluding the USSR, to be about 5 million in 1938. See Hope Simpson, *The Refugee Problem*, pp. 515–16.

73   See Marrus, *The Unwanted*, pp. 170–72.

74   See Sir John Hope Simpson, *Refugees: A Review of the Situation Since 1938*, Oxford University Press for the RIIA, London, 1939, pp. 1–30.
75   Tagil, 'From Nebuchadnezzar to Hitler', p. 9.
76   Nicolai Tolstoy, *Stalin's Secret War*, Cape, London, 1982, p. 112. See also Marrus, *The Unwanted*, p. 197.
77   Marrus, *The Unwanted*, p. 199.
78   Tolstoy, *Stalin's Secret War*, pp. 201 and 222–3. See also Marrus, *The Unwanted*, p. 197.
79   Marrus, *The Unwanted*, pp. 200–2.
80   Kulischer, *Europe on the Move*, p. 305.
81   Michael Marrus, 'The Uprooted: an Historical Perspective', in Rystad, ed., *The Uprooted*, pp. 47–57.
82   See Louise Holborn, *The International Refugee Organisation*, Oxford University Press, London, 1956.
83   The 1951 United Nations Convention Relating to the Status of Refugees, United Nations Treaty Series, vol. 189, no. 2545, p. 137. See also its 1967 Protocol, UNTS, vol. 606. The 1967 Protocol removed the temporal limitation. Texts of the UNHCR Statute and 1951 Convention reproduced in Guy Goodwin-Gill, The Refugee in International Law, Oxford University Press, 1983, pp. 241–6 and pp. 270–74.
84   Despite growing numbers of refugees in other parts of the world over the following years, it was not until 1967 that the temporal limitation was removed by a protocol; the optional geographical limitation was left intact. Over one hundred states have acceded to the 1951 Convention and 1967 Protocol.
85   Note that the first major refugee movements to be experienced in the Third World took place at this time: the partition of India in August 1947 displaced 14 million people, and the formation of Israel resulted in the immediate displacement of at least 700,000 Arabs and subsequent movement of over 750,000 Jews who had been living in Arab countries. See Aristide Zolberg, 'The Refugee Crisis in the Developing World: A Close Look at Africa', in Rystad, ed., *The Uprooted*, pp. 87–8. See also Zolberg et al., *Escape from Violence*, p. 23.
86   Quoted by Dowty, *Closed Borders*, p. 97.
87   Ibid., pp. 100–1.
88   Dowty, *Closed Borders*, p. 116.
89   Jean-Pierre Hocké, 'Beyond Humanitarianism', in Gil Loescher and Laila Monahan, eds., *Refugees and International Relations*, Clarendon Press, Oxford, 1989.
90   See Gil Loescher and John Scanlan, eds., *Calculated Kindness: Refugees and America's Half-Open Door, 1945 to the Present*, Free Press and Collier Macmillan, New York and London, 1986.

Chapter 4

1   Note that colonial ties had already given rise to small numbers of migrants moving from Algeria to France, from the Caribbean to Britain and from Indonesia to the Netherlands during the 1930s. See Alan Dowty, *Closed Borders*, Yale University Press, New Haven and London, 1987, pp. 56–7.
2   No case-study is taken from the new immigration states of Southern Europe (Italy, Spain, Portugal, Greece), since these countries, traditionally sending states, have

only begun introducing coherent immigration policies over the past few years. During the 1980s, however, these states emerged as important countries of immigration (although, it should be noted, Portugal remains a country of net emigration). As noted in Chapter 7, the overall convergence in immigration policies which has taken place in Western Europe since the mid-1980s includes the countries of Southern Europe.

3   'Le problème de la population représente ... le problème numéro un de toute la politique économique française', in 'Documents relatifs à la Première Session du Conseil du Plan (16–19 mars 1946)', Commissariat Général du Plan de Modernisation et d'Equipment, Paris, 1946. Quoted in Georges Tapinos, *L'immigration étrangère en France, 1946–1973*, Institut National d'Etudes Démographiques no. 71, Presses Universitaires de France, Paris, 1975, p. 16.

4   See Tapinos, *L'immigration étrangère*, p. 129, and Catherine Wihtol de Wenden, *Les immigrés et la politique*, Presses de la Fondation Nationale des Sciences Politiques, Paris, 1988, p. 93.

5   2 November 1945. Note also the Ministerial Order of 19 October 1945 establishing the 'Code de la Nationalité Française', including arrangements to facilitate naturalizations.

6   'Au printemps de 1946, un vaste programme d'immigration semblait sur le point de prendre place dans une audacieuse politique de relèvement national, où les exigences démographiques se seraient conciliées heureusement avec les nécessités économiques', in Xavier Lannes, *L'immigration en France depuis 1945*, Nijhoff, Dordrecht, 1953, p. 18, see Wihtol de Wenden, *Les immigrés et la politique*, p. 95.

7   See Dowty, *Closed Borders*, p. 98.

8   Ibid., p. 122.

9   Wihtol de Wenden, *Les immigrés et la politique*, p. 95.

10   Tapinos, *L'immigration étrangère*, p. 28. Accord dated 11 March 1947.

11   See Zig Layton-Henry, 'British Immigration Policy and Politics', in Michael C. LeMay, ed., *The Gatekeepers. Comparative Immigration Policy*, Praeger, New York, 1989, pp. 59–94.

12   Over 100,000 'volunteered' under this scheme, most notably Lithuanians, Ukrainians, Latvians and Yugoslavs. See J. Tannahill, *European Voluntary Workers in Britain*, Manchester University Press, Manchester, 1958.

13   Stephen Adler, *International Migration and Dependence*, Saxon House, Farnborough, Hants, 1977, p. 60.

14   G. Tapinos and Yann Moulier, 'France', in Daniel Kubat, ed., *The Politics of Migration Policies: The First World in the 1970s*, Center for Migration Studies, New York, 1979, pp. 127–43.

15   Wihtol de Wenden, *Les immigrés et la politique*, p. 92.

16   'La constitution de colonies inassimilables sur le territoire national', in ibid., p. 92, quoting Pierre Bideberry, 'Bilan de vingt années d'immigration, 1946–1966', in *Revue Française des affaires sociales*, no. 2, April–June 1967, p. 7.

17   22 February 1946, 24 November 1946, etc. See Wihtol de Wenden, *Les immigrés et la politique*, p. 96.

18   Tapinos, *L'Immigration étrangère*, p. 28.

19   Ibid., p. 33.

20   Wihtol de Wenden, *Les immigrés et la politique*, p. 100.

21 Layton-Henry, 'British Immigration Policy', pp. 61–2.

22 Ibid., p. 62. See Ministry of Labour, 'Report of the Working Party on Employment in the UK of Surplus Colonial Labour', Ministry of Labour Papers 26/226/7503, Public Records Office, 1948.

23 Quoted by Layton-Henry, 'British Immigration Policy', p. 64. See Royal Commission on Population, Cmnd. 7695, HMSO, London, 1949, pp. 226–7.

24 These arrivals were not, in fact, strictly the first immigration flows from the British colonies. By the mid-eighteenth century, several black communities had been established in Britain as a result of the slave trade (e.g. 20,000 immigrants in London in 1764, most of whom were ex-slaves and escapees). During the First World War, 15,000 troops were recruited in the Caribbean, and many other West Indians joined the merchant marine. Many of these settled in existing black communities in Britain or began new settlements in ports such as Cardiff and Liverpool. These ports were the scenes of racial violence in 1919. During the Second World War, over 7,000 West Indians volunteered for the Royal Air Force, factory work (through the Overseas Volunteer Scheme) and the merchant marine. Many settled, and many of those who returned to the West Indies subsequently remigrated to the United Kingdom. According to Stuart Hall, the return migration to the West Indies played an important part in triggering new migration to the United Kingdom beginning in 1948. See Stuart Hall, 'Migration from the English-speaking Caribbean to the United Kingdom, 1950–80', in Charles W. Stahl, ed., *International Migration Today. Vol. 2: Emerging Issues*, UNESCO, Paris, 1988.

25 Note also emigration of British population to the 'Old' Commonwealth at this time. In the late 1940s and 1950s, emigration from Europe overseas accounted for a net loss of 3 million people for the whole of Europe. See Stephen Castles, Heather Booth and Tina Wallace, *Here for Good: Western Europe's New Ethnic Minorities*, Pluto, London, 1984, p. 1.

26 It is worth noting that as a result of past British colonial policies, many Commonwealth immigrants had a good knowledge of the English language, which served as a facilitating factor both in the migration process itself, and in the ease with which immigrants could fill gaps in the labour market.

27 Hall, 'Migration from the English-speaking Caribbean', p. 269.

28 Staff shortages in London Transport persisted well into the 1960s and 1970s. See Paul E. Garbutt, *London Transport and the Politicians*, Ian Allen, London, 1985.

29 Tom Rees, 'The United Kingdom', in Kubat, *The Politics of Migration Policies*, p. 77.

30 Tapinos, *L'Immigration étrangère*, p. 22. Note the lesson that this experience could teach policy-makers today, given the current emphasis on strict control policies which leave little room for the recognition of a demand for immigrant labour, and thus are ill-equipped to manage flows that are taking place irrespective of policies designed to prevent them. This is a theme raised in Chapter 8.

31 'L'établissement définitif et l'insertion des étrangers dans la société française', in Tapinos, *L'Immigration étrangère*, p. 20.

32 Agreements concluded with Greece and Spain 1960, Turkey 1960, Morocco 1963, Portugal 1964, Tunisia 1965, Yugoslavia 1968, further agreements with Turkey 1971 and 1972. See 'Survey of the Policy and Law Regarding Aliens in the Federal Republic of Germany', Federal Minister of the Interior (V II 1-937 020/15), Bonn, 1991, Annex 1. See also Richard Plender, *International Migration Law*, revised second edition, Nijhoff, Dordrecht, 1988, pp. 566–77 and refs. Note the Associa-

tion Agreement concluded between the EC and Turkey in 1963 involving an agreement to step-by-step measures towards freedom of movement between Turkey and the EC to be completed by 1 December 1986. This regulation did not enter into force in 1986.

33   28 April 1965.

34   Marilyn Hoskin and Roy C. Fitzgerald, 'German Immigration Policy and Politics', in LeMay, ed., *The Gatekeepers*, p. 95.

35   Unemployment within the immigrant population increased from 0.2% in 1966 to 1.5% in 1967. See Castles et al., *Here for Good*, p. 145. Between June 1966 and January 1968, numbers of foreign workers in Germany declined by about 31% (nearly one million non-EC immigrants remained). The economic upturn which followed the recession was accompanied by a renewal in immigration streams. By 1974 the number of foreigners legally resident in the Federal Republic had passed the four million mark. See Hoskin and Fitzgerald, 'German Immigration Policy and Politics', p. 151; and OECD, *Continuing Reporting System on Migration (SOPEMI)*, Paris, 1981, p. 33.

36   Note the formal abolition of barriers to free movement of workers within the European Economic Community in 1968 in accordance with Article 3c of the 1957 Treaty of Rome. Since Italy and Germany were both members of the EEC, the Rome Treaty rendered the labour agreement between the two countries obsolete. After 1968 all Italians could enter Germany freely to take up employment. This development did not lead to a large-scale influx of Italian workers, since emigration pressures in Italy had by this time declined to the point where many migrants were returning.

37   By 1969 the proportion of immigrants present in France who had regularized their status after entry had reached 80%. Tapinos and Moulier, 'France', p. 131.

38   Including large numbers of French settlers returning from Algeria, labelled as the '*pieds-noirs*'. This influx had the effect of encouraging subsequent Algerian and other immigration flows as the need for extra housing increased demand for labour in the construction industry.

39   'Il s'agit d'une immigration largement non controlée, caractérisée par la grande variété des pays d'origine et des cadres légaux (ou illégaux) par lesquels ils sont entrés inorganisés, insécurisés, privés de droits politiques, faiblement intégrés dans les organisations ouvrières et peu politisés', in Wihtol de Wenden, *Les immigrés et la politique*, p. 126.

40   Defining Algeria's relationship with France following independence.

41   April 1964. The so-called 'Nekhache-Grandval' agreement, which included a protocol allowing for numbers of Algerians entering France to be fixed according to the labour-market situations in both countries. See Adler, *International Migration and Dependence*.

42   Ibid.

43   'L'immigration clandestine elle-même n'est pas inutile, car si l'on s'en tenait à l'application stricte des règlements et accords internationaux, nous manquerions peut-être de main-d'oeuvre', in Jean-Marcel Jeanneney, 28 March 1966. See Wihtol de Wenden, *Les immigrés et la politique*, p. 161 and fn.

44   Including the UK, the Federal Republic, France, Belgium, the Netherlands, Luxembourg, Austria, Switzerland, Denmark, Norway and Sweden.

45   Castles et al., *Here for Good*, p. 88. Percentages are quoted for 1970. Percentages

as a proportion of the working population would have been higher in every country.

46   OECD, *SOPEMI*, Paris, 1975 and 1976.

47   Roughly 500,000 New Commonwealth citizens settled in Britain between 1955 and 1962. See Layton-Henry, 'British Immigration Policy', p. 69.

48   Category 'A' issued to those with a specific job to come to; Category 'B' issued by the British High Commissions overseas to those with skills or qualifications of which there was a shortage in the United Kingdom; Category 'C' issued to anyone on a first-come-first-served basis. Note that entry of foreign nationals from outside the Commonwealth was still controlled by the Alien Acts of 1914 and 1919 and the rules drawn up under these acts (except, subsequently, EC nationals wishing to enter to take up employment, offer services, etc.).

49   *Sunday Telegraph*, 18 October 1964. Quoted in Patrick Cosgrave, *The Lives of Enoch Powell*, Bodley Head, London, 1989, p. 235.

50   Note the uproar caused by his speech delivered in Birmingham on 20 April 1968.

51   Cosgrave, *The Lives of Enoch Powell*, p. 244.

52   1965 Race Relations Act, followed by a second Race Relations Act in 1976.

53   See Vaughan Bevan, *The Development of British Immigration Law*, Croom Helm, London, 1986, pp. 195–9.

54   Note that this subsequently affected the immigration of Asians from Uganda.

55   Her Majesty's Stationery Office, London 1971. Reproduced in Peter Wallington and Robert Lee, eds., *Blackstone's Statutes on Public Law*, Blackstone, London, 1988, p. 79.

56   Wihtol de Wenden, *Les immigrés et la politique*, p. 160.

57   The second specifying 31 October 1973.

58   See Belkacem Hifi, *L'immigration algérienne en France: origines et perspectives de non-retour*, L'Harmattan/CIEM, Paris, 1985.

59   23 November 1973. This was followed a year later with a restriction on granting of work permits for first employment to aliens residing in the Federal Republic of Germany (13 November 1974).

60   Federal Minister of the Interior, 'Survey of the Policy and Law Regarding Aliens in the Federal Republic of Germany', Bonn, January 1991, p. 49.

61   Note, for example, the European Convention on Human Rights, which calls for respect of family life; the Universal Declaration of Human Rights, which states that 'the family is the natural and fundamental group unit of society and is entitled to protection by society and state' (Art. 16); the International Covenant on Civil and Political Rights; and the Final Act of the Helsinki Conference on Security and Cooperation in Europe, which sets standards for family reunification.

62   For example, France maintained a ban on family immigration from July 1974 to July 1975, and during the late 1970s family immigrants were allowed to enter only on the condition that they would not demand access to the labour market; similarly, the Federal Republic issued dependants and family members residence permits without work permits until 1979.

63   *Immigration Observations on the Report of the Select Committee on Race Relations and Immigration*, Secretary of State for the Home Department, HMSO, London, July 1978, Cmnd. 7287, paragraphs 15 and 16.

64   Federal Minister of the Interior, 'Survey of the Policy and Law', p. 47.

65   OECD, *SOPEMI*, Paris, 1986.

66   Ibid., p. 9.

67   Ibid., p. 28.

68 See Chapter 6 for a discussion of fertility rates among immigrant groups.

69 'L'Europe ... doit s'efforcer de définir en commun des objectives et d'organiser avec les pays un modèle exemplaire de coopération où l'immigration trouve son exacte place', quoted in Wihtol de Wenden, *Les immigrés et la politique*, p. 195.

70 ILO, 'Convention Concerning Migration in Abusive Conditions and the Promotion of Equality of Opportunity and Treatment of Migrant Workers', ILO Convention no. 143, Cmnd. 6674, Geneva, 24 June 1975. See Plender, *International Migration Law*, Chapter 5.

71 Plender, *International Migration Law*, p. 256.

72 Wihtol de Wenden, *Les immigrés et la politique*, p. 224.

73 Gilles Verbunt, 'France', in Tomas Hammar, ed., *European Immigration Policy. A Comparative Study*, Stockholm University Centre for Research in International Migration and Ethnicity, Cambridge University Press, 1985, p. 142.

74 Federal Minister of the Interior, 'Survey of the Policy and Law Regarding Aliens', pp. 6–7.

75 Ibid.

76 Wihtol de Wenden, *Les immigrés et la politique*, p. 124.

77 Layton-Henry, 'British Immigration Policy'. See Bevan, *The Development of British Immigration Law*, Chapter 5, pp. 191–223. Note also the Immigration Act 1988, which introduced a wide range of further provisions designed to restrict immigration.

78 This date was repeatedly postponed until the first parliamentary term of 1982. See Wihtol de Wenden, *Les immigrés et la politique*, p. 281.

79 Ibid, p. 290; and Claude-Valentin Marie, 'L'immigration clandestine in France', in *Travail et Emploi*, no. 17, July–September 1983, pp. 27–39.

80 *Immigration: Observations on the Report of the Select Committee on Race Relations and Immigration*, paragraphs 6 and 24.

81 Note that in France entry of visitors staying for a period of less than three months became subject to stringent conditions in addition to visa requirements, including guarantees of intention to return (proof of sufficient funds to cover period of stay, completion of an arrival card, an attestation of reception signed by the person to be visited, etc.). See Ministère des Affaires Sociales et de la Solidarité Nationale, *1981-1986. Une nouvelle politique de l'immigration*, La Documentation Française, Paris, 1987.

82 See Federal Minister of the Interior, 'Survey of the Policy and Law Regarding Aliens', pp. 51–2. Note the UK 1987 Carrier Liability Act, which allows for air and sea carriers to be penalized in the same way. Reproduced in Wallington and Lee, *Statutes on Public Law*, p. 275.

83 See Presidenza del Consiglio dei Ministri, *Norme Urgenti in Materia di Asilo Politico, Ingresso e Soggiorno dei Cittadini Extracomunitari e di Regolarizzazione de Cittadini Extracomunitari ed Apolidi Già Presenti Nel Territorio Dello Stato*, Law of 28 February 1990, no. 39, converting Decree no. 416 of December 1989, Collana de Testi e Documenti, Dipartimento per L'Informazione e L'Editoria (Istituto Poligrafico e Zecca Dello Stato), Rome, 1990, including English translation, pp. 27–47.

84 Centro Studi Investimenti Sociali (CENSIS), *Immigrati e Società Italiana*, Editalia-Edizioni d'Italia, Rome, 1991, p. 329; CENSIS, *Atti Della Conferenza Nazionale dell' Immigrazione*, Editalia-Edizioni d'Italia, Rome, 1991, p. 484.

Chapter 5

1   D. Papademetriou, 'International Migration in a Changing World', in R. Appleyard, ed., *International Migration Today. Vol. 1: Trends and Prospects*, UNESCO, Paris, 1988.

2   International Labour Office, *Some Growing Employment Problems in Europe*, Report II, Second European Regional Conference, Geneva, 1974, pp. 98–9. Quoted in Philip L. Martin, *The Unfinished Story: Turkish Labour Migration to Western Europe*, Geneva, ILO, 1991, p. 17.

3   Stephen Adler, *Swallow's Children – Emigration and Development in Algeria*, Geneva, ILO, 1980.

4   See John Salt, 'Contemporary Trends in International Migration Study', *International Migration*, vol. 25, 1987, no. 3, pp. 241–7. See also Charles W. Stahl, 'Overview: Economic Perspectives', in R. Appleyard, ed., *The Impact of International Migration on Developing Countries*, OECD, Paris, 1989, p. 362; and Claudio Stern in Appleyard, *International Migration Today*, vol. 1.

5   Papademetriou, 'International Migration in a Changing World'.

6   Ibid.

7   See, for example, E.M. Petras, 'The Global Labour Market in the Modern World Economy', in M.M. Kritz, C.B. Keely and S.M. Tomasi, eds., *Global Trends in Migration: Theory and Research on International Population Movements*, Center for Migration Studies, New York, 1983.

8   Stephen Adler, *A Turkish Conundrum: Emigration, Politics and Development*, ILO World Employment Programme research working paper, Geneva, 1981, p. 82; quoted in Rinus Penninx, 'A Critical Review of Theory and Practice: The Case of Turkey', in *International Migration Review*, vol. 16, 1982, no. 4, pp. 781–818.

9   Note also Turkey's 1963 Association Agreement with the European Communities.

10 'Le Gouvernement français et le Gouvernement turc, désireux d'organiser dans l'intérêt commun le recrutement de travailleurs turcs, sont convenus de ce qui suit: *Art. 1er.* - Le Gouvernement français fait connaître périodiquement au Gouvernement turc ceux de ses besoins en main-d'oeuvre qui conviendraient aux travailleurs turcs....Ces informations préciseront, en particulier, les conditions d'âge, de spécialisations, d'aptitude professionnelle et de santé. Le Gouvernement turc fournit au Gouvernement français des indications aussi précises que possible sur le nombre, l'âge et la qualification des travailleurs turcs désirant travailler en France', Convention de Main-d'Oeuvre Entre La France et La Turquie, 8 April 1965. *Journal Officiel de la République Française*, 15 June 1965, p. 4940.

11 Martin, *The Unfinished Story*, p. 3; (source: Ali Gitmez, 'Turkish Experience of Work Emigration: Economic development or individual well-being', *Yapi Kred: Economic Review*, vol. 3, no. 4, pp. 3–27).

12 Office des Travailleurs Tunisiens à l'Etranger, de l'Emploi et de la Formation Professionelle.

13 I.J. Seccombe and R.I. Lawless, 'State Intervention and the International Labour Market: A Review of Labour Emigration Policies in the Arab World', in Appleyard, ed., *The Impact of International Migration*.

14 Stephen Adler, *International Migration and Dependence*, Saxon House, Farnborough, Hants, 1977, p. 161.

15 Ibid., p. 69.

16 A progressive move away from free circulation as articulated in the Evian Accords:

(i) the Nekhache-Grandval Accord of 1964, which held that arrivals of Algerians in France should be fixed according to the needs of the French (and Algerian) labour market (an annual contingent of 12,000) and which imposed new restrictions òn the entry of Algerian tourists; (ii) the 1968 Agreement concerning the Movement, Employment and Residence of Algerian Nationals and their Families in France, which set a new annual contingent of 35,000, to be renegotiated after 3 years; (iii) the negotatiation of a new annual contingent in 1971 - reduced to 25,000, and publication of a procès-verbal stating the intention to bring the regulation of Algerian immigrants more in line with that of other nationalities (e.g. Spaniards and Portuguese as processed through ONI).

17   In 1968, migrants' remittances were roughly equal in value to tax revenues from oil exports, whereas by 1973 the value of remittances represented only a fraction of the value of oil revenues. See Lawless and Seccombe, 'North African Labour Migration: The Search for Alternatives', *Immigrants and Minorities*, vol. 3, no. 2, July 1984, pp. 151–66.

18   Adopted after a referendum in 1976, the Charte Nationale defined the fundamental principles of the organization of Algerian society. Quoted in Seccombe and Lawless, 'State Intervention and the International Labour Market', p. 81.

19   Adler, *International Migration and Dependence*, p. 77.

20   1976 ILO World Employment Conference, paragraph 42. See Martin, *The Unfinished Story*, pp. 98–9; and W.R. Böhning, *Studies in International Migration*, International Labour Office, London, 1984, p. 9.

21   Barbara Schmitter Heisler, 'Sending Countries and the Politics of Emigration and Destination', in *International Migration Review* (Special Issue: 'Civil Rights and the Socio-political Participation of Migrants'), vol. 19, 1985, no. 3, pp. 469–84.

22   Seccombe and Lawless, 'State Intervention and the International Labour Market', pp. 69–89.

23   See Martin, *The Unfinished Story*, p. 52.

24   And members of the Village Development Cooperatives. This policy was designed to encourage return migration (as it was felt that members of cooperatives would maintain closer ties with their village or region of origin and would have a greater incentive to return). Despite the stated policy aims, the Turkish authorities exercised very little control over worker emigration. Of the 800,000 emigrants processed by the TES, roughly one-third were classed as skilled, and the majority were employed prior to departure. Ibid., p. 52.

25   Allan Findlay and Anne Findlay, *The Geographical Interpretation of International Migration: a Case Study of the Maghreb*, Centre for Middle Eastern and Islamic Studies, Durham, 1982.

26   Moroccan migration policy was largely laissez-faire. See Seccombe and Lawless, 'State Intervention and the International Labour Market'.

27   Emigration out of Morocco was strongly localized. According to Findlay and Findlay, the 'acute localization of Moroccan emigration in certain parts of the country underlines the regional as opposed to national significance of emigration ... [and reflects] the existence of fundamental spatial disequilibrium'. Findlay and Findlay, *The Geographical Interpretation of the International Migration*, p. 39. The geographical concentration of emigrant sources in Morocco also illustrates the importance of 'networks' in determining migration flows.

28   Penninx, 'A Critical Review of Theory and Practice', p. 793. See also Abadan-

Unat et al., *Migration and Development: A Study of the Effects of International Labour Migration on Bogazliyan District*, Ajams-Turk Press, Ankara, 1976.

29   Martin, *The Unfinished Story*, p. 52. Source: Kutlay Ebiri, 'Impact of Labor Migration on the Turkish Economy', in Rosemarie Rogers, ed., *Guests who Come to Stay: the Effects of Labor Migration on Sending and Receiving Countries*, Westview Press, Boulder, Colorado, 1985, pp. 207–30. A similar story is reflected in Stuart Hall's discussion of Caribbean emigration to the UK. Hall cites a number of studies which indicate that 'compared with the population as a whole, the [UK] intake contained a high proportion of skilled workers' – a situation described in some areas as 'a serious "loss of skilled and productive elements in the labour force"'. Hall notes that the percentage of working-age persons in Jamaica declined from 47% in 1943 to 40% in 1960. Stuart Hall, 'Migration from the English-speaking Caribbean to the United Kingdom, 1950–80', in C.W. Stahl, ed., *International Migration Today*, vol. 2 (UNESCO), 1988, pp. 271–3.

30   Bundesanstalt für Arbeit (FRG), *Repräsentativ-Untersuchung 1972, Beschäftigung ausländischer Arbeitnehmer* ('Representative Survey 1972, Employment of Foreign Workers'), Nurnberg, 1973. See Penninx, 'A Critical Review of Theory and Practice', p. 795.

31   The country with probably the most comprehensive return policy was Yugoslavia. According to Zvonimir Baletic, Yugoslav policy was 'designed to keep the migration temporary ... [this was] explicitly defined'. The Yugoslav government sought 'to promote the collective interest of Yugoslav workers in foreign countries ... by organizing their social and cultural life, by attempting to preserve their attachment to their home country and by encouraging them to return home ... the country's economic and social development policy takes into account their return and reintegration into economic and social life'. Zvonimir Baletic, 'International Migration in Modern Economic Development: with special reference to Yugoslavia', *International Migration Review*, vol. 16, 1982, no. 4, pp. 736–56.

32   Findlay and Findlay, *The Geographical Interpretation of International Migration*, p. 19.

33   See Catherine Wihtol de Wenden, 'L'échange de Lettres Franco-Algérien du 18 Septembre 1980 et Son Evolution en 1981 et 1982' in *Les Algériens en France*, CNRS, Paris, 1985, pp. 119–35. The 'aid to return' programmes were dubbed 'useless, ineffective and illusionary' by the Mitterrand administration in 1981. See Lawless and Seccombe, 'North African Labour Migration', p. 154; and G. Simon, 'Industrialisation, Emigration et Réinsertion de la Main-d'Oeuvre Qualifiée au Maghreb – le cas de la Tunisie et de l'Algérie', *Hommes et Migrations*, no. 902, 1976, pp. 4–14.

34   Suzanne Paine, *Exporting Workers: the Turkish Case*, Cambridge University Press, Cambridge, 1974, p. 129.

35   Adler, *A Turkish Conundrum*, p. 43. Quoted in Penninx, 'A Critical Review of Theory and Practice', p. 795.

36   See Martin, *The Unfinished Story*. The Turkish government also supported the Turkish Workers' Companies set up by migrants in Germany.

37   By the early 1980s, most governments of the receiving countries were looking to cooperate more with the sending countries. This was reflected in a greater emphasis on training returning migrants. Note that, at least initially, the interests of receiving and sending countries in encouraging returns did not necessarily coincide, since both were most interested in the most skilled and enterprising migrants.

38 Heinz Werner and Ingeborg König, *Ausländerbeschäftigung: Wiederkehroption für ausländische Jugendliche*, Ausländisches Amt., Bonn, 1988. See Martin, *The Unfinished Story*. The further return incentives introduced by the FRG in 1983/4 encouraged more returns, but again the impact was minimal.

39 See *International Migration*, vol. 24, no. 1, March 1986, which includes a number of papers on return migration (policies, causes, impacts, etc.). See also F.P. Cerase, 'Migration and Social Change: Expectations and Reality. A Case Study of Return Migration from the United States to Southern Italy', *International Migration Review*, vol. 8, no. 2, pp. 245–62. Cerase talks of the return of 'failure', 'conservatism', 'retirement' and the (less frequent) 'return of innovation' in return migration flows. The motivation for return migration is usually not for reinsertion into the industrial sector of the country of origin. See also Böhning, *Studies in International Migration*, p. 178.

40 Many of the agreements reached between sending and receiving countries after 1973 dealt exclusively with questions relating to migrants' living and working conditions and social and economic rights. Note also the mounting concern among sending countries worldwide regarding the treatment of migrant workers. The nine co-sponsors of the first draft text of the UN Convention on the Protection of the Rights of All Migrant Workers and the Members of Their Families (adopted in 1990) were all sending countries, including Algeria, Turkey, Yugoslavia and Morocco. See *International Migration Review*, vol. 25, 1991, no. 4 (special edition on the UN Convention).

41 Adler, *International Migration and Dependence*, pp. 107–8.

42 M. Miller and P. Martin, *Administering Foreign-Workers Programs*, Lexington Books, Lexington MA, 1982. Quoted in Schmitter Heisler, 'Sending Countries and the Politics of Emigration', p. 477.

43 Ben Bella replaced the French Federation with the Amicale largely because the former had sided with the opposition GPRA. Ben Bella was anxious about the possibility of antigovernment action based within the emigrant community (which originated predominantly from the Kabylia region in Algeria). The Amicale was staffed by pro-Ben Bella appointees.

44 See Ali Gitmez and Czarina Wilpert, 'A Micro-Society or an Ethnic Community? Social Organisation and Ethnicity Amongst Turkish Migrants in Berlin', in John Rex, Daniele Joly and Czarina Wilpert, eds., *Immigrant Associations in Europe*, Gower, Aldershot, 1987, pp. 86–125.

45 Penninx, 'A Critical Review of Theory and Practice', p. 797.

46 Author's calculation. *Sources: IMF International Financial Statistics*; and *IMF Balance of Payments Yearbooks 1990*.

47 Ibid.

48 World Bank, *Trends in Developing Economies 1991*.

49 Author's calculation. *Sources*: Ibid.; World Bank, *World Development Report 1991: The Challenge of Development*, Oxford University Press for the World Bank, Oxford, 1991.

50 Penninx, 'A Critical Review of Theory and Practice', p. 809.

51 See, for example, W.R. Böhning, 'Some Thoughts on Emigration from the Mediterranean Basin', *International Labour Review*, vol. 3, no.3, March 1975, pp. 251–77, reproduced in W.R. Böhning, *Studies in International Labour Migration*, Macmillan, London, 1984, pp. 165–90; Heiko Korner, 'The Experience in the Main Geographical OECD Areas: European Sending Countries', in *The Future of*

Migration, OECD, Paris, 1987, pp. 64–85. For a very clear résumé of the main arguments, see C.W. Stahl, 'Overview: Economic Perspectives', in Appleyard, ed., *The Impact of International Migration*; for an authoritative assessment of the impacts in North Africa and the Middle East, see Ismail Serageldin, J.A. Socknat, S. Birks, Bob Li, and Clive A. Sinclair, *Manpower and International Labour Migration in the Middle East and North Africa*, Oxford University Press for the World Bank, Oxford, 1983; for an important contribution to the debate based on evidence from Asia, see Charles W. Stahl, *International Labor Migration: A Study of the ASEAN Countries*, Centre for Migration Studies, New York, 1986. For a detailed study of the effects of emigration on a particular region (Turkey), see Abadan-Unat et al., *Migration and Development*. This research project was part of a larger project called REMPLOD: Reintegration of Emigrant Manpower and Promotion of Local Opportunities for Development (studies carried out in Morocco, Tunisia and Turkey, financed by the Dutch Ministry for Development Coopera- tion).

52   Serageldin et al., *Manpower and International Labour Migration*, p. 107.

53   E.g. 11% on one-year US$ accounts in 1988.

54   Martin, *The Unfinished Story*, p. 33.

55   I.J. Seccombe and R.J. Lawless, 'Some New Trends in Mediterranean Labour Migration: The Middle East Connection', *International Migration*, vol. 23, no. 1, March 1985.

56   Note the expulsions of Tunisian workers from Libya in 1969 (29,356), 1970 (33,939), 1972 (43,251), and 1976 (13,670). See Seccombe and Lawless, 'Some New Trends'.

57   Note that Yugoslavia was also politically well placed to export workers to Libya. In the same month that the Turkish–Libyan agreement was signed, Libya and Yugoslavia signed a technical cooperation agreement which made provisions for the supply of Yugoslav technical and supervisory manpower. In 1982, there were some 12,700 Yugoslavs working in Libya. Ibid.

58   M. Allefresde, 'Migration of Workers from the Mediterranean Countries to the Gulf States', OECD, Paris, 1984 (restricted). Quoted in Seccombe and Lawless, 'Some New Trends'.

59   M. Allefresde, 'The Oil-Producing Countries of the Middle East and North Africa', in *The Future of Migration*, OECD, Paris, 1987, p. 293.

60   Ibid., p. 294; and OECD, *Continuing Reporting System on Migration (SOPEMI)*, Paris, 1987 and 1989.

61   The 'brain drain' or 'reverse transfer of technology' issue received a great amount of attention during the 1960s and 1970s, and is again appearing as a major concern throughout the less developed world. The extent of the problem is indicated by the fact that sub-Saharan Africa lost an estimated 30% of its highly skilled manpower stock to the MDCs of the North (especially the European Community) between 1960 and 1984 (A. Adepoju, 'South–North Migration: the African Experience', *International Migration*, vol. 29, no. 2, p. 211). See also (for example) John Salt and Allan Findlay, 'International Migration of Highly-Skilled Manpower: Theoreti- cal and Development Issues', and D. Chongo Mundende, 'The Brain Drain and Developing Countries', in Appleyard, ed., *The Impact of International Migration*, pp.159–81; and papers presented at the Tenth IOM Seminar on Migration, 'Migration and Development', Geneva, September 1992.

62   Council of Europe, 'Report on the New Countries of Immigration', Document
      6211, Parliamentary Assembly, Strasbourg, 1990. See also John Salt, *Current and
      Future International Migration Trends Affecting Europe*, background document for
      the 4th Conference of European Ministers Responsible for Migration, Luxembourg,
      September 1991 (MMG-4 (91) 1 E), Council of Europe, Strasbourg, 1991, p.15.
63   For a discussion of current demographic pressures in North Africa, see, for
      example, Council of Europe, Committee on Migration, Refugees and Demography,
      'Demographic Imbalances Between the Countries of the Mediterranean Basin'
      (rapporteurs: M. Mota Torres and Vazquez, assisted by Léon Tabah), restricted
      (AS/PR (42) 40), Council of Europe, Strasbourg, 22 May 1991 (AAR40.42). See
      also Raouf Daboussi, 'Economic Evolution, Demographic Trends, Employment and
      Migration Movements', synthesis report for the Mediterranean Information
      Exchange System on International Migration and Employment (MIES), Interna-
      tional Labour Office, Geneva, February 1991.
64   Bimal Ghosh, 'Migration-Development Linkages: Some Specific Issues and
      Practical Policy Measures', paper presented at the Tenth IOM Seminar on Migra-
      tion, Geneva, September 1992, p. 2.
65   Reginald T. Appleyard, *International Migration: Challenge for the Nineties*, paper
      published for the fortieth anniversary of the IOM, International Organisation for
      Migration, Geneva, 1991, p. 83.

Chapter 6

1   Hartmut Esser and Hermann Korte, 'Federal Republic of Germany', in Tomas
     Hammar, ed., *European Immigration Policy: A Comparative Study*, Cambridge
     University Press, 1985, p. 180.
2   For a discussion of immigrant policies in the Netherlands and Sweden, see, for
     example, David Coleman, *International Migrants in Europe: Adjustment and
     Integration Processes and Policies*, paper presented at the United Nations Popula-
     tion Fund/United Nations Economic Commission for Europe Informal Expert
     Group Meeting on International Migration, Geneva, July 1991. Although the
     immigrant policy of the Netherlands was formulated comparatively recently, it is
     the most explicitly multiculturalist in Europe.
3   Czarina Wilpert, 'From One Generation to Another: Occupational Position and
     Social Reproduction – Immigrant and Ethnic Minorities in Europe', in C. Wilpert,
     ed., *Entering the Working World. Following the Descendants of Europe's Immi-
     grant Labour Force*, Gower, Aldershot, 1988, p. 3.
4   Since the term can be understood as classifying descendants of immigrants as
     'foreign' or 'immigrants' on the basis of their parents' status – an inaccurate
     classification for those who have spent all their lives in Britain and are considered
     British by policy-makers.
5   For example, children born in France of legally resident immigrant parents are
     automatically granted French citizenship (on reaching the age of 18) according to
     the principle of *jus soli* (citizenship granted to all individuals born within a state's
     territory irrespective of the nationality of the parents – usually qualified in prac-
     tice), whereas those born in Germany are not, and even the third generation has no
     right to citizenship. (*Jus sanguinis* operates in Germany whereby citizenship is
     inherited from the parents irrespective of the place of birth.) See Tomas Hammar,
     Democracy and the Nation State. Aliens, Denizens and Citizens in a World of

International Migration, Avebury, Aldershot, 1990, especially Chapter 5. See also Anne-Claire Hopmann, *Réflexions sur le futur statut des migrants des pays tiers dans le Marché Unique européen: étude sur le concept de résidence légale, remplaçant la notion de nationalité*, study carried out for DGV of the Commission of the European Communities, Brussels, 22 July 1992.

6   Wilpert, 'From One Generation to Another', p. 3.

7   Those who are clearly identifiable as such, thus excluding, for example, descendants of Irish immigrants in Britain who are to all intents and purposes fully integrated into British society.

8   Note for example that current Eurostat figures are based on census and other statistical sources which range from 1982 (France) to 1990 (Luxembourg).

9   André Lebon, *Regard sur l'immigration et la présence étrangère en France, 1989/90*, Ministère des Affaires Sociales et de la Solidarité, Direction de la Population et des Migrations, Paris, 1990, pp. 25–6. See also David Coleman, *International Migrants in Europe*, p. 4.

10 Note also the relatively high incidence of dual nationality in Britain and France which blurs the distinction further. See Hammar, *Democracy and the Nation State*, pp. 111–13. There is little in the way of statistics on dual citizenship, but Hammar suggests a figure of at least one million dual citizens in France and notes the presence of over 600,000 residents in Britain born in the Irish Republic all of whom are potential dual-citizenship holders. Both countries have a comparatively relaxed attitude towards dual citizenship.

11 Annual reports. Generally provides data on select OECD countries and therefore does not provide comprehensive data for all European countries. See, for example, SOPEMI, *Trends in International Migration 1992*, OECD, Paris, 1992.

12 See, for example, Eurostat, *Demographic Statistics 1992*, Luxembourg, 1992, pp. 152–9. Statistics confined to the EC member states. Less detailed data than that provided by SOPEMI, *Trends in International Migration 1992*.

13 SOPEMI, *Trends in International Migration 1992*, Tables 13, 14, 15 and 17.

14 See *Policies on Immigration and the Social Integration of Migrants in the European Community*, Experts' report drawn up on behalf of the Commission of the European Communities, Brussels, September 1990 (SEC(90)1813 final), p. 7.

15 Including all non-EC nationalities – Old Commonwealth, etc. (and excluding the some 650,000 residents who were born in the Republic of Ireland).

16 OECD, *Continuing Reporting System on Migration (SOPEMI)*, OECD, Paris, 1990; and John Haskey, *The Ethnic Minority Populations of Great Britain: Estimates by Ethnic Group and Country of Birth*, Demographic Analysis and Vital Statistics Division, Office of Population Censuses and Surveys, London, 1990. See also OPCS, *Labour Force Survey*, HMSO, London, 1990.

17 See, for example, Lebon, *Regard sur l'immigration*.

18 Predominantly African (especially North African) and Latin American (particularly in Spain). Figure quoted by John Salt, *Current and Future International Migration Trends Affecting Europe*, paper presented at the Fourth Conference of European Ministers Responsible for Migration (Council of Europe), Luxembourg, 17–18 September 1991 (Council of Europe Document MMG-4 (91) 1 E), p. 15. *Source*: Council of Europe, *Report on the New Countries of Immigration*, Document 6211, Parliamentary Assembly, 1990.

19 According to the 1982 census. See Eurostat, *Demographic Statistics 1991*, Luxembourg, 1991, p. 152.

20 Eurostat, *Demographic Statistics 1992*, Table H-1, p. 152. Data for France based on the results of the 1990 Population Census; for UK, based on Labour Force Survey; and Germany, provisional data only.

21 Percentages for the Community as a whole. See Commission of the European Communities, *Policies on Immigration and the Social Integration of Migrants in the European Community*, SEC(90)1813 final, Brussels, 28 September 1990, statistical annex, pp. 42–8.

22 OECD, *SOPEMI 1991*, Paris, 1992, Table 10, p. 136. No breakdown provided by republic or religion, etc.

23 Estimate for 1985, which includes children born in France to Algerian parents (roughly 300,000), who are French according to French law but considered Algerian by Algeria. Ibid. See also Lebon, *Regard sur l'immigration*, p. 25.

24 OECD, *SOPEMI 1991*, Paris, 1992, Tables 9 and 10, pp. 135–6.

25 Indicative of the recent diversification in immigration flows, characterized by a relative and absolute rise in flows from the Third World generally, particularly from Africa and Asia. See, for example, Salt, *Current and Future International Migration Trends*, p. 10. Note the impact of the 1991 disruptions in the labour markets of the Gulf states on migration flows from North Africa, Asia and the Middle East.

26 Although this distinction is not entirely clear-cut. Note that France actively encouraged European immigration through agreements with sending countries and that North African immigration has also been facilitated by relative geographical proximity. On the other hand, Italian and Yugoslav migration to Germany began before the bilateral recruitment agreements were entered into, reflecting the significance of geographical proximity for migration patterns into Germany. Geographical position is particularly salient for Germany today in relation to migration from Eastern and Central Europe.

27 Eurostat, *Demographic Statistics 1991*. The fact that France and Germany have the largest immigrant populations does not mean that immigrant groups constitute the highest overall percentages of population as compared with other countries. Population of immigrant origin accounts for 15.2% of Switzerland's population and over 26% of Luxembourg's. See SOPEMI, *Trends in International Migration 1992*, and Coleman, *International Migrants in Europe*, p. 1a.

28 Referred to generally as New Commonwealth and Pakistan (NCWP) origin in most statistics, since Pakistan only rejoined the Commonwealth in 1989.

29 On the basis of the OPCS Labour Force Surveys.

30 More accurately American New Commonwealth, including the West Indies, Guyana, Belize and other NCW territories in the Americas.

31 See Haskey, *The Ethnic Minority Populations of Great Britain*, and the OPCS Labour Force Surveys. Since a question on ethnic identity was introduced only into the last census (1991 – no results published at the time of writing), the most reliable source for the UK has been the Labour Force Survey, which is an annual survey covering approximately 60,000 households, the results of which are grossed up to provide national estimates every three years. Note that East African Asians are registered as being of African ethnic origin.

32 The 1986 amnesty (Law 943) led to the registration of roughly 7,000 Senegalese, 3,000 Ghanaians, 1,000 Somalis, 1,000 Nigerians and nearly 500 citizens of the Ivory Coast. It can be assumed that the majority of African immigrants did not come forward to regularize their status (perhaps as many as 90%). See Roger

Blackstone, *The Salt of Another's Bread: Immigration Control and the Social Impact of Immigration in Italy*, Report of a Western European Union Study Visit, Home Office, London, 1989.

33 The rate of Egyptian immigration may increase, particularly as a result of a partial redirection in migration flows resulting from events in the Gulf in 1991.

34 Centro Studi Investimenti Sociali (CENSIS), *Atti Della Conferenza Nazionale dell'Immigrazione*, Editalia-Edizioni d'Italia, Rome, 1991.

35 See OECD, *SOPEMI 1990*, Paris, 1991, Table C1.2. Overall movements are almost certainly under-estimated.

36 On the basis of surveys carried out by CENSIS, the Bocconi University and ISTAT (Central Statistical Institute). See CENSIS, *Atti Della Conferenza Nazionale dell'Immigrazione*. See also OECD, *SOPEMI 1990*, p. 53.

37 See Heather Booth, *Guestworkers or Immigrants? A Demographic Analysis of the Status of Migrants in West Germany*, Monographs in Ethnic Relations, no. 1, Centre for Research in Ethnic Relations, Warwick, 1985. See also OECD, *SOPEMI 1986*, Paris, 1987.

38 OECD, *SOPEMI 1985*, Paris, 1986, p. 63.

39 Percentages and figures from the 1971 Census, the 1977 OPCS Monitor 77/1 and the 1986–8 Labour Force Survey.

40 Eurostat estimate for 1989 is 1.62 children per woman for the European Community as a whole. Italy has the lowest fertility rate in the Community (1.29). See Eurostat, *Demographic Statistics 1991*, Luxembourg, 1991.

41 'Evolution of Fertility of Foreigners and Nationals in OECD Countries', in *Migration. The Demographic Aspects*, OECD, Paris, 1991, pp. 29–41, at p. 39.

42 Stephen Castles, 'The Guests Who Stayed – The Debate on "Foreigners Policy" in the German Federal Republic', in *International Migration Review*, vol. 19, no. 3, Autumn 1985, pp. 517–34, at p. 519.

43 For example, a Turkish fertility rate of over 4 in Sweden cf. a Turkish fertility rate of under 3 in the FRG in 1985. See OECD, 'Evolution of Fertility of Foreigners and Nationals', p. 37.

44 Ibid., p. 39. Low fertility rates also explain the declining numbers of West Indians in Britain during the 1980s cf. high fertility rates for minorities of Pakistani and Bangladeshi origin. High fertility rates within the latter two groups are partly explained by low rates of female labour participation.

45 This is a trend visible in most immigrant groups, at least after two or three decades of settlement. Of course the rate at which fertility declines will vary from group to group. Certain groups – particularly those least integrated and coming from countries with high fertility rates – are likely to manifest slower convergence than others, rates possibly even levelling off at a higher level than that of the population as a whole.

46 OECD, 'Evolution of Fertility of Foreigners and Nationals', p. 40. See also J.J. Schoorl, 'Fertility Adaptation of Turkish and Moroccan Women in The Netherlands', *International Organization for Migration Quarterly Review*, vol. 28, 1990, pp. 477–95. The fact that immigrant fertility rates tend to decline is one of the reasons (leaving aside political or social factors) why immigration cannot be considered to be a potential solution to the problem of ageing in the populations of industrialized countries. The positive effect of immigration on birth rates would not be sustained if yearly inflows were not recurrent.

47   Eurostat, *Rapid Reports, Population and Social Conditions*, no. 4, 1990; and
     Eurostat, *Demographic Statistics 1992*, p. xxv.
48   Eurostat, *Rapid Reports, Population and Social Conditions*.
49   Figures taken from Anton Kuijsten, *International Migration in Europe: Patterns
     and Implications for Receiving Countries*, paper presented at the UNFPA/ECE
     Informal Expert Group Meeting on International Migration, Geneva, 1991, p. 14.
50   Eurostat, *Rapid Reports, Population and Social Conditions*.
51   The recent increase in immigration rates can largely be attributed to four major
     trends: an upturn in labour inflows (predominantly skilled or illegal); the increase
     in numbers of asylum-seekers; the increase in South–North flows into the Northern
     Mediterranean countries; and the sudden increase in flows from eastern Europe
     since 1989. See Salt, *Current and Future International Migration Trends*, pp. 10–
     11.
52   Although the effectiveness of traditional immigration control procedures is now
     being questioned in the light of the recent increase in immigration flows. Ibid., p.
     11.
53   This Act was strengthened by the second Race Relations Act passed in 1968
     outlawing direct discrimination in employment, housing and the provision of
     commercial and other services. Implementation of both Acts was to be secured by
     the Race Relations Board established in 1966 under the 1965 Act. Both Acts
     proved weak, and the RRB had minimal impact. Recognition of race relations as a
     national issue of central importance was also reflected in the establishment of a
     Parliamentary Select Committee on Race Relations and Immigration in 1968. Note
     also the Community Relations Commission established the same year. See Zig
     Layton-Henry, *The Politics of Race in Britain*, Allen and Unwin, London, 1984,
     pp. 122–35.
54   See, for example, Paul White, 'The Migrant Experience in Paris', in Günther
     Glebe and John O'Loughlin, eds., *Foreign Minorities in Continental European
     Cities* (Erdkundliches Wissen, Heft 84), Steiner Verlag, Stuttgart, 1987, pp. 185–
     98, at p. 186.
55   Home Secretary, 1966, quoted in S. Patterson, *Immigration and Race Relations in
     Britain 1960-67*, Oxford University Press, 1969, p. 113.
56   Cf. the explicitly multicultural policies pursued by the Netherlands during the
     1980s. See Coleman, *International Migrants in Europe*.
57   Quoted by Layton-Henry, *The Politics of Race in Britain*, p. 134.
58   The Commission for Racial Equality (CRE) is empowered to investigate com-
     plaints (individual or collective) of racial discrimination (direct or indirect) in all
     areas of housing, employment, education, provision of services, etc., and to take
     cases to court where appropriate (except in employment, where cases are dealt with
     by an industrial tribunal). The CRE received 1,381 applications for legal assistance
     in 1990 (CRE, *Annual Report 1990*, London, 1991, Appendix 6).
59   Commission for Racial Equality, *Review of the Race Relations Act 1976: Proposals
     for Change*, CRE, London, July 1985, paragraph 1.3. Survey carried out by the
     Policy Studies Institute in collaboration with the CRE.
60   Commission for Racial Equality, *Annual Report 1990*, p. 7.
61   R.D. Grillo, *Ideologies and Institutions in Urban France: The Representation of
     Immigrants*, Cambridge University Press, 1985, pp. 289 and 292.
62   Ibid., p. 53.

63   See Gilles Verbunt, 'France', in Hammar, ed., *European Immigration Policy*.
64   See OECD, *SOPEMI 1990*, Paris, 1991, p. 48.
65   'le renforcement de l'action sociale liée au logement des familles immigrées en difficulté, les activités préparant à l'emploi ... la promotion de l'expression des résidents étrangers sur les décisions qui les concernent et tout ce qui touche à l'accueil et à l'information, à l'ecole et à la vie associative', in Lebon, *Regard sur l'immigration*, p. 66.
66   Indeed, Britain stands out in Europe in respect of its comprehensive framework of anti-discrimination legislation and enforcement mechanisms. See UN Centre for Human Rights, *Second Decade to Combat Racism and Racial Discrimination. Global Compilation of National Legislation Against Racial Discrimination*, New York, 1991.
67   See, for example, Esser and Korte, 'Federal Republic of Germany'; and Castles, 'The Guests Who Stayed', pp. 517–34.
68   Stephen Castles, Heather Booth and Tina Wallace, *Here for Good. Western Europe's New Ethnic Minorities*, Pluto, London, 1984.
69   Castles, 'The Guests Who Stayed', p. 522.
70   Ibid.
71   Ibid.
72   Ibid.
73   See Esser and Korte, 'Federal Republic of Germany', p. 183.
74   See Ali Gitmez and Czarina Wilpert, 'A Micro-Society or an Ethnic Community? Social Organization and Ethnicity amongst Turkish Migrants in Berlin', in John Rex, Daniele Joly and Czarina Wilpert, eds., *Immigrant Associations in Europe*, Gower Publishing for the European Science Foundation, Aldershot and Vermont, 1987, p. 107.
75   Federal Minister of the Interior, *Survey of the Policy and Law Regarding Aliens in the Federal Republic of Germany*, V II 1-937020/15, Bonn, 1991, pp. 6–7.
76   Ibid.
77   Ibid.
78   Blackstone, *The Salt of Another's Bread*, p. 58. See also V. Melotti, 'Gli Immigrati Stranieri in Italia: Considerazione dopo la Sanatoria', in *Up and Down*, ISPES, February 1988.
79   Blackstone, *The Salt of Another's Bread*.
80   OECD, *SOPEMI 1990*, Paris, 1991, p. 53.
81   For example, a fear that registration would result in the loss of a job, since the majority of illegal immigrants rely on work in the informal economy. (Many employers using irregular labour would be reluctant to employ legally registered immigrants.) Also significant is the fact that many immigrants in Italy do not intend to stay. According to a survey carried out by CENSIS in 1989/90, only about 30% of immigrants interviewed expressed a desire to remain in Italy. CENSIS, *Atti Della Conferenza Nazionale dell'Immigrazione*, p. 329. See also Salt, *Current and Future International Migration Trends*, p. 16; and OECD, *Comparative Analysis of the Regularisation Experience in France, Italy, Spain, and the United States*, OECD, Paris, 1990.
82   ILO Migrant Workers (Supplementary Provisions) Convention of June 1975.
83   See Blackstone, *The Salt of Another's Bread*, Appendix A.

84 CENSIS, *Immigrati e Società Italiana*, Editalia-Edizioni d'Italia, Rome, 1991, p. 333.
85 CENSIS, *Atti Della Conferenza Nazionale dell'Immigrazione*.
86 CENSIS, *Immigrazione e Diritti di Cittadinanza*, Editalia-Edizioni d'Italia, Rome, 1991, pp. 462–3.
87 See, for example, Annie Phizacklea and Robert Miles, *Labour and Racism*, Routledge and Kegan Paul, London, 1980, Chapter 3; Malcolm Cross, *Migrant Workers in European Cities: Concentration, Conflict and Social Policy*, Working Papers on Ethnic Relations, no. 19, SSRC Research Unit on Ethnic Relations, Birmingham, 1983; D. Massey, *Spatial Divisions of Labour: Social Structures and the Geography of Production*, Macmillan, London, 1984.
88 See for example, John Rex and Sally Tomlinson, *Colonial Immigrants in a British City*, Routledge and Kegan Paul, London, 1979, Chapter 5.
89 Malcolm Cross, 'Ethnic Minority Youth in a Collapsing Labour Market: the UK Experience', in Wilpert, ed., *Entering the Working World*, p. 66.
90 Gilles Verbunt, in Hammar, ed., *European Immigration Policy*.
91 See, for example, Grillo, *Ideologies and Institutions in Urban France*, pp. 117–18.
92 See, for example, Catherine Wihtol de Wenden, *Les immigrés et la politique: cent cinquante ans d'évolution*, Presses de la Fondation Nationale de Sciences Politiques, Paris, 1987.
93 White, 'The Migrant Experience in Paris', p. 195.
94 Attempted for a short period by Birmingham council. See Rex and Tomlinson, *Colonial Immigrants in a British City*, Chapter 5. Note also Ealing Council's attempts to disperse immigrant children by busing them to schools outside the area. See Zig Layton-Henry in Hammar, ed., *European Immigration Policy*. These measures also came in for considerable criticism, not least from immigrants themselves.
95 Note also the recent widespread use of the term '*seuil de tolérance*', or 'threshold of tolerance', in France. See, for example, *Europe: Variations on a Theme of Racism, Race and Class*, vol. 32, no. 3, 1991, p. 50.
96 Helga Leitner, 'Regulating Migrants' Lives', in Glebe and O'Loughlin, eds., *Foreign Minorities in Continental European Cities*, pp. 71–89.
97 Czarina Wilpert, 'Work and the Second Generation: the Descendants of Migrant Workers in the Federal Republic of Germany', in Wilpert, ed., *Entering the Working World*, pp. 126–7. Note that 'young foreigners' rely to a disproportionate extent on irregular and/or casual work.
98 Ibid.
99 Note for example that children of Indian ethnic origin tend to perform above the level of their white peers, whereas children of West Indian descent are more likely to underachieve. See Zig Layton-Henry in T. Hammar (ed.), 1984. Children of Turkish descent tend to underachieve to a greater extent than those of Yugoslav, Greek, Italian or Spanish descent. See Wilpert, 'Work and the Second Generation', pp. 118–19.
100 Women have also been targeted for language training. Note also 'mother-tongue' language teaching, which has often been supported by the state, either (in the past) to promote the preparedness of immigrants and their children to return to their country of origin (especially in the FRG), or to promote cultural identity within

immigrant groups (usually this is left to immigrants themselves, but in the Netherlands, and to a lesser extent in France, the state has taken on direct responsibility for immigrant children's cultural education).

101 Even in the Netherlands, which has hitherto pursued an explicitly multicultural policy, language lessons are now mandatory.

102 Wilpert, 'Work and the Second Generation', p. 127.

103 There is no consistent pattern as to whether the outcome is a de facto displacement of entire communities or whether the result is a break-up of existing concentrations. Immigrant concentration should not be seen as a static or finished process; communities are in a constant state of flux, and one area of concentration may all but disappear only to be replaced by another elsewhere. See, for example, White, 'The Migrant Experience in Paris'.

104 Wilpert, 'Work and the Second Generation'.

105 Tomas Hammar, *Democracy and the Nation State. Aliens, Denizens and Citizens in a World of International Migration*, Research in Ethnic Relations Series, Gower Publishing, Avebury, 1990, p. 3.

106 Ibid. pp. 12–13.

107 Including limited rights in Hamburg and Schleswig-Holstein in Germany; Spain (on the basis of reciprocal agreements); Ireland; the Netherlands; Portugal (nationals of Portuguese-speaking countries only); all five Scandinavian states; and Switzerland (certain cantons only). See Hopmann, *Réflexions sur le futur statut des migrants*. See also Council of Europe, *Community and Ethnic Relations in Europe: Final report of the Community Relations Project of the Council of Europe*, (MG-CR (91) 1 final E), Council of Europe, Strasbourg, 1991, p. 30.

108 Soledad Garcia, *Europe's Fragmented Identities and the Frontiers of Citizenship*, RIIA Discussion Paper no. 45, RIIA, London, 1992.

109 Wilpert, 'Work and the Second Generation'.

110 Uri Ra'anan, 'Nation and State: Order out of Chaos', in Uri Ra'anan, Maria Mesner, Keith Armes and Kate Martin, eds., *State and Nation in Multi-Ethnic Societies: The Breakup of Multinational States*, Institute for the Study of Conflict, Ideology and Policy (Boston), Manchester University Press, Manchester, 1991, pp. 3–32. Based on Hans Kohn's typology, distinguishing a 'Western' rationale and associational version of nationalism from an 'Eastern' organic and mystical version. See Hans Kohn, *The Idea of Nationalism*, second edition, Collier Macmillan, New York, 1967. See also Anthony Smith, *National Identity*, Penguin, London, 1991, Chapter 4.

111 Ibid., p. 13.

112 Note, for example, the terminology used in the recent *Survey of the Policy and Law Regarding Aliens in the Federal Republic of Germany*, Federal Ministry of the Interior, much of which is devoted to a discussion of policy affecting the integration of so-called second and third generations. E.g., 'Approximately 60 per cent of aliens staying in the Federal Republic of Germany have been living here for ten years or more. More than two-thirds of foreign children and juveniles were born in the Federal Republic of Germany. The Federal Government assumes that most of them will stay for a considerable period of time or that some of them will even stay forever. This applies above all to those foreigners who were born and have grown up here.' (p. 5)

Chapter 7

1   Richard Plender, *International Migration Law*, Revised Second Edition, Nijhoff, Dordrecht, 1988, p. 251. The Convention was ratified by Portugal, Spain, Turkey, Sweden and the Netherlands.

2   Council of the European Communities, *Single European Act and Final Act*, Office for Official Publications of the EC (OOPEC), Luxembourg, 1986, Article 8a.

3   Commission of the European Communities, *Commission Communication to the Council and the European Parliament on Immigration*, SEC(91) 1855 final, EC Commission, Brussels, 23 October 1991, p. 8.

4   Note that the Schengen Group has also signed supplementary agreements with Greece and Poland.

5   Note that the Maastricht Treaty transfers certain limited areas of competence to the European Commission and the European Parliament (connected with developing a common visa policy), but most areas remain within the framework of intergovernmental cooperation (the Third Pillar).

6   This Convention had not been signed at the time of writing owing to a dispute between the United Kingdom and Spain over the status of the border between Gibraltar and Spain (the UK government considers the frontier to be internal, Spain considers it an external border). Until the Convention has been signed, the draft is officially confidential. However, a copy was circulated by the European Parliament's Committee on Civil Liberties and Internal Affairs in early 1992.

7   Ministers Responsible for Immigration, 'Signing of the Convention determining the State responsible for examining applications for asylum lodged in one of the Member States of the European Communities', 6941/90 (Presse 87), Dublin, 15 June 1990. At the time of writing, the Dublin Convention had been ratified by only four states: Denmark, Greece, Ireland and the UK. Also at the time of writing, a draft parallel Convention is being considered with a view to including other states, including EFTA countries, in the Dublin regime.

8   Ad Hoc Group on Immigration, *Report from the Ministers Responsible for Immigration to the European Council Meeting in Maastricht on Immigration and Asylum Policy*, SN 4038/91 (WGI 930), Brussels, 3 December 1991.

9   Ministers Responsible for Immigration, 'Signing of the Convention', p. 2.

10 Ad Hoc Group on Immigration, *Report from the Ministers Responsible for Immigration*, p. 12.

11 Ibid.

12 See Commission of the European Communities, *Commission Communication to the Council and the European Parliament on Immigration*, p. 17.

13 Ad Hoc Group on Immigration, *Report from the Ministers Responsible for Immigration*.

14 Council of the European Communities and Commission of the European Communities, *Treaty on European Union* (CONF-UP-UEM 2002/92), OOPEC, Luxembourg, 1992.

15 'Europe may limit influx of migrants', *Independent*, 14 September 1992.

16 'Hurd urges EC to focus on migration', *Independent*, 16 September 1992.

17 Council of Europe, *Final Communiqué of the Conference of Ministers on the Movement of Persons From Central and Eastern European Countries*, Council of Europe, Vienna, 25 January 1991.

18 Council of Europe, Fourth Conference of European Ministers Responsible for

Migration Affairs, *Conclusions and Resolution adopted at the Conference*, 'Conclusions', p. 3.

19 An approach which has already been partially formalized within the Schengen framework, in the form of the agreement reached with Poland in 1991, by which Poland undertakes to readmit rejected asylum-seekers and illegal immigrants who have entered the Schengen area through Poland.

20 Ad Hoc Group on Immigration, *Report from the Ministers Responsible for Immigration*, pp. 3 and 21.

21 Commission of the European Communities, *Policies on Immigration and the Social Integration of Migrants in the European Community*, Experts' report drawn up on behalf of the Commission of the European Communities, Brussels, September 1990 (SEC(90) 1813 final), p. 32.

22 Federal Minister of the Interior, Survey of the Policy and Law Regarding Aliens in the Federal Republic of Germany (Translation), Bonn, January 1991 (V II 1-937 020/15), p. 8.

23 Ibid.

24 See, for example, Institute of Race Relations, 'Race and Class', *Europe: Variations on a Theme of Racism*, Russell Press, Nottingham, 1991. See also European Parliament (Rapporteur: Mr Glyn Ford), *Report of the Committee of Enquiry into Racism and Xenophobia*, Brussels, European Parliament Sessions Document, Brussels, 1989.

25 Commission of the European Communities, *Policies on Immigration*, pp. 37 and 32.

26 Ibid., p. 27.

27 The Work Programme separates action in the area of migration policy from that of asylum policy. Within the first category, the programme lists five broad areas of policy requiring joint action: (1) admission policies; (2) illegal immigration; (3) the migration of labour; (4) the situation of third-country nationals; and (5) migration policy 'in the broad meaning of the term'. See Ad Hoc Group on Immigration, *Report from the Ministers Responsible for Immigration*, pp. 4–6.

28 Ibid.

29 Ibid., pp. 4–6.

30 Commission of the European Communities, *Commission Communication to the Council and the European Parliament on Immigration*, p. 13.

31 Ad Hoc Group on Immigration, *Report from the Ministers Responsible for Immigration*, p. 14.

32 UNHCR, 1992.

33 André Lebon (Ministère des Affaires Sociales et de la Solidarité, Direction de la Population et des Migrations), *Regard sur L'Immigration et la Présence Etrangère en France 1989/90*, La Documentation Française, Paris, 1990, p. 53; and Federal Minister of the Interior, *Survey of the Policy and Law Regarding Aliens*, Annex 1, p. 3.

34 Ad Hoc Group on Immigration, *Report from the Ministers Responsible for Immigration*, p. 32.

35 Note that the European Court of Human Rights has never recognized the right of a family who have never lived together in one country to do so in that particular country, particularly if they can exercise their family unity rights in the country of emigration. The European Convention on the Legal Status of Migrant Workers envisages that the spouse and unmarried minor dependants of a migrant worker

will be permitted to join him/her in the territory of a contracting party, but states are free to make this right conditional, among other things, upon the worker having adequate resources to support the family. See Plender, *International Migration Law*, Chapter 11.

36   Note, however, that an Ad Hoc Group draft resolution on the harmonization of national policies on family reunification was not adopted at a ministerial meeting on 30 November–1 December 1992, since ministers could not agree on a finalized text.

37   Note that Portugal is still a country of net emigration, described as not having yet completed the 'migration cycle'. But it is now also receiving immigrants from Africa and other regions. It is worth noting, however, that immigration into Portugal is far more 'visible' than emigration streams, owing to the ethnic difference of immigrant groups.

38   Gildas Simon, 'Trends and Prospects on the Threshold of the Internal Market', in Commission of the European Communities, Directorate-General for Employment, Industrial Relations and Social Affairs, *Social Europe*, Brussels, 1990, pp. 20–33, at p. 31.

39   The UK's position as an island makes it relatively easy to control entries, which requires little more than controls at ports of entry. The UK's common law traditions, by defining what is prohibited rather than what is required, tend to work against the idea of constant internal checks and controls on the movements and activities of the population (nationals and foreigners).

40   There are, of course, certain mechanisms for internal control, although they do not add up to any form of coherent system. Note, for example, the growing linkage between access to state benefits and services and immigration status, and proposals to fingerprint all asylum applicants for benefit and housing services (1992 Asylum Bill). See papers prepared for the Institute of Public Policy Research on a new UK immigration policy, London, forthcoming June 1993.

41   Note that the Parliamentary Home Affairs Select Committee and policing authorities would seem to support the introduction of voluntary ID cards, whereas the Home Office and immigration service seem to be against their introduction. Support for ID cards may stem more from wider interests connected with crime detection and prevention of terrorism than from a primary interest in immigration control. In addition to the political obstacles, however, the practical difficulties that would be encountered in any effort to introduce a system of ID cards suitable for controlling or monitoring immigration would be enormous. Note also that internal controls have been of dubious efficacy in preventing illegal immigration into countries such as Italy and France.

42   Note that no agreement on the suppression of internal border controls was reached at the ministerial meeting of the Ad Hoc Group of 30 November–1 December 1992. Denmark and Ireland also argued for the maintenance of border controls.

43   Ad Hoc Group on Immigration, *Report from the Ministers Responsible for Immigration*, p. 28.

44   Note also Portugal's intention to carry out a legalization programme in 1993.

45   Commission of the European Communities, *Commission Communication to the Council and the European Parliament on Immigration*, p. 14.

46   Article 17 of the draft circulated by the Committee on Civil Liberties and Internal Affairs of the European Parliament.

47   *Treaty on European Union*, Article 100c.1.

48   See, for example, Joint Council for the Welfare of Immigrants, 'Memorandum of Evidence to the Home Affairs Committee External Borders Inquiry', London, January 1992.
49   Article 17 of the draft circulated by the Committee on Civil Liberties and Internal Affairs of the European Parliament.
50   Joint Council for the Welfare of Immigrants, 'Memorandum of Evidence'.
51   Ibid.
52   *Treaty on European Union*, Article 100c.2. Note also the resolutions adopted at the ministerial meeting of the Ad Hoc Group on 30 November–1 December 1992, the Resolution on manifestly unfounded applications for asylum, and the Resolution concerning host third countries. See, for example, *Migration News Sheet*, no. 117/ 92-12 (December 1992), Brussels, 1992.
53   The Basic Law of 1949. It includes the provision that persons persecuted for political reasons enjoy the right of asylum in the Federal Republic (not open to political discretion). The 1965 Asylum Law extends the right of asylum to refugees within the meaning of the 1951 Convention and of other aliens persecuted on political grounds. Note that the Constitutions of France and Italy also include provisions for the right of asylum, but these have not been interpreted as liberally as that of the German Constitution. See Richard Plender, *International Migration Law*, Revised Second Edition, Nijhoff, Dordrecht, 1988.
54   Commission of the European Communities, *Commission Communication to the Council and the European Parliament on Immigration*, p. 6.
55   Ad Hoc Group on Immigration, *Report from the Ministers Responsible for Immigration*, p. 34.
56   Note, again, the resolutions considered and adopted by and reports submitted to the ministerial meeting of the Ad Hoc Group on 30 November–1 December 1992.
57   As does the Ad Hoc Group's Resolution concerning host third countries, adopted at a ministerial meeting of the Ad Hoc Group on 30 November–1 December 1992.
58   Refugee Policy Group, 'Migration in and from Central and Eastern Europe: Addressing the Root Causes', paper prepared for a Conference on East-West Migration, 'Addressing the Root Causes', RPG and the Aspen Institute, Berlin, June 1992, pp. 20–21. Note, again, the Ad Hoc Group's resolution concerning third host countries, which reflects a concern with refugees and asylum-seekers leaving countries where they have already been granted protection or have had a genuine opportunity to seek such protection.
59   Ad Hoc Group on Immigration, *Report from the Ministers Responsible for Immigration*, p. 6.
60   *Treaty on European Union*, Article A.2 (a) and (b).
61   Commission of the European Communities, *Commission Communication to the Council and the European Parliament on Immigration*, p. 25.
62   Ad Hoc Group on Immigration, *Report from the Ministers Responsible for Immigration*, p. 25.
63   This migration also differs from previous patterns in that movement is generally more transitory or temporary in nature. Much of this migration is regulated through the issue of short-term work permits preventing settlement. See, for example, John Salt and R.T. Kitching, 'Labour Migration and the Work Permit System in the United Kingdom', in *International Migration*, vol. 28 (3), 1990, pp. 267–94.
64   See, for example, John Salt, 'Current and Future International Migration Trends

Affecting Europe', paper presented at the 4th Conference of European Ministers Responsible for Migration, Luxembourg (Council of Europe), September 1991; John Salt and Allan Findlay, 'International Migration of Highly-Skilled Manpower: Theoretical and Development Issues', in R. Appleyard, ed., *The Impacts of International Migration on Developing Countries*, OECD, Paris, 1989, pp. 159–81; John Salt, 'Contemporary Trends in International Migration Study', *International Migration*, September 1987.

65 See Ludwig Hofler (Counsellor, Ministry of Labour and Social Affairs), 'Migration Programmes of the Federal Republic of Germany Aimed at the Training and Short-Term Employment of Workers Originating From Developing Countries or Countries of Central or Eastern Europe', paper delivered at the 10th IOM Seminar on Migration and Development, Geneva, September 1992.

66 Ibid., p. 3.

67 Ad Hoc Group on Immigration, *Report from the Ministers Responsible for Immigration*, p. 24.

68 Commission of the European Communities, *Commission Communication from the Council and the European Parliament on Immigration*, pp. 19–20.

69 Ibid., p. 8.

Chapter 8

1 See Wolfgang Ochel and Kurt Vogler-Ludwig (IFO Institute for Economic Research), 'International Migration: a New Challenge for the Industrialised Countries', paper presented at the Conference of the Tokyo Club Foundation for Global Studies, Tokyo, June 1992.

2 Curt Gasteyger, 'European Security and the New Arc of Crisis: Paper II', in *New Dimensions in International Security*, Adelphi Paper 265, Part I (IISS Annual Conference Papers), Brassey's, London, 1992, pp. 69–81, at p. 69.

3 See also Bimal Ghosh, 'Migration, Trade and International Economic Cooperation: Do the Interlinkages Work?', paper presented at the 10th IOM Seminar on Migration, Geneva, September 1992, p. 14.

4 George Joffé, 'European Security and the New Arc of Crisis: Paper I', in *New Dimensions of Security*, p. 66.

5 Ibid.

6 Jonas Widgren at Aspen Institute/Refugee Policy Group Conference, 'East–West Migration: Addressing the Root-Causes', Berlin, June 1992.

Bibliography

Ad Hoc Group on Immigration, *Report from the Ministers Responsible for Immigration to the European Council Meeting in Maastricht on Immigration and Asylum Policy*, SN 4038/91 (WGI 930), Brussels, 3 December 1991.

Adler, Stephen, *International Migration and Dependence*, Saxon House, Farnborough Hants, 1977.

Adler, Stephen, *Swallow's Children – Emigration and Development in Algeria*, Geneva, ILO, 1980.

Appleyard, R., ed., *The Impacts of International Migration on Developing Countries*, OECD, Paris, 1989.

Appleyard, R., ed., *International Migration Today. Vol. 1: Trends and Prospects*, UNESCO, Paris, 1988.

Appleyard, ed., *The Impact of International Migration*.

Bevan, Vaughan, *The Development of British Immigration Law*, Croom Helm, London, 1986.

Blackstone, *Salt of Another's Bread: Immigration Control and the Social Impact of Immigration in Italy*, Report of a Western European Union Study Visit, Home Office, London, 1989.

Böhning, W.R., *Studies in International Migration*, International Labour Office, London, 1984.

Castles, Stephen, Booth, H. and Wallace, T., *Here for Good: Western Europe's New Ethnic Minorities*, Pluto, London, 1984.

Charles W. Stahl, ed., *International Migration Today. Vol. 2: Emerging Issues*, UNESCO, Paris, 1988.

CENSIS (Centro Studi Investimenti Sociali) *Atti Della Conferenza Nationale dell' Immigrazione*, Editalia-Edizioni d'Italia, Rome, 1991.

CENSIS, *Immigrazione e Diritti di Cittadinanza*, Editalia-Edizioni d'Italia, Rome, 1991.

CENSIS, *Immigrati e Società Italiana*, Editalia-Edizioni d'Italia, Rome, 1991.

Coleman, David, *International Migrants in Europe: Adjustment and Integration Processes and Policies*, paper presented at the United Nations Population Fund/ United Nations Economic Commission for Europe Informal Expert Group Meeting on International Migration, Geneva, July 1991.

Commission of the European Communities, *Commission Communication to the Council and the European Parliament on Immigration*, SEC(91) 1855 final, EC Commission, Brussels, 23 October 1991.

Commission of the European Communities, *Policies on Immigration and the Social Integration of Migrants in the European Community*, Experts' report drawn up on behalf of the Commission of the European Communities, Brussels, September 1990 (SEC(90)1813 final).

Council of Europe, Committee on Migration, Refugees and Demography, *Demographic Imbalances Between the Countries of the Mediterranean Basin* (rapporteurs: M. Mota Torres and Vazquez, assisted by Léon Tabah), restricted (AS/PR (42) 40), Council of Europe, Strasbourg, 22 May 1991 (AAR40.42).

Council of Europe, *Final Communiqué of the Conference of Ministers on the Movement of Persons From Central and Eastern European Countries*, Council of Europe, Vienna, 25 January 1991.

Council of Europe, *Community and Ethnic Relations in Europe: Final report of the Community Relations Project of the Council of Europe*, (MG-CR (91) 1 final E), Council of Europe, Strasbourg, 1991.

Curtin, Philip D., *The Atlantic Slave Trade: A Census*, University of Wisconsin Press, Madison, 1969.

Davis, Kingsley, 'The Migrations of Human Populations', *Scientific American*, no. 231, September 1974.

Dowty, Alan, *Closed Borders*, Yale University Press, New Haven and London, 1987.

European Parliament, *Report of the Committee of Enquiry into Racism and Xenophobia*, (Rapporteur: Mr Glyn Ford), Brussels, European Parliament Sessions Document A3-195/90, Brussels, 1989.

Eurostat, *Demographic Statistics 1991*, Eurostat (Statistical Office of the European Communities), Official Publications Office of the European Communities, Luxembourg, 1991.

Federal Minister of the Interior, 'Survey of the Policy and Law Regarding Aliens in the Federal Republic of Germany', Bonn, January 1991.

Federal Minister of the Interior, *Survey of the Policy and Law Regarding Aliens in the Federal Republic of Germany* (V II 1-937 020/15), Bonn, 1991.

Fried, C., ed., *Minorities: Community and Identity*, Life Sciences Research Report Series no. 27, Springer-Verlag, Berlin, 1983.

Garcia, Soledad, *Europe's Fragmented Identies and the Frontiers of Citizenship*, RIIA Discussion Paper no. 45, RIIA, London, 1992.

Gasteyger, Curt, 'European Security and the New Arc of Crisis: Paper II', in *New Dimensions in International Security*, Adelphi Paper 265, Part I (IISS Annual Conference Papers), Brassey's, London, 1992.

Ghosh, Bimal, 'Migration-Development Linkages: Some Specific Issues and Practical Policy Measures', paper presented at the Tenth IOM Seminar on Migration, Geneva, September 1992.

Grillo, R.D, *Ideologies and Institutions in Urban France: The Representation of Immigrants*, Cambridge University Press, 1985.

Hall, Stuart, 'Migration from the English-speaking Caribbean to the United Kingdom, 1950–80', in Charles W. Stahl, ed., *International Migration Today. Vol. 2: Emerging Issues*, UNESCO, Paris, 1988.

Hammar, Tomas, ed., *European Immigration Policy*, Cambridge University Press, 1985.

Hammar, Tomas, *Democracy and the Nation State. Aliens, Denizens and Citizens in a World of International Migration*, Avebury, Aldershot, 1990.

Joffe, George, 'European Security and the New Arc of Crisis: Paper I', in *New Dimensions in International Security, Adelphi Paper 265*, Part I (IISS Annual Conference Papers), Brassey's, London, 1992.

Johnston, H. J. M., *British Emigration Policy 1815–1830: Shovelling out Paupers*, Clarendon Press, Oxford, 1972.

Joint Council for the Welfare of Immigrants, 'Memorandum of Evidence to the Home Affairs Committee External Borders Inquiry', London, January 1992.

Kritz, M.M., Keely, C.B., and Tomasi, S.M., eds., *Global Trends in Migration: Theory and Research on International Population Movements*, Center for Migration Studies, New York, 1983.

Kubat, Daniel, ed., *The Politics of Migration Policies: The First World in the 1970s*, Center for Migration Studies, New York, 1979.

Kulischer, Eugene, *Jewish Migrations: Past Experiences and Post-War Prospects*, American Jewish Committee, New York, 1943.

Kulischer, Eugene, *Europe on the Move. War and Population Changes 1917–1947*, Columbia University Press, New York, 1943.

Layton-Henry, Zig, *The Politics of Race in Britain*, Allen and Unwin, London, 1984.

Lebon, André, *Regard sur L'immigration et la présence étrangère en France, 1989/90*, Ministère des Affaires Sociales et de la Solidarité, Direction de la Population et des Migrations, Paris, 1990.

LeMay, Michael C. ed., *The Gatekeepers. Comparative Immigration Policy*, Praeger, New York, 1989.

Loescher, Gil and Monahan, Laila, (eds.), *Refugees and International Relations*, Oxford University Press, 1989.

Marrus, Michael, *The Unwanted; European Refugees in the Twentieth Century*, Oxford University Press, New York and Oxford, 1985.

Martin, Philip L., *The Unfinished Story: Turkish Labour Migration to Western Europe*, Geneva, ILO, 1991.

Ochel, Wolfgang, and Vogler-Ludwig, Kurt, (IFO Institute for Economic Research), 'International Migration: a New Challenge for the Industrialised Countries', paper presented at the Conference of the Tokyo Club Foundation for Global Studies, Tokyo, June 1992.

OECD Continuous Reporting on System on Migration (SOPEMI), *Trends in International Migration*, OECD, Paris, 1992.

OECD, *Migration. The Demographic Aspects*, OECD, Paris, 1991.

Paine, Suzanne, *Exporting Workers: the Turkish Case*, Cambridge University Press, 1974.

Phizacklea, A., and Miles, R., *Labour and Racism*, Routledge and Kegan Paul, London, 1980.

Piore, M., *Birds of Passage*, Cambridge University Press, 1979.

Plender, Richard, *International Migration Law*, Revised Second Edition, Nijhoff, Dordrecht, 1988.

Presidenza del Consiglio dei Ministri, *Norme Urgenti in Materia di Asilo Politico, Ingresso e Soggiorno dei Cittadini Extracomunitari e di Regolarizzazione de Cittadini Extracomunitari ed Apolidi Già Presenti Nel Territorio Dello Stato*, Law of 28 February 1990, no. 39, converting Decree no. 416 of December 1989, Collana de Testi e Documenti, Dipartimento per L'Informazione e L'Editoria (Istituto

Poligrafico e Zecca Dello Stato), Rome, 1990; (including English translation).

Ravenstein, E. G., 'The Laws of Migration', *Journal of the Royal Statistical Society*, no. 52, London, 1889.

Rex, J., Joly, D., and Wilpert, C., eds., *Immigrant Associations in Europe*, Gower, Aldershot, 1987.

Rex, J. and Tomlinson, S., *Colonial Immigrants in a British City*, Routledge and Kegan Paul, London, 1979.

Rystad, Göran, ed., *The Uprooted: Forced Migration as an International Problem in the Postwar Era*, Lund University Press, Lund, 1990.

Salt, John, *Current and Future International Migration Trends Affecting Europe*, background document for the 4th Conference of European Ministers Responsible for Migration, Luxembourg, September 1991 (MMG-4 (91) 1 E), Council of Europe, Strasbourg, 1991.

Schmitter Heisler, Barbara, 'Sending Countries and the Politics of Emigration and Destination', in *International Migration Review* (Special Issue: 'Civil Rights and the Socio-political Participation of Migrants'), vol. 19, 1985.

Seccombe, I.J., and Lawless, R.J, 'Some New Trends in Mediterranean Labour Migration: The Middle East Connection', *International Migration*, vol. 23, no. 1, March 1985.

Serageldin, Socknat, Birks, Li, and Sinclair, *Manpower and International Labour Migration in the Middle East and North Africa*, Oxford University Press for the World Bank, Oxford, 1983.

Simon, G., 'Industrialisation, Emigration et Réinsertion de la Main-d'Oeuvre Qualifiée au Maghreb – le cas de la Tunisie et de l'Algérie', *Hommes et Migrations*, no. 902, 1976.

Stanton Russell, S., and Teitelbaum, M.S., *International Migration and International Trade*, World Bank Discussion Paper, no. 160; World Bank, Washington DC, 1992.

Tapinos, Georges, *L'immigration étrangère en France, 1946–1973*, Institut National d'Etudes Démographiques no. 71, Presses Universitaires de France, Paris, 1975.

Thistlethwaite, Frank, 'Migration from Europe Overseas in the Nineteenth and Twentieth Centuries', *Rapports*, vol. 5, 1960.

Thomas, Brinley, *Migration and Economic Growth. A Study of Great Britain and the Atlantic Economy*, Cambridge University Press, 1954.

US Committee for Refugees, *World Refugee Survey 1992*, American Council for Nationalities Service, Washington DC, 1992.

Weiner, Myron, 'On International Migration and International Relations', in *Population and Development Review*, vol. 2, no. 3, 1985.

White, Paul, 'The Migrant Experience in Paris', in Günther Glebe and John O'Loughlin, eds., *Foreign Minorities in Continental European Cities* (Erdkundliches Wissen, Heft 84), Steiner Verlag, Stuttgart, 1987.

Widgren, Jonas, 'International Migration: New Challenges to Europe', report prepared for the Third Conference of European Ministers Responsible for Migration, (Council of Europe), Porto, Portugal, 13–15 May, 1987. Reprinted in *Migration News* no. 2, International Catholic Migration Commission, Geneva, 1987.

Wihtol de Wenden, Catherine, *Les immigrés et la politique*, Presses de la Fondation Nationale des Sciences Politiques, Paris, 1988.

Wilpert, C., ed., *Entering the Working World. Following the Descendants of Europe's Immigrant Labour Force*, Gower, Aldershot, 1988.

Zolberg, A. R., Suhrke, A., and Aguayo, S., *Escape from Violence. Conflict and the Refugee Crisis in the Developing World*, Oxford University Press, New York and Oxford, 1989.

Zolberg, Aristide R., 'Contemporary Transnational Migrations in Historical Perspective: Patterns and Dilemmas', in Mary M. Kritz, ed., US *Immigration and Refugee Policy. Global and Domestic Issues, USA and Canada*, Lexington Books, Lexington MA, 1983.

Index